Walking the Tides
Seasonal Magical Rhythms and Lore

WALKING *the* TIDES
Seasonal Magical Rhythms and Lore

by
Nigel G. Pearson

TROY BOOKS

First North American Edition, 2020
First Printing, 2020
ISBN 978-0-7387-6588-4

Originally published by Troy Books Inc. 2017
ISBN 978-1-909602-29-8
Revised and expanded from the first edition published by Capall Bann in April 2009

Llewellyn Publications is a registered trademark of Llewellyn Worldwide Ltd.

Cataloging-in-Publication Programme data is on file with the British National Bibliography.

Llewellyn Publications
A Division of Llewellyn Worldwide Ltd. 2143 Wooddale Drive
Woodbury, MN 55125-2989 www.llewellyn.com

Printed in the United States of America

Dedication

This book is dedicated with love and in remembrance
to my Father;
Graham Clifford Pearson
1932 – 2017.
A Country Boy At Heart.

Acknowledgements

Gemma Gary & Jane Cox at Troy Books, who continue
to encourage me to write and are brave enough to
publish the resulting work. An especial mention must be
given for publishing this second edition.

Stuart Inman and Michael Howard, who always gave me
encouragement and rare gems of knowledge!

To all those who have read the first edition of this work
and have contributed their comments; you have all been
very kind and helpful. My thanks to you all.

Anthony – you know what for.

Contents

Photoplates
between pages 192 - 193

All photography by the author

Illustrations

Chapter opening illustartions by Anthony Pearson-Moorhouse

Illustartions for the months from *Calendrier des Bergeres*, 1499

Cover illustration by Paul Atlas-Saunders

PREFACE

ᴁᴑᴂᴣ ✤ ᴣᴑᴏᴁ

Behind the seasonal calendar celebrated by most modern pagans is an ebb and flow of natural energies that is seldom mentioned and whose meaning is very little understood. Those that take their practice from a direct experience of the Land and its natural rhythms and tides have always understood and worked with these energies, which gives them a direct connection to the reality behind the modern festivals.

This book aims to give the reader an insight into the great rhythmic tides and flows of energy that animate the Land throughout the year and the natural happenings that occur along the way, thereby giving their practice a validity that it may currently lack.

Walking the Tides describes holy days, celebrations, saints' days, animals, birds, herbs, trees, weather and starlore that are featured in the natural calendar of the British Isles, and the uses to which many of these things are put in traditional practice.

Divided into four sections describing the Winter, Spring, Summer and Autumn Tides (and monthly within these), the author gives the reader a feeling of connection to what is actually going on around them in the natural world, at any given point in the year.

Many books describe the so-called "Wheel of the Year", without giving any context, reason or validation for the practices described; Walking the Tides takes the reader on an intimate journey into the heart of the Land and shows what actually occurs, rather than what is supposed to, enabling the reader to understand the rhythms and tides of the Land around them and to formulate their own celebrations and observances of these tides and their significant points, based on a clear understanding of the world around them.

Much of the information given is taken from Traditional Craft practice, but also from old British folklore, the lore of the Farm, the author's own experience and even Church tradition, the better to give the reader a greater and deeper appreciation and understanding of the seasonal flows throughout the natural year and their place in it.

INTRODUCTION
to the First Edition

❧✿❧

In writing this book, I hope to show and describe the flows and rhythms of energy that inform the natural calendar of the year, those energies and tides that lie behind many of the better-known forms of pagan calendar and some of the lesser-known practices and observances that were – and still are carried on by those people who still have a connection to the Land and its ways today. Whether these practices ultimately originate in our pre-Christian past, whether they are an amalgamation of pagan memory with Christian overlay, or whether they are entirely the product of devout, Mediaeval religious feeling matters not a jot to the Practitioner; it all belongs to the same natural flow of life, from cradle to grave and from one year's round to the next.

I will be covering a range of different practices: from herbs to weather lore, seasonal observances to celestial events, animal lore to tree magic and other oddities that don't fit in happily anywhere. These are the type of things that tend to get left out of most books on modern paganism and the like, because they're a bit too real and dirty for a lot of people's taste. By 'dirty' I mean literally soiled, going out and getting your hands in the earth and coming back with broken nails and grit in your pores, the stuff that really makes you feel alive. This aspect seems to have been lost from many people's practices these days and few are the modern pagans that know where to find a "chicken of the woods" or even what it looks like. (It's a type of edible fungus that grows on trees.)

These practices and observances have been divided up seasonally for ease of reference, and monthly within the given season. My aim is to give a feeling of an overall flow throughout the natural year and its happenings, a sense of an organic whole if you like; so many books describe and give rituals for the festivals of the so-called "Wheel of the Year" without giving any context or explaining why a certain festival is observed at a certain time and this can lead to a vague sense of being 'disjointed', not really connected to an overall pattern within the natural cycle. Indeed, why should a festival be observed at a set time anyway? Like it or not, the formal calendar that we observe today is not the one used by the majority of our forebears, and the impact of climate change is already making itself felt in many and varied ways, not least in the timing of once-predictable seasonal feasts or occasions.

The Equinoxes and Solstices may still be reliably observed on certain dates, as these are empirical, celestial events; however, even the practices that traditionally celebrated them have altered and shifted, due to the change from the Julian to the Gregorian calendar in 1752 (in the British Isles), when we 'lost' 11 days. Therefore, we need to look around the set dates for appropriate observances, maybe under very different names, if we wish to celebrate something real and valid. As for the other festivals generally celebrated in the modern pagan calendar, they really need to be observed when the event(s) that they are purporting to celebrate actually happens. For example, in 2007 the grain harvest in the majority of England was ruined by prolonged and heavy rain, so would one then have celebrated the festival of Lammas (the gathering-in and thanksgiving for the first grain harvest) in the normal way, at the normal time, or even at all? Such things need to be considered when truly practising Natural Religion.

There is also the train of thought that suggests that to practice a truly relevant Land-based spirituality, if it doesn't occur in your area, then you shouldn't observe it anyway. To take our previous example of Lammas; if you don't live in an agricultural area, have no connection to any kind of grain harvest and wouldn't recognise an ear of barley if it bit you on the shin, what are you doing singing songs about John Barleycorn and downing pints of ale in his honour on the 1st August for anyway? All this may seem quite harsh to a modern pagan, used to practicing their trade on set dates quite happily, as they have been taught and read about in books, but what connection does it have to the real world that they profess to connect with and honour?

To a Practitioner of what I shall generally call in this book, Natural Religion or Natural Craft, it is a question of doing things when the time 'feels right' not when some modern, made-up calendar list tells you it's time. (By Natural Crafter or Crafter here, I mean a person that practices a belief system partly derived from, or similar to, Traditional Witchcraft, partly from British folk tradition (which will include outwardly-Christian observances) and partly from either family or personal experience, possibly handed down in a line. The experience and knowledge for when the time feels right comes from the close observation of the natural tides and cycles within Nature itself and being open to the natural energies around you. In general, it can be said that new, fresh energies are generated or released on the astral or inner levels of being at the Equinoxes and Solstices (which tend to be times of great turmoil and chaos on the inner levels, due to the change of tides), and manifest on the material or outer levels (i.e. the physical world that we live in) roughly six or seven weeks later, depending on conditions, hence setting up the situations in Nature and the 'right time' for a festival of celebration or observance.

To put it more clearly, the Winter Solstice can be said to generate the tide of cleansing and purification, which manifests around the beginning of February when the festival of Candlemas can be celebrated. The Spring Equinox can be said to generate the tide of energy, passion and growth, which manifests around the beginning of May with the festival of Beltane or Roodmas. The Summer Solstice can be seen to generate the tide of ripening and maturity, manifesting around the beginning of August when the festival of Lammas may occur. Finally, the Autumn Equinox sets in train the energies of decay, dissolution and death which realise themselves on the outer levels around the beginning of November, when the feast of All Hallows or Hallowmas may be observed, not celebrated; this is not a time for jollity and celebration from a natural point of view, but a time of honouring and reverence. From this point the tides run full cycle and the energies are once more renewed and refreshed at the Winter Solstice. Viewed in this manner, the events occurring throughout the natural year are seen to be part of an ongoing, organic whole, which allows for certain things to happen at certain times. One is not put into the position where unnatural concepts are forced onto dates and times of year that won't support them, but involved in a flow of events that happen naturally and of themselves – and we can be part of it.

Looking at it from a reverential point of view, the Powers that walk the Land are also part of and subject to these same tides and cycles and join with the Practitioner at the high and low points to renew and share the bonds that join them in this cyclic pattern. The "Deities", "Saints" and "Spirits" acknowledged within Natural Religion are even more intimately a part of these tides and cycles, as this is what they are created of and from, and which animates their very Being. Hence in the Spring of the year they may be full of energy and lusty play, but in the Autumn of the year they have expended their energies and are tired, wishing for nothing more than to rest and recuperate, like the rest of the natural world. Therefore, to call on them for great works of magic when they are settling in for a well-earned rest would not only be foolish and unnatural, but completely counter-productive. Many people fall into the trap of calling on their Deities or Powers to do all sorts of things that are completely inappropriate for the time of year and then wonder why they fail dismally. Of course, you can call on the Powers to help you with something that doesn't reflect the time of year, but their influence will not be as great as if you had waited for a more appropriate time. If it's worth doing, it's worth waiting for!

I have not attempted to include any mythological cycles of the Deities throughout the year, in any more than a cursory way; this is a separate study in itself and, although part of the natural year, deals more with the Male and Female Mysteries, which are a different and more intimately individual thing altogether. Likewise, I have not dealt specifically with the phases of the Moon in this book, as it is essentially a solar-based work; the Moon's tides do not accord with those of the Sun and must be followed in their own cycles, which is not the theme of this work. I have included the Sunrise and Sunset times for the beginning of each month at the start of each chapter however, for two reasons; firstly, to give an idea of how the courses of light and dark actually run throughout the year and secondly, on a more practical level, so that the reader may plan for the timing of specific rituals or observances, based around these points. The times I have given are necessarily approximate, as the Sun, contrary to the modern insistence on conformity, does not rise and set at the same time everywhere throughout the country. Check your local times to be absolutely accurate.

I have also included some traditional images for each month at the start of the chapter, which may be used as a focus for meditation and contemplation for that time. They are taken directly from a small book entitled Queen-like Closet, or Rich Cabinet by Hannah Wooley (dated 1681) and were originally intended as designs for samplers to depict the natural year month by month.

So, let us begin the journey through the year together and take that first step upon the path that will have us Walking the Tides.

Nigel G. Pearson
Suffolk, England
Hollantide 2008

INTRODUCTION
to the Second Edition

✤✤✤ ✤ ✤✤✤

In preparing this second edition of Walking the Tides I have changed very little of the text. There has been some minor restructuring of some sections, I have rewritten some passages and made additions and sometimes deletions in other places. I have added a few recipes and instructions/ suggestions for practical workings, but overall I haven't 'tampered' too much. Basically, I have you, the reader, to thank/blame for this. The comments and reviews I received after the first edition was published were overwhelmingly favourable and most people felt that the text needed little amending, if at all. I have therefore complied with that advice and not changed too much.

The aspect that I would most like to stress for this second edition is the whole idea behind the book, which some people seem to have missed. I have written this book in an attempt to describe the overall flows of the energy tides etc. of the year, from the point of view of a Crafter or Witch living in the British Isles. This is because that's where I live; I was born and brought up here and this is the area that I know the best. I therefore describe the flows and energies through the magic, folklore, flora and fauna and seasonal activity of these Lands. I do not have any practical experience of living or working in other areas, so I thought it wise to stick to what I know best. However, as I have tried to stress throughout the book – and I reiterate here now – what I consider to be the central theme and message of the work is that the core principles herein are applicable – and should be applied wherever you live.

We all live and work magically by the seasons; it is inevitable if you work with natural energies in any genuine manner. Therefore, we should all look to the ways and manners that those natural energies manifest themselves in the Lands that we live in, wherever we are. The customs, rites, folk-practices and magic that I describe herein will not be applicable as they stand to all places on the planet, but the core message will. Each reader needs to look at the place on the planet in which they live and see how they can apply the things that I describe in their own place. As an obvious example, when it is the Summer Solstice in the Northern hemisphere, it will be the Winter Solstice in the Southern hemisphere. Therefore, in places like Australia, Brazil or South Africa, you will need to observe the things that are going on at that time and incorporate them into your practice, rather than slavishly follow what it says in some book, written by a fellow in another place.

Many practices in this book will be perfectly suitable to other lands, but many others will not. The Witch or Crafter throughout the world will be familiar with many folk-practices originating from the British Isles or the European mainland, because of the past colonial history of those places and the cultural heritage they have received because of it. However, there is a risk in that case of ignoring the valuable indigenous traditions that have grown up in those other places over centuries, possibly millennia, and that are more appropriate to that part of the Land. I stress here that I do not mean that I advocate what has come to be called "cultural appropriation", that is the deliberate theft of other cultures' traditions without any right to, or proper knowledge of them – this is disrespectful at best and a continuation of colonial exploitation at worst. No, what I mean is that we can learn from the native knowledge of seasonal lore, customs, traditions, energy tides and flows and apply that intimate knowledge to our own practices and workings. As I say in the book; if a seasonal practice or celebration – such as a corn harvest – doesn't occur in your area, why are you celebrating it? Look at what actually happens where you are and work with that.

This may take a lot more effort on the part of practitioners in Lands that don't have as full a written history of customs and lore as the British Isles, but that then makes it all the more interesting to find out. Go out into the Land and see what is actually happening at any given season or time and work with that accordingly. If the leaves are falling from the trees, don't work magic for Spring! Wrong timing! Get in tune with the place in which you live and you will be richly rewarded, as your practice will work with the natural flows and energies, rather than against them. Keep diaries of what happens at a particular time of year and use them as your own resource in years to come. Look back on them and see the patterns that you need to work with and adjust your workings accordingly. These may then become a resource for others that you work with, or those that follow after.

In addition to noticing the patterns of the energies and tides, take note also of the cultural traditions of your area. What do people habitually do at certain times of the year? How do they celebrate the seasons and points in between? These observations will all give you clues as to what is actually happening at any given time and enable you to plan your own workings appropriately.

I therefore hope that this book can act both as a resource for people in the British Isles and as a template and inspiration for people in other Lands. In either case, use both your outer and inner senses and abilities to find what is appropriate for you, in your local area and the Land that you live on, and you will be working in tune with your Land and the Powers and Spirits that inhabit and enliven it.

Nigel G. Pearson
Suffolk, England
Candlemas 2017

THE WINTER TIDE

꧁ ❄ ꧂

Although due to climate change and other man-made and environmental factors Winter can be a moveable feast these days, it is still a recognisable season in the British Isles and people, plants and animals react to it as such. On an inner, energetic level this is even more true and we are all 'programmed' to react in a certain way at a very basic level of our psyches. At the first hint of a frost or slight chill in the air a thousand different reactions start to take place to prepare us, both mentally and physically, for the long dark ahead. In the animal kingdom, there has already been much secreting away of food for the dark months and many wild beasts will now begin to prepare for hibernation. Those that do not hibernate will be checking up on their stockpiles and putting on as much extra weight as possible to see them through the lean times. The trees, if not already shedding their leaves, will now drop their canopies of gold, red, bronze and green to carpet the ground underfoot and they too will begin to shut down for a long sleep. Other plants and herbs, if annual, will simply wither and die away; if herbaceous and/or perennial they will withdraw their vital energies down into their roots and shed their top foliage, to wait out the long, cold and dark months ahead.

On a human level we too are primed to react in certain ways, if we allow ourselves to be dragged away from our hectic, '24/7' lifestyle and acknowledge a more natural rhythm. We tend to become more sluggish in our thoughts and actions, slowing down like the rest of the natural world around us in an attempt to conserve energy. We feel as though we want to get up later and go to bed earlier, which is triggered by the much shorter days now, particularly after changing the clocks at the end of October, which can lead to quite a shock to the system; by the time we've adjusted it seems like it's dark all day! Some people are particularly affected by this seasonal darkening (usually called SAD these days – Seasonal Affective Disorder) and can become quite ill. Luckily Nature has the answer in the St. John's wort plant (Hypericum perforatum), which is best taken as a tea or tincture and which releases a welcome dose of sunshine into the sufferer's body, but more of that anon.

As the Northern hemisphere tilts further away from the Sun in its annual orbit, certain stars and constellations move out of our range of appreciation and others move into it, bringing in different energies to encounter and with which to work. The influence of Orion the Hunter is strong during this season, as is that of the Seven Sisters, and there are also major meteor showers to be seen. The night sky is often easier and clearer to see during the darker, colder and fresher months – certainly there are more hours of darkness to see it in! – especially if you move away from densely-inhabited areas where the light pollution often obscures much of interest. The heavens seem to be closer to earth at this time of year and you feel as if you could just reach out and pluck down a star or two, all the better to feel the influences of the stellar energies.

Of course, it is also during this, the darkest time of the year, that we celebrate the largest festival dedicated to Light and renewal, that of the Midwinter, call it what you will; the Midwinter festival has absorbed much in its long history – and continues to do so – but still brings a smile to the faces of many in the midst of the darkness, promising as it does a slice of hope that all will not remain as it now is. Many traditions and customs are celebrated at this time, some secular, some not so, and a little bit of magic can easily be included in most things that you do around now, just to make the season a little bit more special and powerful.

However, to start the Winter Tide, we begin with the earthing of the energies released at the Autumn Equinox: those of dissolution, decay and death. Before any renewal can take place we must deal with the energies and residue of the past and that means confronting certain things that we may not wish to see or remember. The spirits of yesteryear see and hear more than we would sometimes wish and it is better to make our peace with and to honour them than to sweep them under the carpet of the year just passed; 'rear' and 'bite' come all too readily to mind!

November

✤✿✤ ✤ ✤✿✤

The Sun rises at approximately 6:55 a.m. and sets at approximately 4:32 p.m. at the beginning of the month.
The image for November, traditionally known as the Black Month, is as follows:

> *In a Garment of Changeable Green and Black upon his Head, a garland of Olives with the fruit in his Left hand. Bunches of Parsnips and Turnips in his Right. His Sign Sagittarius.*

Times & Tides
At the entrance to the Winter of the year comes the darkest feast of all, that of Hallowmas, All Hallows or Hallowe'en.

This is the earthing or manifestation of the energies that were 'released' or commenced on the inner levels at the Autumn Equinox: those of decay, dissolution and death. It is one of the pivotal points of the year and the greatest of the three "Spirit Nights" (the other two being May Eve and Midsummer's Eve). From time immemorial the feast of the Dead or the Ancestors has been observed – not celebrated – around this time of year, finally becoming fixed in our current calendar on the 31st October or the 1st November. Originally the feast would have taken place at various times in different parts of the country, depending on local custom. Some would have observed this time at the Dark of the Moon or after the first frosts, while others would wait for a Full Moon at the end of October or beginning of November, and still others would have waited for an appropriate astrological point. Be that as it may, originally it would not have been a fixed calendar date and those who follow a Natural Religion or Craft still wait for their own certain signs in Nature before observing this time; essentially it must feel right for the Crafter, and particular occurrences and energies must have been observed and sensed, so this feast may actually occur anytime from mid-October to mid-November. Nowadays of course, the Church also has its festivals of remembrance at this time, namely All Saints on November 1st and All Souls on the 2nd. This is shortly followed by St. Martin's Day or Martinmas on the 11th of this month, which is now more usually observed as Armistice Day (although this is often held on the nearest Sunday). St. Martin of Tours, in France, was an avid anti-pagan in the early years of the Church and was instrumental in destroying many sacred groves of the Old Faith, paving the way for the rule of Rome to take its place. It is maybe fitting therefore, that he is remembered at this time of year. Having said all this, what exactly are all these dates commemorating or observing?

Essentially, the observances held at this time are recognising and honouring what has passed, what has gone before, generally, and our own connection to this, specifically, through our own flesh and blood, our Ancestors. All cultures at one point or another in their evolution have practised ancestor-worship in one form or another. It may be that some people deified their ancestors, or turned them into mythical figures of reverence and awe. It may be that some became ghosts or spectres to be feared and warded against. It may also be that they were remembered as heroes or saints to be lauded and emulated. However the people of the past are regarded, they all hold a certain something over us and that is that they have passed beyond this material plane, into that world that is normally veiled and hidden from mere mortals during their lifetime. It is at this time of year, specifically, that we remember what has gone before and honour and respect those who have passed through the veil, in whatever manner, and seek to commune with them in some way, the better to retain some link with our departed kith and kin and to keep hold of or regain what was considered of value. The link may not necessarily be of blood either; we may remember those of our religious belief, faith or practice with whom we wish to retain a link. We may remember those of an organisation or educational establishment, as well as those of the armed forces who, willingly or not, died as a sacrifice to our way of life (which in itself may be considered a magical act). It is at this point in the year – the entrance into the dark and reflective tide – that our minds naturally turn to those who have already passed this way. Seeing the tides of Life ebb and grow dim, observing the drawing back of the energising light of the Sun, the death of plant and not a little animal life, our own mortality seems that much more of a reality and we are both entranced and horrified at the thought. This goes a long way to explain the ambiguous nature of this time of year; part of us is fascinated by the idea of continuing life in another form … and terrified that it might be true and come and get us. Hence the two sides to the type of rites observed now: those of protection and placation, and those of delving into unknown realms.

This is the time when the gates of the Otherworld open up and communion with those of the past may take place; the borders between Life and Death temporarily disappear and the Good Folk, the Fay, ride out on their ritual procession across the Land. It can be a time of initiation for some, when knowledge obtained may advance the individual on their quest into the Mysteries and add to their store of knowledge and experience. There is a strong tradition at the heart of many branches of Natural Craft that the Lordly Ones are actually the spirits of our departed kin in their post-mortem guise, our Ancestors transformed. Their rules, morality and ethics, however, are not ours and they have little interest in our doings and care even less about their effects on us; if they notice us at all it will be in passing, but if we get in their way, their reactions can be dire and terrible. This is one of the reasons that this time of year is feared by most folk – beware lest you attract the attention of the Fay! It is not for nothing that offerings and libations are left out at night and, if they are spoken of at all, the People of the Hills are spoken of by euphemism and with respect, lest they become offended. Approach them in certain ways however, and they may teach and guide the Crafter along the path into the deeper Mysteries and reward them for their efforts and dedication. The tradition of Guising or "disguising" also originates in the attempt to escape the notice of the Other People; by cross-dressing, dressing in spirit, demon or otherworldly manner, it was hoped that their attention would not be attracted and people would be left unharmed. "Fairies" are not nice people in general and can do serious harm, so be warned.

On a slightly different note, it is customary amongst those who keep to a natural path to observe this time of year with a feast or gathering. As said previously, it is not a time of celebration — but of remembrance of what has gone before. To do this many people prepare and consume a special meal, in company with others of their kind, or by themselves, but never "alone". This meal is called by some the "Dumb Supper" and can actually be used as a magical rite of evocation of the Shades of the Dead if performed in a certain way, but for Natural Craft it is a coming together, literally a 'communion', with those who are already gone, to honour and remember them. It can be observed in the following manner.

Lay your table in your usual way, as for a special family dinner or gathering of friends, using your best crockery, cutlery and any natural and seasonal decorations that you may feel appropriate. Set enough places at the table for each person who will be attending, plus one extra setting. This is for the "Unknown Guest" and should be set at a place of honour, or with a special chair. Light a single candle and set it by this place; this represents the essential soul-principle that is being honoured on this night and acts as a beacon to guide and welcome the Spirit Guest. Serve a special meal which reflects the likes and tastes of your guests and time of the year, i.e. use seasonal vegetables and fruits from as local a source as possible and some locally-reared meat or poultry; serve as many courses as you feel appropriate. As each course is served, also place some on the plate or in the bowl of the Unknown Guest, as well as any drink being served in a separate glass, and treat that place as if it was for a V.I.P. guest at the gathering. The conversation should not be dour or funereal, nor should it be frivolous and jolly, but centre mainly on things that have gone before, without remorse or sadness. You may wish to speak of family members who have passed on, or other relatives or friends and people you have known. Members of a group – of whatever nature – may wish to recall past members and speak of the times and things they shared together. If you are alone, this can be an especially poignant communion with the past, giving you pause to think of all that has gone before in your life and put it into perspective. In this case the Unknown Guest may be treated as a best friend or confidante, to whom you may reminisce in safety. As you move through your courses, leave them intact in front of the special setting and do not clear them away. Once you have finished, clear all else away and leave only this setting, set with a single, lighted candle and leave this for the night. This is a symbolic sacrifice to the Ancestors and the Spirits who care for your house and family line and is a powerful connection with the past, whatever our view of it. You may wish to sit up with your group, or alone, and commune with the Powers and Spirits on this night, performing whatever other rites are customary for you, either before or after the meal. Sometimes the Shades called upon or remembered at the meal may take on visible or semi-visible appearance and join you in your observances; if this happens, consider yourselves blessed and touched by Otherworldly fortunes. It is possible that some form of communion may take place during this night; if you are given the opportunity to ask questions, consider carefully before asking and value the answers and knowledge given. In the morning, the remains of the meal should be taken out and left somewhere in the wild, as a physical offering to the Land and our connection to it (it will also help feed any local wildlife that may not have put enough away as well!).

The 11th of this month, as well as being Martinmas, is also given to the remembrance and respect of the spirits of the Blackthorn tree, called by some the "Lunantishees". It is fitting that these spirits are honoured at this tide of the year, as theirs is a dark reputation. The wood of the Blackthorn, well known for its viciously sharp and dangerous thorns, has for centuries been used for clubs and stout staves, used both for defence and offence. Its sinister reputation for things dark and dangerous is enhanced by the fact that it is traditionally the wood from which comes the renowned "blasting rod" of malefic Witches and it can also form the Stang of the Master of a Traditional Witchcraft coven. It is used, when necessary, for cursing or ill-wishing those that have caused the Craft harm or who have betrayed their oaths; not in retribution, but purely in self-defence and in protection of the Craft ways and practices. If one breaks a solemn oath, given before the great Powers, one must expect some comeback, as these oaths are not given lightly nor do they deal in fairy dust; great energies can be invoked from them. However, the Blackthorn is also the provider of that great fruit, the sloe, which has been used for many years as the basis for sloe gin, a much-relished liqueur. Historically, this has also been used both as a laxative and a digestive (hence drinking a small glass of sloe gin after a large meal) and also, confusingly to many, as a cure for diarrhoea! It needs to be remembered, however, that it is the fruits that are used as a laxative and the leaves that are used to cure diarrhoea; don't get them the wrong way around! It is a very astringent and sour fruit, which can act in either direction and is best picked – carefully! – after the first frosts have softened it up a little, making it easier to digest and/or extract the juice from it. A libation of sloe gin or, failing that, of milk and honey to sweeten their temperament, is very welcome to the Blackthorn spirits at this time and goes a long way towards getting them on your side in any emergency, as they are woefully neglected by most people.

November 20th is St. Edmund's Day, the alternative – and original – patron saint of England. He was ruler of the ancient kingdom of East Anglia and was martyred by an invading Danish army on this day in the year 869 CE, for refusing to give up both his (Christian) faith and his crown. He was tied to a tree, speared and shot full of arrows. After being killed, Edmund was beheaded and his head was thrown into a nearby thicket; his followers later returned to recover the body and found the head being guarded by a Wolf. This was one of the sacred animals of the royal East Anglian line (known as the Wuffingas) and this instance added to the sacredness of the event. Known also as Deadman's Day, this time is still honoured and acknowledged by many Crafters and Witches as being a sacred day of one of the ancient sacrificial kings, who died for their Land and People irrespective of the Faith that they held.

The tide of All Hallows can cast a long shadow during the month of November, depending on when the observation occurs, and much time can be taken up with its aftermath. It may bring up long-forgotten memories and emotions that must be considered and dealt with, or other facets of the life-cycle that need due examination, but eventually its time fades and other occasions arise. Near the end of the month, on the 23rd, the feast of St. Clement is celebrated and this brings to mind different, if associated, energies. St. Clement was one of the first martyrs, dying early in the Christian era, some say 1st century, others say 4th century, who has become the patron saint of both sailors and blacksmiths, although it is with the latter that he is most generally associated. Not much is known about him, certainly little if any historical evidence survives, but the fact that he shares his day with the Anglo-Saxon deity Wayland, and was himself a smith, makes him particularly connected with the horse trade. Called "Old Clem" in rural areas, he was particularly honoured with parades where his image was carried around the local area whilst money was collected, and later he would be feasted and toasted by a gathering of the local smiths. His association with Wayland and the fact that they share a day may suggest that he took over the celebrations of the Saxon deity, or similar, at some point and that is why he is now particularly associated with horses and their trade. The "Society of the Horseman's Word" is certainly known to reverence him and, although his symbol is officially an anchor, it is with the horseshoe that he is most associated. This symbol was once to be seen hanging over many a forge with its points downwards to pour out the luck, and also over many a cottage door with the points up to keep in the luck. If any horseshoe were to be seen hanging outside a gatepost with the "heels" downwards, it was and is often considered an error; however, it is a little-known sign to a travelling smith (there were many once upon a time) that a horse needed shoeing and not necessarily a mistake on the part of the occupant. The water that the horseshoe was quenched in, once forged in the sacred fires of the forge, itself the subject of much enquiry into its composition, was known as "Thunder Water". This is still greatly valued by Practitioners of Natural Craft to this day for its power and use in magic and spells. It is of great use in calling upon the Underworld shades and in communicating with their Lord, the great horseman Himself and leader of the Wild Hunt, especially during the Winter Tide. It adds power and potency to all forms of aqueous potions and can be sprinkled around the compass, both as a protective measure and to further enhance the workings within.

Andermass or St. Andrew's Day, on the 30th, rounds off the feast days of November. The patron saint of Scotland, St. Andrew the Apostle, never actually set foot there, unlike in Greece and Russia where he is also patron. He was crucified on the X-shaped cross which is his symbol, in or around 64 CE at Patras in Achaia, where he was buried. However, his remains were later taken to Constantinople (modern Istanbul), and then removed in 1210 CE to Amalfi in the South of Italy, where they are reputed to remain. Relics of the saint were said to have been brought to Scotland around 732 CE by Bishop Acca, after he had been banished from Hexham and sought refuge with the Pictish King, Angus MacFergus; some time later the King had a vision the night before a battle of a great X-shaped cross flaming over the sky, and subsequently won the battle the next day. This began the devotion of the Scots to the saint, which continues to this day. His Day was, and still is, honoured with great feasting and merrymaking, the high point being the Andermass Dinner which, of course, includes haggis and whisky. Although not a native of these Isles, St. Andrew has found a ready home in the North and continues to elicit much support amongst those of a natural spirituality.

Flora

I mentioned earlier that at this tide many people start to suffer from depression, due in part to the lack of light, and that this could be greatly alleviated in most by the use of a tincture of St. John's wort (*Hypericum perforatum*). Whilst I intend to go into the details of this herb elsewhere (see Summer Tide – June), as it is essentially a herb of sunlight and Midsummer, I would like to spend some time here on the making of herbal tinctures for medicinal purposes. They are of great benefit in many, many conditions, cost very little to prepare, use the natural energies of the plants and the Land and often succeed where orthodox medicine fails – I know this from years of personal experience of working with herbal preparations and in taking them myself. A tincture is essentially plant material that has been infused in high-proof alcohol for a period, the residue filtered off and kept, and the plant material being returned to the Land. The benefit of a tincture over an infusion (tea), is that it is stronger; the alcohol extracts more of the active ingredients and, being alcohol-based, it gets into the bodily system more rapidly. It also has the advantage of being able to be used topically on the skin and can also be used in healing baths; in both cases it is absorbed directly through the pores into the body. Tinctures of course may be bought from reputable herbalists and high-street shops these days, but there is something much more comforting and magical in making your own and the technique is very simple. You also have the added advantage of collecting the plant material in season yourself and knowing where it came from, and also being able to request the aid of the plant spirit and give thanks and offerings in its place. So, the method is as follows.

Decide what volume of tincture you are going to make and obtain a vessel to hold that much. You don't want any metal to come into contact with the liquid, so a jam jar is out, or any metal-topped container. I find that an old fashioned, glass Kilner jar is best (the old, hinged-lid pickle jar) as it has a wide mouth and no metal contacts on the inside. Pack the jar with a third of the amount of plant material as the amount of liquid you are going to use. Although I abhor metric systems, they are easier to use than imperial in this case and I will give an example. Suppose you have a half-litre jar (500ml), you will need a third of that in weight of dried herb, so just under 170 gm. (If using the fresh herb you will need double the amount of dried). Put the herb in first, then pour over the liquid. Any high-proof alcohol will do, but I find vodka to be the best, as it is totally clear and has no taste or smell of its own to mar the finished tincture. Give the jar a good shake and put it away somewhere warm and dark to do its work; somewhere like an airing cupboard is ideal. Leave it for 10-14 days, giving it a good shake once or twice a day. Use your instinct to 'feel' when it is ready, then filter the whole lot through a jelly bag or a few layers of clean cotton or muslin into a clean bottle of appropriate size (give the material a good squeeze to get out as much of the liquid that has been absorbed by the plant as you can). Make up to the original volume with fresh, spring water and screw on the cap securely. Do not just discard the remains of the plant material; put it on your compost heap or, better still, take it back and place it at the foot of the plant that gave it, with a few words of thanks. You now have your tincture ready for use. This will keep well for a long while, a year or two, as it is an alcohol-based substance and this acts as a preservative. The dosage for any given person will vary as we are all individuals; this will depend on size, age, weight and gender, but here are some guidelines. If using a pipette to measure the dosage in drops, the standard dose is 40 drops for a 1:3 ratio tincture (this equals 2½ml) If using a 5ml (standard) teaspoon, give half a teaspoon per dose for adults and half that (20 drops) for children under teenage and you should be fine. For very small children check with a qualified herbalist first. You need two doses per day for a chronic condition and three for an acute one. Continue treatment for a week to 10 days after symptoms have disappeared to ensure a clean bill of health.

During this month is a prime time to be picking rosehips (Rosa canina), as the first frosts will have softened them and made them ripe for plucking and using in various preparations. I recommend using them first in tincture form and secondly in a syrup. Rosehips are a very rich source of vitamin C and have been used for fending off and curing colds and Winter sniffles from well before the time when people knew what vitamin C was. Weight for weight, rosehips contain 20 times the amount of vitamin C as oranges, they are native to the Land, are free to pick and their production causes no harm to the environment. Collect all you can, but be careful of the thorns. They lend themselves well to being dried; cut them lengthwise in half and lay on some paper in a baking tray. Place them in an oven at about 100°C and leave the door open slightly to allow the moisture to escape, otherwise they can become rotten. When they have dried thoroughly you need to place them in a sieve and shake them hard, as the hips contain small hairs which can irritate and enflame the throat if swallowed and need to be got rid of. (This irritant ability is often made use of by children who want a natural 'itching powder'; a small pinch of the fresh or dried seeds down the back of the neck can cause hours of amusement!) When sieved, store them in a clean, dry airtight container, ready for use. They will keep for a year or two if properly dried, but best to collect fresh each year. I have already given the method for making a tincture and rosehips lend themselves well to this, fresh or dried (but mind the little hairs), so I will explain how to make the syrup.

This is excellent not only for colds and 'flu during the Winter, but also those irritating sore throats and coughs that go with them. Collect as many rosehips as you want, put them in a pan and just cover them with fresh water. Let them simmer gently for about 20-30 minutes and then filter off the liquid through a fine sieve or cloth, making sure to extract all the hairs. For every pint of liquid you have remaining, add one pound of demerara sugar or local honey. Gently heat these ingredients together until they are well dissolved and combined and bottle in clean, warm jars to store. To use, place one tablespoon of the mixte in a mug and add hot water. This not only makes a delicious drink, but does you good as well!

Another plant that is especially useful around now is the Burdock (*Arctium lappa*). Also known as "Gypsy Rhubarb" and "Thorny Burr", the tall, branching spikes can be seen standing in ditches and by waterways at this time of the year, with their furry, sticky burrs etched against the skyline on a bleak and frosty morning. Children love theses burrs and often employ them in games of catch and chase, pelting one another with the burrs that stick all over them – and on dogs' fur too, as I know to my own cost; it's a devil to remove them once they get deeply embedded in the fur. Burdock can be a great tonic at this time of the year, for various complaints. Although the leaves can be used in medicine also, it is the root that concerns me here.. It is now that most of the foliage above ground has decayed and rotted off – apart from the burrs of course – and all the essential nutrients and goodness have been withdrawn below ground into the roots, as with many other perennial herbs. The roots can be quite large and extensive, so make sure you have a good strong spade with you if attempting to dig them up. However, only take one at a time, from a large area where they grow in profusion, as digging up the root obviously kills the whole plant, as opposed to just taking foliage. Once obtained, washed and scrubbed gently, the root can be used fresh or dried and chopped, but I would advise the latter as it keeps much longer. Use the drying method given above for rosehips. Once prepared Burdock can be used for treating many ills that occur at this time of year. It is one of the most powerful and reliable blood tonics in herbal medicine, which is ideal for cleansing the system of any impurities as we head into the dark season. It is also an ideal liver tonic, which should help with all the excesses of the coming season. Mostly it is used for conditions such as arthritis, gout and boils, all of which can become a problem in the Winter Tide. As it contains high doses of iron, sulphur and B-vitamins, it is also excellent in combating anaemia, which many people are prone to at this time. It is better taken in small doses over a longer period, than large doses over short periods. You can take it as an infusion (tea), as a tincture, in which case make sure you have some prepared well in advance of when you need it, or as a decoction, which I shall explain in detail later on. As a tea, take half a cup twice daily. As a tincture take half a teaspoon twice a day and as a decoction, half a cup once a day. Continue this through the Winter Tide and you should be free from most aches and pains.

Rosemary (*Rosmarinus officinalis*), or "Dew of the Sea", is also an appropriate plant to look at now, as, being an evergreen, it is one of the few plants that still retains its foliage at this time of year. This is an especially potent plant for this tide, lending strength to searches into the past and beyond the veil as it does, and is a particular favourite of many Crafters, having a wide range of uses. "Rosemary for remembrance" is a well-known adage and, although used by the Sue Ryder Foundation in its fundraising campaigns, harks back much further. It was a Roman custom to place bunches of Rosemary in the coffin at funerals and it would be planted around tombs later on. During the Mediaeval period in England it was used as an antidote to the Black Death – unfortunately not overly successfully – and so its association with death and remembrance has a long history. In some forms of Natural Craft to this day, Rosemary is one of the plants woven into a wreath that is used to garland the Stang, representing the Lord of Death, at the Hallowmas rites. Its strong and pungent smell is a distinctive addition to incense at this time of year and it may also be used in rites of divination for the clarity of thought it brings. It is sometimes baked into cakes to be eaten during the Hallowmas observances and is hung up around the ritual area in honour and remembrance of the Ancestors at this time. It is also dedicated to the Virgin Mary in Christian tradition and was hung up in the home as a ward against witches and evil spirits, and against the Night Mare when placed under pillows. Its strong and fragrant smell makes it exceedingly attractive in any warding or protective actions and it has been used for centuries in this manner, retaining its scent long after the leaves have dried out. Medicinally it is used for a variety of purposes. It is a very strong antiseptic, so a wash (weak tea) made of the leaves can be used to bathe cut fingers and hands after the heavy pruning often needed in the garden at this time of year. Its actions include increasing the amount of oxygen in the bloodstream and for that reason it is often used as a tea for migraine and severe headaches, sipped at regular intervals throughout the day. Its antidepressant qualities lead it to being used by those who suffer from the lack of light at this time of year and, as a strong circulatory tonic, it aids in keeping fingers and toes warm, aids the heart in its action and fends off some of the pains of arthritis in the joints, as well as warming the muscular ache that is associated with it. The pure essential oil of Rosemary may also be used for any of the above purposes, and also a couple of drops in a warm bath work wonders for tired and aching bodies and stuffy heads, but do not use it neat on the skin, always dilute in a vegetable-based oil first.

Seasonal Skies

Ushering in the Winter Tide in the night sky is the great constellation of Orion, second only to The Plough or Big Dipper in brightness in the Northern latitudes. After a long absence from our skies for the Summer, Orion returns around the end of October and beginning of November and reaches its height during December. With its main stars Betelgeuse, Rigel and Bellatrix and the lesser, but still bright stars of its belt, Orion, surnamed "the Hunter", announces the season of the Wild Hunt; that chaotic race of damned and lost spirits which cross the night sky, pursued by the horses and hounds of the spectral warriors, led by the Lord of the Dead Himself. It is a great and beautiful thing to stand beneath this constellation on a clear night and gaze up with awe at its mighty stars, feeling the pull of the wild energies as it leads you on in an ecstatic chase that can last half the night. There are many myths about Orion, most revolving around his death – appropriate for this time of year. It is said that the great hunter often boasted of his skill and claimed that he could kill all living beasts. This enraged the Earth Mother, who sent a scorpion to sting and kill him and this can be seen borne out in the stars; as the constellation of Scorpius rises in the East, Orion sinks despatched into the West. In an alternative version of the story, it is said that the Maiden Huntress was tricked into mortally wounding Orion with one of her arrows whilst he was swimming and, in remorse, placed him in the heavens for all eternity. He has been compared to the Anglo-Saxon mythic figure of Earendel who was also a warrior and huntsman, and also to Wayland the Smith, whose feast day is appropriately in this month. This connects the energies of the constellation of Orion both with the celestial forces of internal illumination or enlightenment and also with the darker energies of the fires in the Underworld, themselves a symbol of internal or personal spiritual illumination and advanced knowledge. Continuing the themes begun at Hallowmas, Orion's stellar energies are of great use in initiatory rites held at this time, enabling the postulant to delve deeper and travel further into the Mysteries than would otherwise be possible, riding the train of the Wild Hunter and His pack. For the Egyptians, he represented Osiris, Lord of the Underworld, who ensured that the previous pharaoh would be reborn as Horus, to continue his reign as his successor. It can therefore be seen that this constellation has long and close links with the dead, the Underworld and this time of year and is well worth marking and studying by those who follow a natural system.

Around the 16th-18th of the month, seek out the constellation of Leo in the South-East and, after the middle of the night you will be rewarded with a rush of spectacular shooting stars. This is the Leonid meteor shower that puts on a great show every year.

Towards the end of the month, around the 21st, the Sun enters into the astrological sign of Sagittarius, which, by coincidence, is also a constellation of a hunter. It can be seen low down in the West and, pictorially, it is imaged as aiming an arrow straight at Scorpius; the hunter defending the hunter? Although this constellation is known as "the Archer" and is associated with war and fire, it has also been linked with the wise centaur Chiron (although properly this is the constellation of Centaurus). It can be seen here that although the warrior 'ethic' is strong at this time of the year, with two martial constellations significant to the presiding energies, the principle of wisdom is also present, which tempers and balances it. The energies of November, although redolent of death, decay, the hunt and the Underworld are not totally wild and mindless; there is a pattern and a knowledge behind them – one might say a natural order and design – which leads the discerning seeker onto further depth and knowledge than would immediately be apparent.

The night sky is not the only interesting natural phenomenon at this time of year; the weather itself can be exceedingly changeable and eye-catching. The initial and general feeling that November brings to mind is often dank, dark and dismal and this can certainly be true. Taking a walk around now can indeed be a dismal experience with the overriding smell of wet, rotting vegetation and the omnipresent threat of a cold burst of rain, or something worse. Chilly fogs abound and the harsh frosts around dawn can seem personally directed at you as you take the dogs for their morning walk, not to mention the biting winds. This may all have given rise to the country rhyme that goes as follows:

> *No warmth, no cheerfulness, no healthful ease,*
> *No comfortable feel in any member –*
> *No shade, no shine, no butterflies no bees,*
> *No fruits, no flowers, no leaves, no birds –*
> *November!*

However, this is not always the case and we are often surprised by a sudden burst of warmth, bright sunny days and a lift in the spirits that can last nearly a week. Indeed, despite his rather desperate and gloomy reputation, as already described above, St. Martin's Day is often known as the "Little Summer" (see also St. Luke in October) when the weather turns back for a brief spell. Not so long ago this day was celebrated with feasting and drinking and much merry-making and was also known as "Pack-Rag Day". This was because, as the weather was still fine and employment was often arranged in the country on a yearly basis, if they were not content where they were the servants packed their possessions and left the farms to find employment elsewhere, the roads still being fit to travel – just. St. Martin, however, may not have looked with favour on all this jollity, as he is the patron saint of reformed drunkards! As an alternative to this, it is said that if the wind is from the South-West on MartinmasDay it will remain in that quarter until after Christmas: "On St. Martin's Day, Winter is on the way." This was the season when cattle were killed and dried in great brick chimneys, for Winter use, because of the lack of fresh fodder (this has been practised for very many centuries). The meat was known as Martinmas beef or mutton and whole sides or flitches of pork were cured likewise, giving rise to the saying: *'It's Martinmas will come, as it does to every Hog.'*

Whatever the weather, there is always a saying to go with it: *'If November be fine we'll have a cold Winter. If November be bad, the Winter be fine!'* and 'You can't brush away a November fog with a fan!'

Hearth & Home

On a more domestic front, it is time to look ahead and prepare for the coming Midwinter celebrations. The third Sunday in the month is often known as "Stir-up Sunday"; this is supposedly from the church collect of that day, which states, "*Stir up, we beseech thee, O Lord, the wills of Thy faithful people.*" However, it is remembered much more for the fact that this is the traditional day for the making of Christmas puddings and young lads would go around the houses singing: *'Stir up we beseech thee, the pudding in the pot, And when we get home, we'll eat the lot!'* A much more welcome meaning I'm sure you'll agree!

This is also the time to look to the protection of your own home and hearth. The dark time may not be filled with evil spirits and demons out to get you at every moment, but there are beings and energies abroad, particularly at this time, that can be detrimental to the good working and harmony of the home and it is a wise person who puts precautions in place before there is any trouble. In times gone by each town and village would have its own "Ward". This was the protection of a place at night by spiritual guardians, both human and non-human. Often this was a job carried out unknown to the local population, usually by members of a certain family or families who passed the responsibility down through the generations. They would join with the local Land spirits and 'stand guard' each night against any malignant energies or spirits or against spiritual attacks by ill-wishers. Sadly, this tradition has now lapsed in most places, but it is ideally adapted for the protection of the home, either by an individual or by a group of family members. It is fairly simple in design, but powerful in execution and effect, but does take a lot of effort and control on the part of the operator(s). It also takes some familiarity with your local Land Wights (spirits) and an ease of communication with them, which does take some practice (for advice on how to go about this, see my previous work, Treading the Mill; details in the Bibliography). Assuming this familiarity, here is the procedure to adopt.

After going to bed at night, lie flat on your back, arms at your sides and compose yourself as for deep meditation. Breathe deeply several times and relax all the muscles in your body, releasing all your tensions and cares of the day. DO NOT FALL ASLEEP! Once you are perfectly at ease and have obtained that 'between' state, rise up from your body and through the ceiling, until you are floating just above the roof of your house. (If you are able to achieve full projection then so much the better. However, a strongly-visualised image of doing this is just as effective). Go to the Northernmost point of the boundary of your property and face outwards. Raise your arms and make this Call, either out loud or mentally, but do project it strongly.

> *Northwards stand I,*
> *To the great Powers of the Land I make this Call.*
> *By your power,*
> *May this Place be kept safe from all foes,*
> *Guarded against all ills.*
> *Joined together, your power with mine,*
> *May no evil have the cunning,*
> *No man nor spirit have the power,*
> *To pass through this Ward.*
> *By your power and mine do I set this seal.*

Bow respectfully to the North and move round to the East, then South, then West and repeat the Call and bow at each direction. (Whilst bowing, it is as well to wait for some form of acknowledgement that your Call has been answered.) As you pass from direction to direction, see yourself leaving a strong trail of burning, blue-white fire, flowing in your wake and surrounding your property. Finish by returning to the North to complete the circle of protective fire. Finally, position yourself at the centre of your protective circle and raise your arms above your head, as you do so 'pulling' the boundary fire into a cover above your home. Lower your arms now to shoulder level and from there, 'push' the fire down to cover you below. This must be done with total concentration and visualisation to be fully effective. Once achieved to your satisfaction you may allow yourself to drift off to sleep, secure in the knowledge that your home and loved ones are protected through the time of darkness. This is a very powerful method of protection when performed properly, but it does rely on a good working relationship with your local Land Wights, so do make every effort to contact them. Work on a level of mutual respect and make frequent offerings to the spirits of the wild in gratitude for their help.

Fauna

With the darkening of the year, we turn our minds also to our furred and feathered kin and the preparations they too are making for the Winter. Not all will be preparing in the same way as some hibernate and some do not, others even journeying from distant lands to be with us for this time.

In the case of the Red Deer (*Cervus elaphus*) preparations take on a decidedly 'robust' nature. It is the time of the annual "rut", the mating of the stags with the hinds that are in season. The Red Deer is the largest, native British land mammal and the second largest in Europe. They tend to grow larger in England than in Scotland, but the Scottish deer are purer stock. A lot of the English animals have interbred with the introduced Sika deer (Cervus nippon) over the years to create a somewhat hybrid animal; it is thought that not long into the future, the only pure-blood Red Deer left will be in the Highlands and Islands. The main habitat of this animal is either woodland or patchy heathland, where they feed mostly on the shoots of trees and shrubs, or heather, grass and other low-growing vegetation such as mosses, although in hard Winters they resort to the bark of certain species of trees. The male deer is called a "stag", which used to refer to the males of many other species as well but has now become more specific and after its fifth year it can also be referred to as a "hart". The female is usually referred to as a "hind" and the young as "calves"; the male calf in its second year with its first antlers is called a "brocket". The word "rut" is Middle English, coming from the Latin "rugire" meaning "to roar", and this is certainly the sound that is heard at this time of year. The rut begins in late October, when the males start to collect together their harems of females, but reaches its climax near the middle of November, when the competition really heats up. The roaring of the stags is both a declaration of ownership of their group of hinds and also a challenge to other males to come and try their luck. The fighting can be ferocious and can sometimes lead to the death of one or even both contenders. Before the rut, the adult males who will be in competition gain many pounds in weight and the neck muscles enlarge in preparation for the head-to-head battles. The soft velvet that has covered the antlers all Summer is now scraped off and these fearsome weapons are revealed in all their glory. Many stags in Britain can claim antlers of 12 points or "tines", but on the continent 20 or more is not uncommon. These bony swords are thrashed and sharpened on the ground by tearing up huge chunks of grass and soil, sometimes even the bark or branches from trees. The fighting can be fierce and will only stop when one contender backs down or is so injured as to be unable to continue. The victor then mates with the hinds that are in season and passes his genes on to the next generation. Contrary to much common belief, the antlers are not dropped after the rut, but retained during the Winter and dropped the next Spring, around March/April time. The branching horns are of great use during the Winter if it snows, to brush it away and get at the moss and grass underneath, or as a defence against predators that may try to attack, although natural ones are now almost non-existent. When the antlers drop in the Spring, they are often chewed and eaten by the deer, to regain some of the vitamins and minerals it took to grow them originally, especially if their diet is deficient in those things. This explains the lack of antlers just lying around each year. The young are born between mid-May and early June, and stay with their mothers for up to three years, if male, and in the group of hinds if female. Red Deer are often called "Faerie Cattle" in the Highlands, as they are under the especial protection of the Good Folk and they are believed to be milked by them on the tops of mountains, above the snow line. The mythical White Hart is actually not quite so mythical, white being a not uncommon colour amongst the stags. However, a White Hart is representative of the Male Powers below the Land, the Lord of the Mound in the Underworld, and should be treated with caution if encountered; he may lead you on a merry chase from which you will never return quite the same! The Black Stag is seen by many Traditional Crafters as a symbol of the Horned Lord in His Winter guise, who takes over from the White Stag at this time of year; their combat, which has many mythical overtones and parallels, is seen in the annual rut, the winner leading his "herd" through the dark times ahead.

The Badger (*Meles meles*), is another large native of these Isles and may be glimpsed in its foraging at dusk at this time of year. Also known as the "Badget", "Bawson", "Burran", "Earth Dog", "Grey", "Gripper", "Guisard" and, most commonly by the Old English (from Old Celtic) term, "Brock". The Badger is generally a much-loved and admired animal, being considered as wise as the owl and as a kindly creature. The male, known as a "boar", can be up to one metre in length and weigh over 12 kg; the larger of the females ("sow"), being not much smaller. They are fairly common in the South-West of the country, less so in the East, East Anglia and Scotland. They are almost entirely nocturnal, coming out at night to forage for their principle food, which consists of earthworms, slugs and snails, although they are omnivorous and will eat most things, including carrion, young birds and other small animals. They particularly like wasps and bees' nests, which they will dig up for the juicy larvae, being protected from the stings by their rough and shaggy fur. They live in burrows, known as "setts", which are usually to be found in woodland, but any sheltered spot is sufficient. Setts can be very extensive indeed, including separate sleeping, nursing and lavatory sections and these are kept exceptionally clean and tidy. Strangely, Badgers often share their setts with other animals and Foxes, Rabbits and Badgers can all be found in the same sett at the one time. Although much respected by most, Badgers have been persecuted for centuries for no particular reason and have often been subject to the cruel 'sport' of Badger baiting, where a lone animal is placed in a confined area and set upon by one or more dogs. It can take a long time for the Badger to die, as, when cornered these are fierce and dangerous animals, having powerful jaws and shoulder muscles, not to mention wickedly sharp talons and teeth. A Badger can easily maim or kill a single dog, can bite clean through a man's foot and its teeth can leave an imprint on a steel spade. Although never killed for this reason when being baited, Badger meat makes very good eating, especially the thighs which can be smoked like hams or used in stews. The fat was used until very recently for oils and salves which were used to relieve lung conditions and shortness of breath. Badger fur is famously used for shaving brushes, and also for sporrans, in which case sometimes the whole pelt is used, the head included which is folded over the front as a closing flap. Recently there has been much concern over them being the cause of the spread of bovine tuberculosis in cattle in the West Country; whilst it is true that some Badgers do carry the disease, many are shot and killed in other less savoury manners, just to find out if they do – most do not. Cattle are only culled when it is proven a herd has been infected. It is a little-known fact that Badgers can mourn for and bury their own dead, this being known as a "Badger funeral". One or more animals have been observed to excavate a shallow grave and then drag the deceased to it and cover it over, all the time making short sniffing and whining noises; many Badgers from road kills have been known to disappear in this manner. Linked closely with the Underworld powers, the Badger is a caring and powerful spirit animal to work with when investigating the Otherworldly realms, particularly at this time of year.

A migrant visitor to our shores at this time of year, in large numbers, similar to flocking starlings, is the Redwing (*Turdus iliacus*), the smallest member of the Thrush family.

Most closely resembling the Song Thrush, it is also known colloquially as the "Pop", "Swine Pipe", "Whindle", "Winnard" and "Little Feltfare",and it often accompanies this bird in its migrations. Living mostly in Scandinavia, where it numbers in the millions, over 750,00 can migrate here at this time for the Winter, although only about 60-80 pairs tend to breed here, mainly in Scotland but recently also in Kent. The flocks arrive in November in vast swarms and can be identified by the orange-red patches on their flanks and underwing areas, although the buff stripes over the eyes and through the moustache are often more noticeable. As they cross the North Sea they make an eerie 'rushing' noise, which is known as the "Herring Spear" or "Herring Piece" which can be quite unnerving when heard on a dark, moonless night. This has sometimes linked them with the flying Wild Hunt as it rushes on its way and is a clear indication that the dark times have once more arrived.

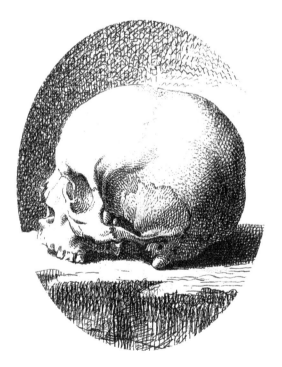

December

✤✤✤ ✤ ✤✤✤

The Sun rises at approximately 7:45 a.m. and sets at approximately 3:53 p.m. at the beginning of the month.

This is the image for December which, like November, is traditionally also known as the Black Month:

A horrid and fearful aspect, clad in Irish-rags, or coarse Freez girt upon him, upon his Head three or four Night Caps, and over them a Turkish Turburt; Its Nose red, his Mouth and beard clog'd with Isicles, at his back a bundle of Holly, Ivy or Mistletoe, holding in fir'd Mittens the Sign of Capricornus.

Seasonal Skies

As the Winter Tide moves into December, we enter the darkest period of the year. Although the length of the days and nights are roughly the same as in January, December always seems to be darker and bleaker, which is probably why most attention is focused on the festivities towards the end of the month; but more of that later. The night sky is normally particularly clear at this time and is good for observing the heavens and the celestial images to be found there.

The constellation of Draco the Dragon is rather large and shapeless, coiling randomly around the North Celestial Pole. It has four major stars, the brightest being Thuban in its body and Rastaban and Eltanin at its head. Thuban was at one time the Pole Star, around 3000 BCE, but has since been displaced by precession. The Dragon was also once winged, when it was first named by the Mesopotamian cultures, but had its wings 'lopped off' by the Greeks later on, to create the constellation of Ursa Minor (the Little Bear), just above it. Draco reaches its culmination around June 22nd, about the time of the Summer Solstice, so now it is at about its lowest point in the night sky, just above the horizon when looking North. In ancient cultures, the Dragon was associated with the Titans, the ancient Powers that were displaced by the younger, incoming deities, and also with the depths and guardianship. It was overcome only with great effort and placed among the stars in honour of its great struggles to protect those things which should not always see the light of day. The Dragon or Serpent has always been linked with the Land and treasure, energy or secret knowledge in this country. The fact that it is now at its lowest ebb speaks loudly of the quiescence of the energies in the Land and of the rest that the Earth Powers are enjoying at this time. The link with the Land energies and the Underworld can perhaps be intimated by the loss of its wings, hence making it a constellation connected with more worldly energies, rather than transcendent ones. It is, however, a time when knowledge and mysteries may be sought in the dark, hidden places that are little visited by most people, as opposed to the bright and obvious things that are heralded by the light of the Summer Tide. In the brightest of lights, everything is obvious and clear; it is in the dark where things must be sought out and are more rewardingly won! Use the energies of Draco, gently, to look within at whatever project you may be working on at this time, be that magical, mundane or even yourself. Quiet, inner contemplation on a thing often brings more to light than was originally apparent. The stellar energies of the Dragon can also be linked with the inner, serpent fire that all humans possess and which, at certain times and with certain techniques may be roused. Profound inner contemplation on the nature and correspondence between these two energies would be well advised during the Dark time, prior to actual use of these energies in the Summer of the year.

During this month, there is another meteor shower, around the 13th/14th, appearing to originate from the 'head' of Castor in the Gemini cluster and named after it – the Geminid meteors. If, as is often the case, you have a series of clear nights at this time, it is well worth staying up to watch this phenomenon; it is like a pre-Yule fireworks display, created especially for this time of year!

Although for most of this month the Sun resides in the sign of Sagittarius, around the 21st it passes into the astrological sign of Capricorn. This sign is known as the constellation of the Sea Goat, first conceived of by the Assyro-Babylonians in the Middle-East and connected with their deity Oannes, purveyor of wisdom. Later the Greeks associated it with Poseidon, calling it his offspring, and also with Pan, the deity of Arcady and the uncontrolled and wild powers of the natural world, frequently represented as a totally chaotic force. Normally associated with the element of Water, there is a strong Earth link here, which connects strongly with the Land at this time of the year. Capricorn, the Sea Goat, is known to have two natures, the other being the Mountain

Goat. Poseidon, whose symbol is the trident, was originally an Earth deity, known as "Earth-Shaker" because of his liking for creating earthquakes. Pan is the chaotic Power of unregenerate nature, whose character Capricorn takes on in this guise. It will now be understood that far from being of a watery nature, this constellation represents the chaotic energies that are unleashed at this time of year, as the Winter Solstice changes the inner tides and the Lord of Misrule, the Jester, the Fool presides over the festivities. Contact with these energies at this time can lead to some interesting insights into the nature of reality, if you really let go and follow the unrestrained energies that this time represents.

This month is subject to every type of weather which is fatal to plants of a tender nature, however on a slightly lighter note, although December has not much weather lore related to it, it is interesting to see that according to folklore *"a green Christmas means a fat churchyard"*. This seems borne out by experience as if the weather is mild then there are no frosts to kill off the viruses that abound at this time of year and many elderly people are carried off by Winter chills and 'flu. The so-called "Winter-vomiting bug" has been virulent in recent years and, unfortunately, many hospital mortuaries have been full to overflowing. On this theme, it is important that Christmas Day be fine, warm and bright to ensure a good Spring and few late frosts. Frosts ruin apple blossom and blight crops, so, according to tradition, a sunny Christmas leads to a frost-free May and a bumper harvest. However, fickle as ever, traditional lore also states that if the fruit trees are covered in snow on Christmas Morning, they will be covered with fruit in the Summer, betokening an early fruit harvest. Take your pick!

Flora

Generally speaking, at this time of year most greenery has disappeared and there are few, if any, flowers about in the wild. The only things available are the evergreens and fromr time immemorial people have brought what greenery there is inside their homes to brighten the dark days with the promise of Spring and fresh life to come. I have already talked about Rosemary in the previous chapter and this is one of the time-honoured plants that is used not only to decorate the home at this time of year, but also to give it a sharp and fresh fragrance. The use of essential oils is increasingly popular and this is an excellent one to use to give the whole house a bit of a 'lift'. There are, however, many other evergreens – apart from the well-known and traditional Holly and Mistletoe – that can be used to decorate the home around now.

Box (*Buxus sempervirens*), is a much-neglected plant for decoration these days, being used mainly for hedges and topiary outside, but it has a venerable heritage for indoor decoration and was much used in the Middle Ages for this purpose. It is a native tree and, despite its supposedly foul smell (reminiscent of Foxes it is alleged) has been associated with Midwinter festivities for hundreds of years. At other times of the year it is normally associated with funerals and burials – precisely because it is an evergreen – but now it has a double purpose, both to remind us of the death of the old year and the promise of renewal and fresh greenery to come. Its scent, not much noticed by humans it has to be said, is excellent at repelling moths, fleas and other bugs, which is another reason it was used indoors in yesteryear, before the 'advent' (sorry!) of modern pesticides. Animals in Britain will not eat its leaves, but it is said that camels will readily chew on them, even though it poisons them! The folk-name for Box is "Dudgeon" and under this name the herbalist Gerard recommended its root for use as dagger hafts, boxes and wood turning.

The Bay Laurel, or simply Bay (*Laurus nobilis*), has likewise been brought indoors for decoration at Midwinter. Also known as "Sweet Bay" and "Sweetleaf", the Bay is well-known for its use in topiary and culinary preparations. It is a plant of fire and the Sun and for this reason alone is ideal for decorations at this Solstice. Although all parts of the Bay contain medicinal properties it is dangerous to take internally as it is easy to 'overdose' on it, and even a small amount can cause potentially serious vomiting. Having said that, the leaves were anciently chewed by the wise folks to bring on visions and prophecies and seven berries were given to bring on childbirth – not recommended! Heroes, poets and warriors were anciently crowned with Bay as a symbol of their achievements and we still remember this in the appointment of a "Poet Laureate" as our nation's wordsmith. Inside it is hung up to guard against lightning strikes and Witches and to invoke the beneficial powers and properties of the benevolent, reborn Sun.

Surely one of the best known and loved of Winter decorative plants, beside the Holly and Mistletoe, is the Ivy (*Hedera helix*). Like Bay, its leaves and vines have been used for poets' crowns and its leaves have been chewed for visions and prophecy. Its trailing growth is well-known and the fact that it can cover any unsightly ruin and make it look beautiful in a relatively short time makes it an eternal favourite. Its flowers do not come out until late in the year, sometimes as late as November, and its berries are not fully formed until the Spring; this makes it an ideal source of nourishment for late lived insects at the end of the year and for birds and other small creatures at the beginning of the new, before anything else has come out and food is short. Its habit of growing by throwing out suckers and climbing up walls and trees is well-known, but it is a fallacy that it ruins buildings in so doing; the roots adhere to the wall, they do not, generally, penetrate and destroy the wall, although when growing up trees it can suck the nourishing fluids from the stem and wither the growth of the tree. In times past it was bound round the forehead of revellers as it was said to prevent drunkenness – ideal for Yuletide celebrations – and is said to keep the mind focussed and clear. Ivy is seen as feminine and as sacred to the Female Powers, an ideal counterpart to the harsh maleness of the Holly tree, especially at this bleak time of year. A sprig of

Ivy may be left as an offering at any outdoor rite dedicated to the Lady, and Ivy tendrils wrapped around the room at Yule will invoke the blessing and protection of the Mother – again, very appropriate at this time of year. The Ivy Wreath that some Crafters make at Hallowmas may now be taken down and burned in the Solstice flame, to effectively demonstrate the turning of the tides, or may be kept throughout the Winter Tide and abandoned only at the beginning of the Summer. Medicinally, Ivy has traditionally been used in various ways. It may be used in cases of Whooping Cough to liquefy and express bronchial phlegm. The berries were macerated in vinegar to form an acid tincture used to relieve symptoms of the Plague and it may also be used topically, in poultice form, to help reduce swollen glands and relieve chronic leg ulcers.

Hearth & Home

To counterbalance the feminine nature of the Ivy plant, it is as well to have some Holly hung up around the house during this period. I will not go into the symbolism of this particular plant here as it is far too well-known, but I will give an idea for a Holly and Mistletoe ball, which not only looks good, is simple to make, but also invokes the blessing of the Male Powers on the Midwinter festivities. Take a large potato and tie a length of ribbon around it, leaving a long end to hang it up by. Sharpen the ends of some Holly and Mistletoe sprigs and push these in all around the potato, including through the ribbon so that you don't have a bare 'band'. Push smaller pieces in between the larger ones to totally hide and cover the potato, until you have a completely round shape of foliage. Hang the ball from a suitable place in the house, preferably where it can be well seen or act as a centrepiece, and it will last well past the New Year, the juice in the potato keeping the greenery fresh until Twelfth Night.

Having now decorated the home, it is a suitable practice to honour the spirits and beings that guard it and to say 'thank you' for their care, help and protection during the past year. The Eve of the Winter Solstice, the longest night, was called in the Anglo-Saxon calendar "Modra-niht", "Mothers' Night" or the "Night of the Mothers" and it was at this time that the Female Guardian Spirits of the family – the "Disir" – were honoured and remembered. With all the focus on the return of the Child of Light, it is as well to remember the Mothers too! "The Mothers" are closely linked in lore with the "Faere Folk", the "Good Neighbours", and all the spirits who assist with household concerns; it is well to remember them also, lest you incur their displeasure at such ingratitude. A simple ceremony of thanks and appreciation may be performed as follows. Gather all those living in the home around the hearth, or whatever is your central focus of the house (at this time of year, it may be the Christmas tree). Place a smallish, empty bowl in the hearth. Each person present should have a cup of milk and a small piece of bread or mince pie. Have the room in darkness or subdued light and turn of all sources of noise, like the T.V. or stereo. Light a single, white candle and place it near the bowl in the hearth-place and one person (the Mother of the House or the oldest woman is best), should say the following words or something similar, slowly and from the heart:

> *On this, the longest night of the Year, we honour the Mothers, the Divine Ancestors, those that have gone before and given birth to us all. Those who have clothed and fed us and watched over us during this past year, the Spirits of Family, Hearth and Home. Before the Light is birthed anew, we give thanks and respect to those Ancient Ones, from Time Immemorial, whose aid and succour have nourished our home and all it contains this year past. Please accept from us these offerings of Gratitude and Respect.*

Each person in turn should come forward and pour a little of their milk and place a piece of their food into the bowl, whispering such words of thanks and respect as they think fit. All present should now consume the rest of their food and drink in companionable silence, whilst thinking of the Mothers and the help they have received from them during the past year. When all have finished, simply make a slight bow to the hearth and walk away. Leave the offering bowl in the hearth overnight and, next morning, pour the remains out on the Earth outside. The candle may be left to burn out overnight if you consider it safe; if not, leave it to burn for as long as possible, then put it out before going to bed, but leave it in the hearth. This simple ceremony works on many levels; it honours the Spirits of the Home, the Female Guardian Spirits of the family and ensures their continued concern and watchfulness in the year to come. It also brings the people of a shared house together – be that a blood family or one of friendship – and strengthens the bonds that bind them. It is an ideal rite for children to be brought into as well and paves the way for stories of Winter, the Solstice and Christmas, or whatever you like.

Fauna
Whilst we are all cosy and warm indoors, it is a good thing to bear in mind what is going on in the (probably) cold and wet world of outdoors. Many creatures do not hibernate all Winter, at least not fully, and it is still possible to see a lot of activity if you look carefully.

The Squirrel is one type of creature that is active most of the Winter, foraging for the nuts and cones that they have hidden away earlier, although they do take periods of extended sleep in between. They don't have particularly good memories however and often forget where they have hidden their Winter stores; it is reckoned that the Squirrel is responsible for planting most of our native woodland, as the food they store away tends to sprout and grow if forgotten. The Red Squirrel (*Sciurus vulgaris*) is our native animal, the Grey (*Sciurus carolinensis*) being the North American import. Apart from the obvious difference in colour, the Red is smaller and daintier than the Grey and has much more prominent ear tufts, giving it the children's favourite nickname of "Tufty"; other dialect names include "Puggy", "Scorel" and "Squaggy". The Red is sadly in great decline these days, being rapidly overtaken in numbers by the Grey, which are bigger and carry a virus to which they are immune, but which can be deadly to the Red. Contrary to received opinion, Reds and Greys rarely meet directly, and when they do there are no great and bloody battles. For some time, prior to any contact with the Greys, the Reds have been leaving certain areas and the Greys tend to colonise the deserted areas later, having no opposition or competition. No one really knows why the Reds leave an area, but they are now found in less and less of the country, their strongholds being mainly Scotland, Wales, parts of East Anglia and the Isle of Wight. The name "Squirrel" has been with us for a long time and is Late Middle English, coming from the Old Greek term meaning "Shade Tail", for obvious reasons I would think. The nest is known as a "drey" or "dray", the Reds excavating a hole on a branch near to the trunk of a tree, the Greys preferring one further out along the branch. Our native Squirrel has not always been seen in such a benevolent light as it is today and was frequently persecuted in the past. It was reviled for its harsh, chattering and scolding tongue and persecuted because of the perceived damage to trees that it apparently perpetrated. They were often stoned to death by gangs of youths who considered it great sport and in many areas there were organised "Squirrel Hunts" on Boxing Day; these often turned into great chaotic and riotous festivals, with the hunt being just an excuse for wild abandon, but many were killed and much damage was done to landowners' property besides. Squirrel meat makes good eating, being somewhat like rabbit in taste and texture and, in some areas, it is making a great comeback, particularly where the Grey population is becoming a nuisance! The Red is a very good swimmer, strangely enough, often climbing onto floating logs and branches, where according to folklore it uses its tail as a sail; this is totally false!

One of our most majestic, native animals is the Mute Swan (*Cygnus olor*). It is also the largest of the three types of Swan that we see in the British Isles, the other two being migrant birds. The name "Swan" is Old English for "sound", so it seems like a contradiction to call an animal a "Mute Sound"; however, this bird used to be called the "Tame Swan", up until the 1700s, when its name was changed to distinguish it from other, domesticated birds. The male is known as a "Cob", being Middle English for "big" or "stout", the female being called a "Pen". No one is quite sure where this name came from, but it is thought it has something to do with the use of the feathers as quills for writing. The Mute Swan is well-known as being a Royal bird and all wild Swans are indeed owned by the Crown, although they make claim only to those on the River Thames these days. Other institutions also have a claim on the Swan, being allowed ownership in certain cases by the Crown, and this has led to the strange-sounding practice of "Swan Upping". This annual practice simply concerns the catching and marking of Swans to show their ownership. The two main English Universities, Oxford and Cambridge, each have their own mark, but the Crown no longer makes a mark, relying on the fact that everyone knows an unmarked Swan belongs to it. One of the reasons that the ownership of Swans was so hotly contested is that they make very good eating and in days gone by were second only to Venison and Boar on the royal tables at Yuletide. Certain colleges are still allowed the privilege of serving Swan at the Christmas dinner and a few are kept expressly for this purpose, but only in England. In Scotland and Ireland, Swans are believed to embody human souls and there are many native tales of people being transformed into these beautiful creatures. Around the world also there is an association between Swans and beautiful maidens, which has given rise to such wonderful creations of music and art as the ballet "Swan Lake". The faithful birds mate for life, but that is not unusual in the avian world; what is unusual is that the Swan is one of the few birds that possesses a true penis. The old saw that Swans are very dangerous and can break a man's limb with one blow of its wing is totally false. Like most birds the Swan needs to be as light as possible for its size, in order to fly; its bones are honeycombed with small gaps and pockets to cut down on its weight and would easily break if hit against a man's more solid limb. Although called "Mute" they do make a hissing noise if threatened, or if defending their nest or young. The word "Sound" is most aptly applied to this magnificent bird when it is in flight, particularly as it flies over your head and you hear a kind of 'whooshing' noise that is almost impossible to describe otherwise. Try to get out and see these beautiful creatures at this time of the year and perhaps have a crust of bread in your pocket, just in case they're hungry.

There are two birds that are most often associated with this time of the year: the Robin and the Wren. Much has been written already on the Robin, but very little seems to be heard of the Wren, so I shall attempt to remedy that, in however small a way, here. The Wren (*Troglodytes troglodytes*), is our second smallest native bird, the smallest being the Goldcrest. Colloquially known variously as the "Cracket", "Guradnan", "Jenny", "Scutty", "Stumpit", "Tope", "Wirann" and "Wrannock", the word "Wren" comes from Middle English "Wrenne" and means "Little Tail". It is the commonest nesting bird in Britain, the male building several nests from which the female then makes her choice and lays typically five to eight eggs. The Wren is a Winter singer whose song is very loud for such a tiny bird; it is a very clear and jubilant trilling. This bossy, little brown bird with its characteristic erect tail, scurries around in the undergrowth or flies for short distances close to the ground. Although normally unsociable and aggressive, at this time of year the Wren will roost communally for warmth in some shared cavity. Despite its tiny size, Wrens are fearless birds that will mob predators such as small mammals and larger birds with a loud, rattling alarm call. Apart from "*The Robin and the Wren, God Almighty's Cock and Hen*", the Wren is also known as the King of the Birds, having won the title by trickery. According to legend, the birds made a great parliament to decide which one of them should rule all the others, but could not decide. Finally, it was agreed to have a flying contest and the one that flew the highest would be King of the Birds. They all took off and flew as high as they could, one by one gradually dropping away. At last there was only the Eagle left who shouted that he must obviously take the title. Just then, from his back where he had hitched a ride, the Wren flew up and over his head, declaring himself the winner. The birds were so impressed by his cunning and skill that they let him keep the title and he is King to this day! Alongside this, most lore revolves around the "Hunting of the Wren" on Boxing Day, December 26th, which has given rise to a traditional song, mainly referred to as "The Cutty Wren".

The wren, the wren, the King of the Birds
St. Stephen's Day was killed in the furze
Although he is little, his family's great
And I pray you good people please give us a treat.

'The Cutty Wren', as depicted here, is the re-enactment of an ancient wren hunting ceremony, now performed annually (after an interruption lasting nearly a century) on Boxing Day evening, by Old Glory Molly Dancers, at 'The Bell' public house in Middleton, Suffolk. Wren hunting, a very ancient custom with origins possibly dating back to Neolithic times, has been found all over Europe with diverse explanations as to significance. For many, the ritual symbolises the annual fertility cycle of death and regeneration, also characterised in Mummers Plays. In some enactments, a wren is captured, and then either killed and placed on a long pole, or housed alive in a 'wren-house' decked with ribbons and surrounded with holly and ivy. In their re-enactment of the tradition in Suffolk, Old Glory have substituted a carved wooden wren for the live one. On Boxing Day evening, Old Glory, bedecked with greenery, process by torchlight and in silence, carrying the wren-house from Middleton Village Hall to 'The Bell', where the wren ceremony is enacted and there is much music and Molly Dancing. Afterwards, into the pub for more songs and stories." (As described by Colin Cater of Hedingham Fair)

The Wren has been linked with the old Underworld Power, Bran the Blessed, whose 'totem' bird this is. It is emblematic at this time of year of the quiescence of the Otherworldly Powers and also of the change of the inner tides around the Solstice; this is very much a liminal time, of crossing and recrossing boundaries – as is shown in many Mummers Plays by the cross-dressing of the dancers – indicating the shift from one tide to another and the corresponding chaos involved. It is interesting that after this period, there is a very strict taboo on the Hunting of the Wren, when it would be very bad luck to kill one. There is also a train of thought that further links the Wren with Bran thus; "Cutty Wren" is actually a corruption of "Cuddy Vran", the word "Vran" meaning "Raven", which is also the meaning of "Bran", or even the very word itself. There are echoes here of ancient sacrificial rites that once marked the change of seasons and the replacement of one form of 'energy' with another. So, the Wren, although a tiny bird, embodies within itself a very large amount of symbolism, history and lore indeed.

Times & Tides

We now come to the main focus of events for this month and that is the festivities surrounding the time of the Winter Solstice. This is not a book that is expressly concerned with particular, individual festivals and celebrations, but more specifically with the overall pattern of the flow of the natural energies throughout the year. However, this necessarily involves descriptions of how people mark these flows and tides, so some description of specific celebrations is appropriate. The point around which everything revolves this month is the Solstice, occurring around the 20th/21st/22nd of the month. It is a natural turning point in the year, independent of man-made months or other political or secular divisions and so has attracted many separate traditions, which it has retained in some form or another, up to the present day, often despite fervent opposition from both religious and other leaders. The main celebrations of concern for a person following a natural belief system are obviously the Solstice itself, and Christmas and the observations following it. However, there are a few traditional dates running up to these that are of note in themselves.

It has recently come to my notice, that the first Sunday in the month is kept by some Traditions as "Elf Day". On this day it is their custom to bring in the greenery and put up their Yuletide decorations, especially honouring the Elven Spirits who both come in with the fresh boughs and who already live in the home. Great merriment is the norm, with much fun and laughter and many toasts being made to the Elvish companions on this day. I have not been able to get to the roots of this tradition, but it is possible that for those that celebrate it, it may be a displaced version of the Norse "Alfablot". Whatever its origins, it is a fun-filled day for all concerned, but with particular care made to honour and make offerings to the Elvish folk.

St. Nicholas' Day, celebrated on the December 6th, is named after the patron saint of Children and Fishermen who gives rise to all the later versions of Santa Claus/ Klaus. He was historically the Bishop of Myra in Turkey in the 4th century around whom many legends of acts of kindness grew up. He could grant special wishes on his day and people would light a candle in his honour (a common theme at this time of the year) which they would leave burning all night, so that the saint could see his way. He would bring small gifts to those who had been good all year and leave them in their stockings to be found in the morning. This tradition has obviously now been transferred to Christmas Eve. His image of a large, jolly man has been revamped and combined with other mythic figures over the years – notably the CocaCola 'reinvention' of Santa Claus in America in the 1930s – and is now the archetypal picture of Father Christmas, the gift-giver at Midwinter.

St. Lucy's Day was formerly much celebrated on December 13th in Britain, but is much neglected nowadays; however, it is still very popular in Scandinavia and on the European Continent –. Historically, Lucy was a young Sicilian Christian maid, who refused to marry a pagan husband and gave her dowry away to the poor. When she was arrested and sentenced to death for her beliefs and actions, the flames of the pyre on which she was to be burnt refused to harm her and she had to be stabbed to death instead. Because of this she has become associated with the Powers of Light, particularly those that ward off evil and darkness, and is patron saint of the blind. On her feast day, young girls are dressed in white, wearing wreaths on their heads which are set with nine lighted white candles, and visit local houses at Sunset to bless the neighbours, flocks and crops. The 'jingle' that is repeated on her day, *"Lucy light, Lucy light, shortest day and longest night"*, at first appears out of time with her feast day, until you take into account the calendar change in Britain of 1752. Lucy's day was December 13th in the old Julian calendar, which was then the Winter Solstice; when the change to the current Gregorian calendar took place, the date was retained but obviously the loss of days now makes it out of alignment with the Solstice it is talking about. This discrepancy has never been addressed or corrected. It is possible that Lucy represents one of the old, pre-Christian Female Powers representing the Sun, who returns at this time and bestows blessings upon the Land and her worshippers. However, this direct link has now been lost, although it is still acknowledged by many Crafters in their rites.

St. Thomas' Day is still celebrated on December 21st and retains the correctlydated – if somewhat pessimistic

– jingle of *"St. Thomas grey, St. Thomas grey, the longest night and the shortest day"*. The Thomas in question is Thomas the doubting Apostle, who needed physical proof before he would believe in the Resurrection. He is now the patron saint of the elderly and on his day people would go "A-Thomasing", which meant distributing small amounts of alms amongst the poor of the parish; this supposedly bestowed spiritual grace on the givers which would help them on their journey to heaven. It was also traditional to ring loud peals on the church bells on St. Thomas' Day, both to announce the longest night of the year and also to ward against the powers of darkness that were believed to be abroad at this time.

I would now like to look at the actual Solstice itself and some of the history around its observation and those festivals that have become attached/associated with it. The acknowledgement of the Winter Solstice in these Lands has a long and ancient history. We know from megalithic remains that it was recognised and observed at least as long ago as 3500 BCE, from remains such as Newgrange (Bru na Boinne) in Eire, Maeshowe in Orkney, and Stonehenge in Southern England.

The stunning, megalithic mound of Newgrange in the Boyne valley is directly orientated to the rising Sun of the Winter Solstice. Above the doorway is an aperture that lets the Sun shine through and down a narrow passage, at Sunrise for a few days either side of the Solstice, which then illuminates a spiral pattern cut into the rock in the centre of the internal chamber. It is truly a spectacular feat of engineering and a most wondrous sight to behold, but we have absolutely no idea what rites accompanied this event, or what was going through the minds of the participants at the time. But the fact that they were celebrating or acknowledging the Solstice is obviously significant.

Likewise, at Maeshowe on the Orkney mainland, a "passage grave" roughly contemporary with Newgrange and sharing many design features, the Winter Solstice is accurately plotted. Again, the light shines through a gap above the blocked-off doorway, directly down the main passage into the central chamber; this time however, it marks the Solstitial Sunset rather than Sunrise. This orientation is also shown in another megalithic building, directly adjacent to MaeshoweMaes and contemporary with it.

Possibly the most famous stone circle in the world, Stonehenge, was 'adjusted' around 2100 BCE to create different alignments relating to Solstitial events. Most people are aware of the commonly accepted alignment to the rising Sun at the Summer Solstice, but the alignment is not exact, even allowing for the shifts in positioning during the intervening millennia. Recent investigation has reasonably confirmed that the actually intended alignment is to the Winter Solstice Sunset, through the uprights of the central, largest "trilithon". Again, we do not know the rites accompanying this event, but the alignment is significant.

Apart from a few ancient "cursus" constructions in the South of England that have Midwinter alignments, there are no other known significant connections to the Winter Solstice in ancient monuments. This lack of evidence applies also to our immediately pre-Roman forebears, the Iron Age peoples of this Land. In almost all the remaining mythology and legends from this period, there is little, if any, mention of activities at Midwinter, let alone evidence of major festivals or celebrations. It may have been that the Iron Age culture was predominantly pastoral and hence was not tied so specifically to the Equinoxes and Solstices, or it may just be that these events were not important to their way of belief; we do not know for sure. However, despite this lack in the mythological and legendary record, we do have the evidence of St. Patrick who, in his writings railed against the Irish of his time, calling them inveterate Sun worshippers. It is a mystery. Incidentally, the 'well-known' account written by Pliny, of the Druids cutting mistletoe at the Winter Solstice is totally invalid in this instance; Pliny does not mention any season of the year in his account, stating only that it was on the sixth day of the New Moon, and he was writing specifically of the Druids in Gaul. We do find later though, in the early Mediaeval period in Welsh and Norse literature, that a supposedly ancient Midwinter festival is celebrated, so the puzzle continues.

It is not until we come to the Romans that we have any direct evidence of Midwinter or Solstitial celebrations. Saturnalia, so-called after the agricultural and fertility deity Saturn, began on or just after the 17th of the Roman December and officially continued for three or four days thereafter, although many diehards continued celebrating longer. The 17th itself was reserved for religious rites, but afterwards all sorts of revelry and feasting went on. Gambling was allowed at this time of year; masters would wait upon servants at table; gifts were given to friends and family and, among young noblemen, a kind of "King of Misrule" would be elected, who gave all sorts of idiotic orders that had to be obeyed. There was some confusion in Roman times as to when the actual Solstice occurred – anything from the 23rd to the 26th was stated – so the period surrounding the Solstice itself was left clear of celebration and was quite quiet. The confusion is understandable as the Sun does appear to rise and set in the same places for a few days either side of the Solstice and, indeed, our word "Solstice" comes from the Latin meaning "Sun stands still". The feasting and revelry would pick up again after this period and fresh celebrations would take place at the "Kalends" of January, from the 1st to the 3rd of the month. The festival of "Sol Invictus" (the "Unconquered Sun") was celebrated during this period also, although, unlike Saturnalia which was an ancient Roman festival, this was a relatively recent addition to the Roman calendar, having been introduced in the 3rd century as a state occasion to unify the Empire. It was a smaller affair than Saturnalia and was mostly celebrated with private religious rites by the family at home.

It was not until the Viking invasions of this Land, from the 9th century onwards that we get the introduction of the word "Yule" for the Midwinter period. This is normally translated as "Wheel", but may also come from the same root that gives us the word "Jolly"; the derivation is unclear and there is no definitive answer. Yule is normally described as a time of great feasting, agreed upon by both the Venerable Bede and Snorri Sturluson in their writings, and the pagan nature of the festivities incited great anger in the Christian bishops of the period. From the 4th to the 11th centuries they issued condemnations against the common folks' activities – particularly dressing up as animals or in animal skins at the New Year period – but also against such practices as leaving offerings to stones and trees, various divinatory practices and worshipping at wells and springs. The Norsemen are also credited with the introduction of the custom of burning or bringing in the Yule Log and it is also possible, however remote, that they would set up a tree or a wooden pole at this period, indicative of the World Tree. Sacrifices would be made for good harvests in the following year and oaths and pledges given to Lords and local Masters would be renewed. (A note concerning what we now know as the Christmas Tree here. Although this is generally agreed to have been introduced into Britain, either by Prince Albert or by German immigrants in the 19th century. there is another possible origin. The late Michael Howard records in his *Liber Nox* (see Bibliography) that there is a reference concerning a tree from the 15th century. Apparently, this tree was set up on the Cornhill in London and was decorated with Holly and Ivy, specifically to celebrate Christmas. It was considered to be noteworthy as it was destroyed in a thunderstorm on Candlemas Day, the traditional time when the festive greenery was originally taken down and burned. Could this be a remnant from the old Norse "World Tree" poles?)

The festival we now know as "Christmas" has a long and chequered history. It is obvious from a reading of the canonical gospels that no date is given of the event at all, or even hinted at. The "Feast of the Nativity", as it was originally called, was not fixed to the present date until 354 CE and was not universally adopted in the Christian world until much later, spreading out from Rome after that period. Until then, there had been various dates upon which people had celebrated the festival, most favouring a date in Spring, but there was no certain consensus. The date of December 25th was picked, famously, so that Christians could celebrate their holy rites unmolested, whilst the pagans were celebrating their unholy ones. Unfortunately for devout Christians, the Nativity absorbed many elements of pagan ritual and practice from its very outset and the Church Fathers frequently had to issue reminders that it was the birthday of Jesus that they were celebrating and not the rebirth of the Sun, as many of their flocks seemed to be celebrating both! The term Christmas, as "Cristes Mæssan", was first recorded as an alternative to the ecclesiastical "Nativited" and it has stuck in English-speaking countries ever since. A period of 12 days of feasting had gradually evolved around this time, encompassing many saints' feasts and other holy days, and leading up to "Epiphany" on the 6th January. By the Middle Ages this was firmly fixed, King Alfred the Great issuing laws freeing all servants from work during this time. These customs have, in general, continued until the present day with essentially the same meaning attached.

It can be seen from this very brief history of Midwinter customs in these Lands that it would appear to have always been a very special and important time, however little written history we have of its origins. But what does it mean to a Practitioner of Natural Religion in this day and age, and how can it be acknowledged or celebrated? I would like to give some suggestions to answer each of these points and I will leave the reader to make up their own mind as to which, if any, to accept and act upon.

I would firstly like to look at what the Winter Solstice actually means, in the context of the tides of the year and I offer three interpretations below, which I hope will prove useful.

On an obvious, physical level, it is the point in the year when the Land is at its furthest point from the life-giving and warming Sun – hence Mid Winter. Due to the elliptical orbit of our planet and the tilt in its North-South axis, this event varies by a day or two each year, but each year we can say we have travelled the furthest from our source of heat and light and it is now time to start the long journey back. (Paradoxically, the Earth is actually at its closest point to the Sun at this time and it is only the tilt in the planet that gives us our Winter in the Northern hemisphere). We know that from this point onwards, the days will stop getting shorter and, ever so slowly, will start getting longer again and we can look forward to the seemingly far-off Summer. The weather may not yet have given of its worst and there is still a long way to go until Spring, but we can rejoice that the seasons have turned again and there is fresh hope. This is the feeling, surely, that people first had when they realised that the years were not random events and that they could rely on the days getting longer again, instead of huddling together in the cold, fearing the end of the world. It is the realisation that life goes on and all does not end in the dark.

Leading on from that point and going somewhat deeper, the Winter Solstice period is the celebration of the incarnation of the Light once more. It matters not a jot what you call this Light: Jesus, Yeshu, Mithras, Sol, Lucifer, Balder, Belenos. Nor does it matter what you call its Mother: be that Mary, Maria, Marah, Frigga or the Eternal One. (The exception to this is if you are forming a personal relationship with a single aspect of Deity, to act as a Patron or Patroness, but that is rather different to the present context.) They are all myths and symbols to embody the same thing, namely that at this time we appreciate that some Divine Spark incarnates in physical matter – whether literally or esoterically – and that we are the better for it. In the deepest Darkness the brightest Light is to be found, for it is from and through this Darkness that the Light is born, the source and secret of all true magic. It is a mirror for our own divine natures and a reminder that we must look inwards into our darkest selves to find that spark of divinity and bring it out into the daylight. Remember – it is only the Light that casts a shadow, the Darkness is sufficient unto itself!

On yet another level, it is the release of a fresh tide of energy on the inner or astral planes, which will ultimately manifest itself on our physical level around the end of January or the beginning of February. This is the tide of Cleansing and Purification, of Renewal and Rebirth. It sweeps away all that is dead, rotten and decayed, the end of the old year just gone, and makes a fresh start. We know this has happened because we instinctively feel its effects at this time of year and celebrate it. However, this is not necessarily a gentle tide, as cleansing and purification of that which is old and outworn can often be extremely painful, especially if the individual or situation is unwilling to let go of the past and the outmoded forms it clings to. It can be as easy as a gentle Spring rain, or as devastating as a Winter flood in its effects.

Having looked at some possibilities surrounding the meaning of the Winter Solstice/Christmas, I would like to suggest some ways of marking it in a slightly more meaningful way than usual. Obviously, Practitioners of a Natural Religion will have their own rites and customs and will join in the various activities and festive events of their families and friends at this time of year, but there are a few things that may be done to mark this time out as even more special for the individual or group/family.

The custom of bringing in the Yule Log, as already mentioned, was probably begun by our Norse ancestors and it not only gave heat and light at a time when it was sorely needed, but it also had a symbolic aspect too. The blazing log, set to burn on the hearth on the Eve of the Solstice and tended for the 12 days thereafter, never being allowed to go out, reflected both the tide of cleansing and purification that had begun, but also the return of the Sun and the inherent Light within all present. The days of large, open hearths are gone for the vast majority of people, but the practice can still be enjoined in a smaller, adapted form and held as being just the same and just as special. Obtain a log about 18 inches long and 6-8 inches in diameter; Ash wood is best if you can find it, otherwise Pine or Birch. If you have a fire grate fill it with Pine cones and Holly leaves, otherwise find a suitable receptacle and fill it likewise, placing it wherever is best suited. Drill three holes along the top of the log, of a size suitable to hold candles of your choice. Alternatively, knock in three nails at equal distances along the top of the log and cut off the heads, then use them as spikes to hold the candles. Place the log with its candles on the decorated holder and light the candles on the Eve of the Solstice. Put these out before going to bed, but light them again each evening, for the following 12 days. It is up to you what ceremony, wording or actions you use to light the candles, but you may like to light them after performing the rite to the Mothers, given previously, on the first night, then with a few simple words each night thereafter.

Another custom which may be kept is the lighting of the "Yule Candle". This is called a "Christingle" in one of its forms by Christian folk, but the symbolism would appear to precede that religion and has been used in my household for many years, being known simply as the "Orb"; my husband reverently calls it "the Sputnik"! Take a large orange or golden apple and three hazel twigs. Sharpen one end of each of the twigs and push them into the fruit to form a tripod stand. Cut a small hole in the top of the fruit, large enough for a taper candle and push one in (red is the traditional colour). Wrap a red ribbon around the middle of the fruit, tying it into a bow, and stick three equidistant sprigs of Holly or Rosemary into the top of the fruit, surrounding the candle. Get a suitably sized bowl, blackened on the inside, fill it with water and stand the "Orb" in the bowl. Place the bowl in the centre of a wreath of Ivy, as the central display at your Yuletide meals. This may be lit, with or without ceremony, at the start of each meal you have during the feasting season, to remind you of the reasons for keeping this time of year. The symbolism is fairly obvious, but a few points may need clarification. The fruit with the candle obviously represents the reborn Sun/Son, the light of the candle being the divine spark in physical matter. The foliage has the usual meaning of its type and the ribbon represents the blood of life. The blackened bowl (which some people fill with fragrant Winter greenery instead of water), represents the Darkness of chaos and night from which the Light – and all of us – are reborn; the Ivy symbolises the Feminine Principle which gives birth to the Light once more.

Finally on this point, here is a small rite for the individual or family to perform. This may be done on the Eve of the Solstice, or Christmas Eve, whatever suits you and your Way best. Take a lighted, red candle and go to stand outside, facing the West as the Sun sets. Raise your candle in salute and watch the Sun go down, beginning the longest night. Put out your candle once the Sun has set and stand a few moments in contemplation. Try to think of all those things from the past year that you wish to let go of, that you do not wish to carry forward with you after the turning of the tides. Make a determined mental effort to cast these things off and leave them behind you. Turn around then and go back home without looking back. Once home, perform your usual seasonal activities. Go to bed knowing that you have cast off all that you do not wish to keep and enjoy a deep and refreshing sleep. Determine the time of Sunrise the next day and arise in plenty of time before it (this should not be too difficult at this time of year as the

Sun rises quite late). This time take a white candle and go to stand outside, facing East. Wait for the Sun to rise and, as it does so, light your candle and raise it high in salute. Watch it rise, contemplating all the new things that this new tide will bring and what the new Sunrise of this tide means to you personally, or as a family. Keep your candle alight and return home to enjoy the festivities of the day. Give the candle a place of honour, perhaps in your personal or family shrine or on your special table and let it burn out completely through the day. You have lit the light of the new tide both within your home and within yourself; nurture it well until it comes to full fruition.

The remainder of this month is generally given over to celebration and holiday, until at least the calendrical New Year and frequently beyond, although these days we probably don't quite keep the 12 days as people of yesteryear once did. Basically, what all the celebrations are about, in one form or another, is the turning of the tides of the year. This is one of those great liminal times, a time when tides and energies change and we are caught in that in-between time where rules are reversed and societal norms are turned topsy-turvy. One very good example of this is the traditional Pantomime, beloved of most English people and not understood by most others! Here we have girls playing boys' parts, grown men dressing up as women, talking animals, magical happenings and all sorts of other outlandish events. It is literally fantastical and well-placed in the calendar to reflect the great tide of the year. Similar roles are enacted by Mummers and Morris Dancers in the streets of towns and villages at this time. These displays of 'ancient ritual' often involve a Fool, a man dressed as an animal or in animal skins and usually a "Shemale" character who weaves in and around all the rest, causing chaos and mayhem. There are killings and beheadings, miraculous cures and resurrections, all enabled by the "Wizard" or "Doctor" of the group. This all describes in graphic detail the very borderline nature of this period and people's reaction to it.

Probably the most liminal time of all is at the end of the month, New Year's Eve itself, when most people seem to have public approval to lose all forms of restraint and anything goes. Historically, this was a time of fear and uncertainty surrounding the future and therefore an excellent time for divination; looking into the future at this 'threshold moment' to determine the fortunes of the coming year, just as previously happened at All Hallows.

There are many customs and traditions surrounding the moment of New Year, far too many to encompass here where our focus is on the flow of the seasons and the tides. I shall leave this chapter with the advice I was given by a very wise person many years ago. Just before midnight, on the cusp of the Old and New Years, throw open your back door to let the Old year out. Then, go to your front door and fling it wide open (weather permitting!) to let the New year in. Stand well back and accept what comes through …

January

The Sun rises at approximately 8:08 a.m. and sets at approximately 3:59 p.m. at the beginning of the month.

The image for January, traditionally known as the Cold Month, is as follows:

> *Clad all in White as the Earth looks with the Snow, blowing his nails; in his Left Arm a Billet, the sign Aquarius.*

Times and Tides

And through the door the New Year comes rushing in. It was and is always considered very important exactly what, or who, comes through the door first after midnight on New Year's Morn. The first thing(s) through the door would have a determining effect on what fortunes the home and family had in the coming seasons. This practice gradually evolved into the tradition of "First Footing", mostly now associated with the Scottish lands and folk, but once widespread throughout the British Isles. Originally, the first person through the door would have been the local priest, or equivalent, carrying the holy things to bless the house and its occupants. Nowadays this rarely happens and much emphasis is placed on the symbolism of the first entrant(s). There are many taboos in this practice, chiefly among them things which are deemed to be malefic and unlucky – anyone who is deformed or has a disability and people with red hair (although in parts of the country people with red hair are considered to be lucky) and also women; a red-headed woman coming first through your door must be avoided at all costs! (No accounting for taste in folklore is there!) Basically, the luckiest and most beneficial things to come/be brought into the house first are all the good things that people would wish to enjoy in their lives. This normally involves food, wealth, warmth, security and love or good companionship, or the representatives of the same and this has been whittled down over the years to an almost clichéd, set formula. The luckiest person over the threshold is traditionally a young, tall, dark, handsome, virile man, bearing food, drink, light and often a piece of coal; all things symbolising the blessing of the home for the coming year. Different parts of the country have their own local variations on this theme, but this is the norm. On entering, the bringer of good fortune must be greeted warmly and immediately offered the best seat in the house and some food and drink; if this is not done, despite the blessing just arrived, all good fortune will be negated. In many communities a distinct individual was in great demand for this role and one wonders how he made the rounds all in one night, without becoming exceedingly drunk or incapable of moving due to an overstuffed belly.

However, be that as it may, this tradition is enjoying a revival these days and has never been forgotten by those practising a Natural Craft; everything must always be done to ensure the prosperity and security of the home and the family and to avoid or omit this small – but important – ceremony could be courting disaster. At this liminal time, all actions, symbolic or otherwise, are deemed to have a great effect on the future and must be carried out with extreme care and caution.

In many areas fire ceremonies were, and in some cases still are, carried out in the fields on New Year's Morn. Circles of 12 fires or flares would be made, with a thirteenth in the centre, which would then be taken up and whirled around the fields, to the sounds of much rejoicing and laughter. The reasons for this are twofold. Firstly, the fires are lit to fend off the spirits and old energies of the year passed; no need for stagnant and stale energy if you wish to sow fresh crops. Secondly, the fires betokened and welcomed or beckoned the new light of a new year, refreshing and fertilising the Land for this season's crops. The fertility of the Land is of paramount importance if one is to eat, in any day or age, chemical fertilisers or not (actually, specifically if you use chemical fertilisers!). This ceremony would all be rounded off with a hearty feast and toasts to the landowner and family, accompanied by various forms of blessing and divination for the farm and the year ahead. This practice was also carried out at the time of the next celebration, described below.

The festivities continue apace, if on a much lesser scale now, until the effectual end of the Yuletide festivities, Twelfth Night, the evening of January 5th. This is Christmas Eve in the Julian calendar and was still observed as such until recently by the Orthodox Church of Eastern Europe. It is also seen by those of a more 'earthier' belief system as the high tide of the ride of the Wild Hunt and Old Yule by another name. The Wild Hunt first rides out at Hallowmas and returns to its Otherworldly abode at Candlemas; its peak time of operation comes at the period of liminality from Yule/Winter Solstice to Twelfth Night/Old Yule. It is the ride of both the ancestral spirits, who are let loose to join in the revels of this dark period of reversal and chaos, and also of the Old Powers from time immemorial, who bring both illumination and enlightenment for those with the senses to perceive them. It is not for nothing that the month of January is named for the old deity "Janus", the double-headed and dual-faced Being who looks both ways, both forwards and back, and presides over the changing of the inner tides; from darkness to light He turns His head and all is changed in the blink of an eye. Madness is to be found if you are un/fortunate enough to be swept up in the train of the furious Hunt, but whether this is the madness of the divine or the madness of fools, only the one so caught up can tell.

It is now that most consider it time to take down the Yuletide decorations, the greenery and tinsel that have kept hope alive over the darkest period and have accompanied us through to the other side. The evergreens are now starting to fade and dry out and who knows but that they might still harbour some dangerous energies from the Old Year; what devious or malicious sprites might he hiding amongst the crumpled and fading leaves to cause mischief if left behind? Originally these decorations were kept up until Candlemas time, the true end of the Winter period, but with Victorian practicality came a drive to revamp old traditions and so the decorations had to come down as a herald of a return to work. These were generally taken outside and burned, the ashes being kept to spread on the fields at sowing time, as a blessing on the Land, retaining the link with the past and utilising their energies anew for future harvests.

The next day is the January 6th, being Twelfth Day and the final end of the Yuletide holidays. This is generally celebrated by the Church as Epiphany, the day on which the baby Jesus was visited by the three Wise Men, who presented Him with Gold, Frankincense and Myrrh. There is actually no mention of the date of their visit in the gospels, like Christmas itself, and also no mention of the number of Wise Men. The number three has been taken from the number of gifts presented and the names Caspar, Balthazar and Melchior have become sanctioned by tradition, but there is no scriptural basis for this. Be that as it may, this date and association has now been long established and marks the end of the twelve days of celebration. It is also, obviously, Christmas Day by the Old calendar, as was celebrated as such right up until the 19th century in some areas of rural Britain, and until even more recently by the Orthodox Church again. (A short note here on the dating of Twelfth Night and Day. If one counts from Christmas Eve, which is the norm, then Twelfth Night comes out at January 5th and Twelfth Day at the 6th. This dates from the times when people counted evenings first, as the start of a new day and this custom continues in our use of the term a "fortnight" for a period of two weeks. If you do not count Christmas Eve, then Twelfth Night comes out atJanuary 6th and Twelfth Day the 7th. The former method of dating is the usual, but there are areas which follow the latter. This actually makes no difference for a follower of a natural system, as 24 man-made hours mean nothing in this case of a natural flow of timing and energies.)

The Monday after the first Sunday after Twelfth Day is known as Plough Monday and it was on this day that the men were supposed to go back to work in the fields, turning the soil ready for the Spring planting. In fact, precious little work was done on this day, as it was again given over to revelry and tomfoolery. The plough would be decorated, often elaborately with horse brasses and ribbons, and dragged through the fields by boys and young men, similarly decorated and disguised in various costumes, sometimes dressed as witches and sprites. After this, the plough would be drawn through the village and there would often be a Shemale accompanying the throng, known as the "Bessie" or "Betsy" and 'she' would carry a box into which 'contributions' would be placed from the locals. (This under threat of having your garden ploughed up otherwise, so contributions were often healthy.) This money would originally have been given to the local church by the Ploughman's Guild, to support the Plough Light that was kept burning there all year round. This tradition ended with the Reformation and donations were made to the local poor instead. The current ceremony of "Blessing the Plough", which is currently gaining popularity again, is the descendant of this tradition and garden implements of all kinds are often taken to the church to be blessed also; what goes around comes around!

The next day, the first Tuesday after "Twelfth", is known as Distaff Day and is the day when, traditionally, the women went back to work after the Yuletide break (although who did all the work over this period with everyone off celebrating is beyond me – maybe the Faere Folk lent a hand?!). The term "distaff" refers to the implement used as part of the process of spinning thread or yarn(the distaff is the wooden bit that holds the unspun fibres) and was always a woman's tool, which she would have ever by her. The distaff also links this to the Old Powers of Fate and Destiny, who would spin and weave a person's life pattern on their loom, using the thread wound on the distaff. It was an old European tradition that the Feminine Powers who ruled this work demanded that all women suspend this task over the liminal Yuletide period and only take it up again once the festivities were over; there were heavy penalties from the Fates if any woman disobeyed this rule and carried on spinning during this time. It can be clearly seen that spinning was, and is, considered to be a magical practice, involving the warp and weft of a person's life – to perform this operation during a time when all was in chaos would be to seriously jeopardise a person's life and hence the activity was banned until the energies had reasonably returned to 'normal'.

On the 17th of the month it was, and most certainly still is, time to Wassail the Apple orchards. Wassail comes from the old Anglo-Saxon "Wes Hal" or "Wes Hael", which literally means "Be Whole" or "Be Healthy" and was a practice much observed over the Winter Tide. Essentially it involves toasting a thing or person with much ceremony and celebration. Wassailing the Apple orchards has been a custom since Roman times and probably before, to ensure a good crop in the coming year. Cider, made from last year's apples, is taken out to the orchards and poured around the roots of the trees, and pieces of toast or cake soaked in the cider are placed in the forks of the branches. Normally then, the oldest, largest and most venerable tree is singled out, more toasts are made to it and a song is sung. This varies from district to district, but here is an example which is fairly widespread and gives the essential points:

> *Here's to Thee, Old Apple Tree,*
> *Whence Thou may'st bud and whence Thou may'st blow,*
> *And whence Thou may'st bear Apples enow.*
> *Hats full, caps full, bushel, bushel sacks full,*
> *And my pockets full too*

More toasting follows and then a great racket is made. Shotguns are commonly used these days, preferably old ones that make lots of noise, and fired through the branches of the trees, but originally it would have been drums, horns, pipes, anything that made a large and scary sound when beaten or blown. The whole idea of this exercise is to scare away any malignant spirits that may be hiding in the trees and might blight or curse the fruit and to wake up the trees from their Winter slumber, ready to start growing the blossoms – and later the fruit – for that year's harvest. The louder the noise, singing and toasts, the better the harvest was deemed to be. It is essentially honouring the pirit(s) of the Apple tree(s) and requesting their help in the coming year, whilst giving back some of what they have already provided, in gratitude and thanks. This ceremony has never gone out of fashion and is still practised today, in all seriousness, mostly in the South and West of Britain, but originally it covered most of these Isles and was not just limited to Apple orchards either. Many different types of fruit crops were treated to this honour and still are in smaller ways today. If you wish for a bumper harvest from your own fruit trees, there is no reason why you should not adopt this ceremony and honour your own 'orchard', even if you only have one tree. However, I'd warn the neighbours first, or maybe invite them to join in!

Soon after this time, on St. Agnes' Eve, January 21st, it is time for young, unmarried girls to attempt to find out who their future husbands will be. St. Agnes was a teenage Roman girl who was raped and murdered for refusing to marry the son of a centurion; she subsequently became the patron saint of chastity, girls, rape victims and virgins. On the Eve of her festival, young women would make a "Dumb Cake", so called because no one must speak during the making and baking of it. The girl's initials were then pricked into it and it was left out overnight. She must retire to bed in silence without looking over her shoulder, whence she would dream of her future husband, who would eat with her and kiss her. In the morning, his initials would appear pricked into the cake next to hers. John Keats once wrote a very long poem on the subject, which is still considered to be one of his best pieces of work. It is never reported as to how successful this little ritual is, but it must have brought comfort to many and have some efficaciousness to be still performed today, as I am assured it still is!

Hearth & Home

Most domestic activities this month will centre around the celebrations and festivities already described above, but there are a few different aspects that can be looked at here and added to the overall celebrations. When taking your decorations down, be they the modern tinsel variety or especially the traditional greenery, give a thought to the spirits of the house; either those that live there all the year round, or those who have taken shelter in the decorations over the Yuletide period. Not all sprites who have hitched a ride on a piece of Holly or a green bough of Bay or Box are malignant, and indeed they may be persuaded to stay if they are friendly, and become valuable and honoured additions to the family members. So, before you finally take out the remains of the dried-up old leaves and boughs, pause a moment and whisper a few words of thanks to the green sprites who have given their energies to the jollifications of the season. Maybe you would like to sprinkle a few drops of milk or honey-water over the greenery before it is cast away, or place a larger bowl of offerings in the hearth. If you have had a live tree in your home, you should certainly give thanks to the spirit of the tree for lending its energies to your celebrations, and make sure that it receives a good libation to its roots before it is taken outside once more. Treat it well – either replant it with care and love, or keep it well-tended in its pot until next Yule; never anger domestic or wild spirits – they are of limited intelligence and sensibility and can easily lash out in anger or misunderstanding.

Something you may like to add to your Twelfth Night or Day observances is the creation of the "Bean King". Traditionally this time was a point of huge merriment, the last real bash of Christmas – even if some did continue the observance until Candlemas – as work would begin again soon. A large cake, called the "Twelfth Cake", would be baked, or a number of smaller ones, into which would be baked a dried bean (sometimes also a dried pea for the "Pea Queen", although this was less common). The person who had the piece of cake containing the bean then became the "Bean King" for the rest of the revels, even selecting a deputy to help him in his role. He would be the Lord of the feast, dictating what was done when, what was served when and even giving forfeits as he chose to those that offended him. This tradition obviously has a long ancestry, going back to the Fools and Lords of Misrule of Saturnalia and underlines the last echoes of the time of chaos just past, when everything was turned topsy-turvy and roles were reversed, as anyone could be elected the King or the Fool, irrespective of station or condition. However, these days it can be seen as simply a piece of fun, just to wind up the more serious aspects of practice that have gone before.

As part of your "Twelfth" celebrations, or anything else for that matter, you may like to make use of the traditional Wassail, discussed above in association with the Apple orchards. When not Wassailing the trees, a different mixture of drink is used, which I will go on to describe soon, but first I would like to mention the vessel that the drink is held in, namely the Wassail Bowl. Examples of this type of bowl have come down through history and are generally held in high regard and can also be very valuable, often being edged or bound with silver chasework. The bowl itself is often fashioned from Maple wood and in this form goes back to the toasting bowls of the Anglo-Saxon period. It is perhaps the only traditional use for the native Maple tree (Acer campestre) as there is practically no other lore extant concerning it. The name Maple comes from the Anglo-Saxon word "Mapldur", the "dur" part maybe deriving from the same root as the French word for "hard" or "enduring", which is probably why this wood was chosen for the Wassail bowl. Some surviving examples are hundreds of years old and are treasured family possessions. They are the precursors to the modern punchbowls, their nature, shape and function deriving directly from the older original. The original Wassail bowls can often be of great size and are capable of holding up to a gallon of liquid, which I shall now describe. There are many recipes for the Wassail "punch", but all follow a general rule of hot, spiced ale, with apples and sugar; here is one with a bit more 'kick' to it that you might like to try.

Ingredients:

6 cooking apples
soft brown sugar
½oz dried, ground ginger
½ grated nutmeg
pinch powdered cinnamon
8oz demerara sugar
3 pints mild or brown ale
½ bottle raisin wine
½ bottle sherry
1 lemon
sugar cubes
a few slices of hot, buttered toast

Method:

Core the apples but do not peel them and fill the holes with soft, brown sugar. Place them on a baking tray and roast in a medium oven for 45 minutes to one hr. making sure that they do not burst their skins by making a few light cuts in the surface of each apple. Meanwhile, mix together in a saucepan the nutmeg, ginger, cinnamon and demerara sugar, adding one pint of the ale and bringing just to the boil. Stir well to dissolve all the ingredients. Add the rest of the ale, the wines and 10 lumps of sugar that have been rubbed hard on the lemon rind. Heat the mixture through till all is dissolved, but do not boil. Place the roasted apples in the Wassail Bowl, pour over the hot liquid with half the sliced lemon and float the slices of toast on the top. Serve immediately in small mugs and stand well back!

If that doesn't cure any cold or 'flu bugs that are hanging around, or if it gives you a sore throat or a cough, then try the following recipe which is a tried and tested remedy from my local countryside at this time of year. Dice one large onion and slice a few large cloves of garlic. Take a large jam jar and cover the base to about half-an-inch deep with good-quality brown sugar. Add a similar layer of the onion and garlic and cover with another layer of sugar. Continue this layering process until the onion and garlic are used up and top with a final layer of sugar. Screw on the lid tightly and leave the mixture to soak in a warm, dark place for three to four days, by which time the sugar will have dissolved and absorbed the beneficial qualities of the onion and garlic. After this time, strain off the liquid through a few layers of cotton, muslin or a fine sieve, into a pan and warm through gently on a low heat. Stir in an equivalent volume of honey to the sugar liquid and continue stirring on the heat for about five minutes. Remove the pan from the heat, but continue to keep stirring for another minute or two until the mixture cools, then transfer into clean, sterilised glass bottles. Stopper tightly and keep out of the light. Take one or two teaspoonfuls when the need arrives. An unusual taste but an effective remedy!

Seasonal Skies

The weather in January is notoriously unreliable. Considering that the length of the days is roughly the same as in early December, the variation in temperature can be remarkable; it can be very warm or surprisingly cold and there are many traditional sayings which give evidence to this:

> *If the grass grows in January, it grows the worse for all the year.*
> *A January Spring is worth nothing.*
> *If the birds begin to sing in January, then frosts are on the way.*
> *March in January, January in March!*

As I write these words on the 15th of the month, the rain is pouring down and the wind is at gale force, but it is really quite warm, 12^0 C.

There are also traditional ways of forecasting the weather for the following months, according to the weather in January. The type of weather we get in the first three days of the month are said to indicate the weather for the first three months of the year and the last 12 days of January are said to forecast the weather for the whole of the 12 months, each day representing the respective month. Obviously, this is not always totally accurate, but these old sayings are not just superstitions, they are based on the collected observations of generations of people who were close to the Land and were aware of its moods. The patterns of weather would be remarked upon and remembered and gradually a set of sayings would develop which would help to foretell what weather would be likely in the coming year. The fact that many of these old saws contradict each other need not necessarily concern us either, they just need to be looked at for their place of origin; the type of weather that would occur in one place at one time of year would not necessarily be the same as that in another place at the same time and this must be remembered. For example, the 13th day of the month, the Feast of St. Hilary, is often said to be the coldest day of the year, yet I can remember far colder within the same month and yet no more than 50 miles away from me the temperature was 10 degrees colder. On the 25th of the month, *"If St. Paul's Day be fair and clear, then it betides a happy year."* This will only be proven much later and the weather on St. Paul's Day needs noting and comparing with what happens later. It is a good practice to begin your own notations of weather and climate for your own part of the country; not only will this begin to give you some observations to look back upon for future comparison, but you will also begin to develop a feel for the tides of your own part of the Land and this can only help you to develop a closer bond and association with it.

The first meteor shower of the year can be seen around the 3rd-4th of the month. This is the Quadrantid meteor shower, coming from the area of the constellation Boötes and so named for an older galaxy – Quadrans Muralis – which has now been displaced. It is one of the strongest showers of the year, supplying up to 80 meteors an hour for its duration, but cannot be seen for long. As it reaches its peak, dawn breaks and observation becomes impossible. This shower actually begins in late December and ends on January 7th, but is practically unobservable at its beginning and ending dates. Start watching the Northern sky after about 11:00 p.m., just above the horizon, and you should catch this amazing spectacle.

Late on a crisp January night, the saucepan-like shape of The Plough, part of the Great Bear (Ursa Major), climbs away from the North-Eastern horizon. Its 'pointers', Merak and Dubhe, indicate the position of our current Pole Star (Polaris, part of the Little Bear, Ursa Minor) around which all the other stars appear to circle throughout the night. Polaris is a little over 400 light years away; when you watch it you are seeing light that left the Pole Star about the time that the great Spanish Armada was approaching the British coasts! The Plough has long held a central role in British mythology and starlore and has been known by many other names as well, among them "Arthur's Wain", "Our Lord's Wain" (referring to the Old Male Power of the Witches) and "Gabriel's Wain". "Wain" means "wagon" and refers to the shape of The Plough, otherwise called saucepan-like. As well as pointing the way to the Pole Star, The Plough, the Nail of the Heavens, is seen as the vessel and container of the Old Powers, always 'watching' the constellation of Orion, with which it shares many connections. Its name of "Gabriel's Wain" links it with the Gabriel Ratchets or Hounds and hence to the Wild Hunt which rides high, fast and furious at this time of the year. Because of this association perhaps, it has also been linked to a funeral bier in its role of conveying the spirits of the deceased to their celestial abode in the Otherworld, which is, conversely, seen as being inside the sacred Land. It is also linked in natural lore with the "Seven Whistlers", those supernatural beings (said by some to be Geese!) that presage the individual's death when heard high overhead at night. It is the one constellation that is immediately identifiable by most people and hence the most important and – literally – central to British lore. It can be observed at any time of year, but has, perhaps, more connection with the Winter Tide than others, and can always be used to orient oneself and one's actions correctly. That it is important further afield is borne out in that it is named as some kind of Wain in most other Northern European countries, variously being "King David's Chariot" (Eire), "La Roue" or the "Great Chariot" (France), "Karl's Vagn" (referring to Thor in Denmark, Sweden and Iceland), "Irmines Wagen" (Saxony) and the "Himmel Wagen" (referring to Odin/Wotan in Germany). It is a constellation essentially of transformational energy (mainly of a masculine nature), and is worked with to great advantage at this pivotal time in the year.

Around the 20th of the month the constellation of Aquarius comes to the fore and in traditional astrology its influence is felt for about the next four weeks. Seen throughout recorded history by most cultures as primarily connected to water, it is an appropriate constellation to view at this wet and often dismal time of year. The star system has variously been viewed as a water jug, a jar, a bucket, a man or boy carrying or pouring water and a donkey with water jars in its panniers. It has no essentially bright stars and can be difficult to pick out but should be looked for on the North-Western horizon from the latter part of the month onwards. Its main stars are Sadalmelik (from the Arabic for "Lucky stars of the king") and Sadalsuud ("Luckiest of the lucky") and may refer to its association with the myth of the youth, Ganymede. He was the son of the King of Troy, the most beautiful youth in the world and was much desired by the Greek Zeus. The Olympian carried him off to the top of the sacred mount, home of the Greek Powers, in the form of an eagle (Aquila the Eagle is another constellation nearby) and installed him there as his cupbearer. This angered Hera, whose daughter Ganymede had displaced, which in turn enraged Zeus, who glorified the youth by setting him up among the stars. All the 'liquid' and emotional overtones of the associations makes this a beneficial constellation to work with, but one that must be treated with caution lest you be 'carried away' yourself! It is appropriate for this constellation – with its watery nature – to be prominent at this time, as it heralds the earthing towards the end of the month of the cleansing and purificatory energies, released on the inner planes at the Winter Solstice and which manifest at Candlemas time. Research into the deeper meanings underlying these myths and energies would be well rewarded.

Flora

One of our most well-known and loved native trees is the Yew (*Taxus baccata*). Its evergreen leaves stand out sharply against the wasted backdrop of an English wood at this time of year, especially with the slight silvering on the underside of the prickly, spiny leaves. This immensely shaggy tree can grow up to a height of 40 or 50 feet or more and is the longest-lived species in Britain, outdoing even the Oak by many centuries. It is difficult to judge exactly how old individual specimens can be as the heartwood dies after about 400 or 500 years, the tree becoming completely hollow, and hence the ring-dating technique of dendrochronology is impossible. The usual method after this time is by measuring the girth of the tree and extrapolating the date from previous measurements. It is estimated by this method that trees of 30 feet in girth are approximately 2,400 years old, of 33 feet are 3,000 years old and those of 35 feet exceed 4,500 years. This takes into account the queer habit of the tree of suspending its own growth rate in later life and even of periods of shrinkage in girth! The leaves, fruit and seed are all highly poisonous, except to birds who love the fruit, and are the main instrument in propagating the species by passing the seed through their droppings. We get our word "toxin" from the Greek word "Taxus", meaning "poison", which is the genus name of the tree. However, recently the drug "Taxol" has been extracted from leaf cuttings and has proved to be highly effective in combating ovarian and other types of cancer. Incidentally, the folk name "Snottygags" also comes from the sticky berries, which adhere to almost anything they touch once squashed. The wood of the tree, far from being poisonous, has been famously used for the English longbow for centuries, although, surprisingly, Spanish or Italian Yew wood was preferred and imported in the Middle Ages, as the British variety was too brittle. The branch wood however, is a beautiful wood to carve, very white, smooth and strong, almost like bone and makes excellent walking sticks, staffs and particularly wands. It is said that seasoned Yew wood outlives iron and a 250,000 year-old Yew spear, uncovered in Essex, is the oldest-known wooden artefact yet discovered. The Yew tree is notorious for growing in churchyards and this must now be addressed. Many reasons are given for this, the two main ones being that it was a royal decree to plant the tree to grow the wood for bows and that by growing them in walled churchyards it would keep them away from the cattle, who would otherwise eat them and be poisoned. The first of these explanations can be safely dismissed for a few reasons. The age of the vast majority of Yews pre-date the churches by which they grow; Yews are only generally found in ones and twos in churchyards, which would not produce a great stock of bows; only about 28% of known Yews grow in churchyards so many people must have disobeyed the royal decree in that case. Finally, the wood for longbows was usually imported as we have already seen. The arguments for protecting livestock also fall down when you consider that most Yews were planted or are found outside of the protective walls of the churchyard. Although the Church did make use of the branches as substitute "Palms" at Easter, it would seem that the churches were built on already-existing, sacred places, hallowed by long practice and association and by the sanctity and awe in which the tree was — and is — held. Because of its longevity and the fact that it is an evergreen the Yew has always been seen as a symbol of immortality and eternity – it is even seen as the original Nordic World Tree "Yggrdrasil" by some, instead of the more commonly-accepted Ash tree – and has been venerated as such for centuries before the Christian era. However, because of its toxic nature, it is also seen as a tree of death and the Underworld; this has been the tradition for many centuries and Yews were planted over graves in churchyards later on, to protect and purify the dead. What better symbol then for the eternally-cycling tides of life and death, of renewal and growth, of decay and decline, only to be renewed again? The Yew was revered long before Christianity came to these shores and the newer beliefs fell in with the patterns of worship of the older faiths, as with so much else. There is no need to look any further for the explanation.

One of the early signs that life is returning to the wild is the flowering of the Lesser Celandine (*Ranunculus ficaria*) otherwise more commonly known as "Pilewort" (other less well-known names being "Figwort", "Golden Guineas", "Foalfoot" and "Spring Messenger"). Not to be confused with the Greater Celandine, which flowers much later and with which it shares no relationship, this delightful little plant puts forth bright yellow star-shaped flowers, on the top of spindly little stalks about three inches long. The flowers open and close, depending on the amount of sunlight during the day and the temperature of the air surrounding them. The leaves are heart-shaped when young, turning ivy-shaped later and are often spotted or blotched with darker markings. This plant grows profusely in moist areas, such as ditches, stream banks and the corners of fields, and also in drier areas where there is plenty of shade to conserve the moisture that it loves. Although commonly supposed to flower from February onwards, reaching a peak in March and April, I have often seen it flower in January; indeed, I saw many blooms this morning, January 19th and have even known it to flower profusely before the Winter Solstice. More evidence of global warming? The name "Celandine" comes from the Greek "Chelidon" meaning "Swallow" and referring to the harbinger of Springtime. But the Lesser Celandine flowers well before the return of this welcome bird and the term has probably become confused with the Greater Celandine, which does indeed flower when the Swallows return. The common name, Pilewort, comes from the shape of the roots, or more exactly tubers, which take the shape of clusters of little haemorrhoids. According to the "Doctrine of Signatures" 'like cures like' and Pilewort has for centuries been used as an herbal remedy for the cure and ease of this complaint. Either a tincture is made from the tuber and taken internally or an ointment is made from the expressed juice and applied topically, the astringent action being to cause the haemorrhoids to shrink and hence ease the pain of the sufferer. The ointment applied to varicose veins will also relieve this condition and, in my experience, is used for this purpose even more than for piles. If it works, use it; it doesn't matter why! The tubers break readily from their attachment to the plant and spread rapidly in any area where the plant is found. After May, however, the conditions generally become too dry for it and the above-ground portions wither and die, leaving no trace it was ever there. The below-ground tubers though, continue to harvest moisture and to swell, reaching a peak in late Summer and Autumn. They then lie dormant until fresh growth is triggered in the New Year, or earlier; the retaining of the moisture underground is the reason why they are so ready and eager to flower so early and bring a welcome splash of colour to the dull and dreary woodlands of late Winter.

Another native evergreen is the Juniper bush (*Juniperus communis*). I say bush, but the growth of this plant is so varied that it can often appear as a tree, growing up to 17 or 18 feet tall. It prefers to grow on well-drained, rocky, acidic, limestone soil. In the North of the country it will be found on cold, rainy moorland, near bilberry and other berry bushes; in the South it prefers hot, dry chalk downlands. It can grow from a low, spindly prostrate bush, much shaped by wind and animal low-browsers, to a tall, conical column, much like a Mediterranean Cypress. Male and female are separate plants, the female having both unripe green berries and ripe blue ones on its branches at the same time, the fruit taking two or three years to be mature. Once picked and dried, the berries tend to lose the blue colour and turn blackish, which is how we generally know them. The branches have long been used for firewood, producing a piney/cedar smell which is not unpleasant, and also for the bases of hayricks, the resinous nature of the wood making it resist rot well. The exceedingly spiky branches – a sharp green in colour above with a silvery sheen beneath – have in the past often been used as a cheaper substitute for barbed wire ... and it works just as well! The berries are well-known as the distinctive flavouring for the spirituous drink Gin and have been used as such for centuries. British Juniper has not been used for this purpose for over a century though, the berries being imported from Eastern Europe, mainly Hungary, as they produce a better flavour. The folk name "Bastard Killer" comes from the common and infamous use of Gin as an abortifacient, deriving from one of the properties of the berries themselves. Taken in small doses in infusion the plant is an aid to digestion and a carminative to the system; taken in larger dosages by pregnant women it can cause miscarriage and haemorrhage. As late as 1993, Juniper pills were being advertised in certain magazines as *The Lady's Friend* and were apparently in great demand. On a lighter note, Juniper is an excellent diuretic, having an irritant action on the lining of the kidneys and hence helps in the case of kidney and liver complaints and in water retention. It was also used in the delightful sounding complaint of "dropsy" (a build-up of fluid around the heart) to release the liquid and hence the pressure on the essential organ. In animal husbandry an ointment was made from the leaves and berries, for wounds and to keep flies away from the injury. It was also used in very small amounts in horses' feed to perk up an ailing animal and give it a bit of spirit. The main folk use for this helpful plant was in its aromatic smoke when burned; it has been used for centuries as a purificatory agent in the case of hauntings and spirit possession, of ill health when supernatural agencies were suspected and for general ghostly hauntings and infestations. In the Highlands of Scotland it was the custom for the young men at Hogmanay (New Year's Eve) to go into the hills and collect Juniper branches, which would then be left out overnight by the fire to dry. In the morning, all the doors and windows would be closed, the dried branches lit and the whole house fumigated with the aromatic smoke. This was to banish any lingering, negative influence from the past year and to cleanse and purify the home for the New Year just begun.

Fauna

A colourful and sprightly creature that is highly-visible at the moment is the Goldfinch (*Carduelis carduelis*) whose common names are equally as eye catching: "Goldie", "Gool", "Proud Tailor", "Jack Nicker", "King Harry", "Linnet", "Red Cap" and "Thistle Finch". "Finch" comes from the Old English and originally referred only to the Chaffinch, but subsequently became extended to include the whole family. The colouration of the Goldfinch is both striking and beautiful, especially when seen against the backdrop of the bare trees of the season and the Thistle and Teasel heads, the seeds from which are its main food.

It looks like an exotic escapee from some Victorian aviary and indeed many thousands were once caught and sold as cage birds. The attraction of the birds' plumage was enhanced by their sweet and melodious voices and hence they became highly desirable. The collective noun for the Goldfinch is a "charm", by derivation from the 16th-century meaning of "a blended noise", but the root word is Middle English, from the Latin "carmen" meaning an "incantation or spell", and refers to the magical, twittering sound that they make when flocking together. Many of their folk names refer to their gorgeous plumage – "Proud Taylor", "King Henry" – and reflect the resplendent colours and the costumes of the old monarchy. The Goldfinch has long been depicted in religious art and painting, second only to the Dove, where it was used to represent the Resurrection. The golden wings were seen as highly symbolic and important, as was the red cap, hence the name "Red Cap"; many red-marked birds, like the Robin, were associated with the blood from the crown of thorns at the Crucifixion and as the Goldfinch was strongly associated with the prickly Thistle seed heads, this was seen as highly relevant. There is a long tradition of using the bird in literary allusions too, going as far back as the time of Chaucer; in *The Cooks Tale* is this reference to the apprentice: *"Gaillard he was as goldfinch in the shawe"*. The bird is also used in the later poem attributed to Chaucer, called *The Flower and the Leaf.* As well as a symbol of virtue the Goldfinch was used to denote wealth in literature, as in the Wedding of Cock Robin and Jenny Wren: *"Who gives this maid away? / I do says the goldfinch/ And her fortune I will pay"*. Inevitably for such a striking bird, the Goldfinch has also found medicinal use; the flesh, if particularly fatty, was used as a restorative in consumptives and, mixed with other ingredients, it was used to clear obstructions of the bladder and urinary system.

A more down-to-earth creature is the native Stoat (*Mustela erminea*). This notorious small mammal is larger than the Weasel, although frequently confused with it, even sharing the same name in Eire (Weasel that is; there are no native Weasels in Ireland). Other common terms are "Clubster", "Ermine", "Futteret", "Puttice" and "Whitteret". It has had the common name "Stoat" since 1460, but the origin is obscure and there is no known meaning. During the Summer the Stoat is chestnut in colour above, having pure white underparts and a black tip to its tail; in Winter it changes to pure white all over – except the tail end – which then gives it its main alternative name of "Ermine". This small hunter is quite a vicious little creature and fearless to boot. They occur throughout Britain, eating mainly rodents and voles, although larger males will take rabbits if they can. They kill by a sharp bite to the back of the neck, kill for seeming pleasure as will a Fox and can devastate a hen-house easily if it is not well protected. It is said that they have been known to suck the blood from babies left outside to sleep, from a bite under the ear and, although it is untrue that they gang up on and attack lone boys, they will leap upon humans if cornered and can deliver a nasty bite in the process. These days they themselves are under threat from the predation of introduced Mink that have escaped into the wild, or been deliberately released by well-meaning "animal liberationists", and who themselves are now causing havoc to the native wildlife. Stoats nest in small burrows or hollows in trees, often taking these over from their prey, if to their liking. The males always mate with females that are still suckling from their mothers and the implantation of the fertilised egg is delayed until maturity is reached, hence the females grow up pregnant and ready to start their own families! The use of Ermine as a fur was first mentioned in 1138 and has always been linked to royalty and nobility, commoners being forbidden to wear it – even if they could afford it. Peers' robes are still made from Ermine (although these days it is more likely to be synthetic unless they have inherited them), the number of lines of 'dots' on the robes (the tail of the Stoat), denoting the rank; four is the highest, denoting a Duke. The white fur symbolises purity and chastity and was much used by Queen Elizabeth I in her perceived role as the Virgin Queen, having various portraits of herself painted wearing it and even being accompanied in one by a very curious, tiny representation of the creature itself – not very accurately rendered. The fur itself can appear to change colour in a few days, depending on the temperature and location of the animal; all Stoats in the North of

Britain turn white, but for those in the South the change can be only partial. The reason for the apparently abrupt change in colour is that the new coat grows gradually under the old fur; when the temperature changes, the old coat is shed and out pops the new.

On the subject of dark and light colouring, there can be no more obvious bird in the British countryside, and one that most people will instantly recognise, than the Magpie (*Pica pica*). Essentially a black and white Crow, this member of the Corvid family goes by many pseudonyms, amongst them being "Chattermag", "Haggister", "Madge", "Marget", "Ninut", "Pyat" and "Tell Piet". Many of the folk names derive from the Latin term "pica" meaning "piebald", and denote the main feature of this bird, referring to its distinctive black and white plumage (although the black is actually a very beautiful blue-black iridescent colour when seen up close). Probably the first thing that comes to mind when anybody thinks of a Magpie is the rhyme associated with it, beginning "*One for sorrow* ... ". This rhyme is known throughout the British Isles in many different versions, often varying quite widely, but all containing the essence that the Magpie is a bird not quite of this world and closely connected with the Other. Often known as the "Devil's bird", meeting one unexpectedly could often be a shock if not an ill omen and had to be dealt with in various ways; one should doff one's cap/hat/bonnet, bow and wish it a good day. Alternatively, one should bow, turn around, spit on the ground and walk away. Whatever was done, however the perceived threat was dealt with, the main ingredients were respect and politeness; in this way, one should always approach and treat the Other. As a bird, the Magpie is aggressive and omnivorous and, despite persecution, has trebled in numbers in the last 40 years. It has an unjustified reputation for the decline in British songbirds, according to recent research, but it can and will take both their eggs and young. It has a harsh, chattering call that is particularly apparent at this time of year, when it congregates in large numbers in the bare fields and leafless branches of the trees, in a kind of "parliament", seemingly discussing their next moves on the defenceless wildlife around them; this of necessity adds to its sinister reputation. Maybe because of its garrulous reputation, folklore claims that if the tongue of a Magpie is scratched with the edge of a silver sixpence and a drop of human blood dripped onto the cut, the bird will acquire the power of human speech; I wouldn't advise trying it! The Magpie has a nasty reputation for bad luck, based on totally spurious Biblical references, but these do not hold water when examined closely; however, this does reinforce its association with the Other and the Old Powers. A variant of the well-known rhyme concerning the number of Magpies one sees, from my home county of Suffolk, also reinforces this:

One for Anger
Two for Mirth
Three for a Wedding
Four for a Birth
Five for Rich
Six for Poor
Seven for a Witch, I can tell you no more!

On the other hand, it's nice to know that this much-maligned bird was also reputed to have healing powers too. The dried and powdered flesh was used as a cure for epilepsy; eating a Magpie leg would help someone who had been bewitched and the flesh, when eaten, would cure melancholy, vertigo and poor eyesight. So that's all right then!

And so, we come to the close of the Winter Tide. As I have said before, these divisions are not hard and fast and already the signs of Spring may have been apparent for a few weeks, the snowdrops out, the sun warmer. However, working with a natural rhythm, it is probably time to put the things of the Dark Time behind us now and look forward to the brighter and longer days that are ahead of us, make plans for the future and observe the next phase of the natural cycle – the Tide of Spring.

THE SPRING TIDE

≈℧ᘓ ✤ ᘓ℧≈

The feel of the energies that flow from Candlemas to Roodmas is markedly different to that of the Winter Tide. Whenever the Spring Tide may begin – and this will vary from year to year as we follow a natural rhythm, watching and waiting for the signs and sensations that tell us that Spring has truly arrived – the feeling is on a much more optimistic note than that of the preceding dark days. Despite the fact that the weather may still have a few surprises in store for us, in that some of the coldest, wettest and windiest days may yet still be ahead of us, there is a certain lightness in the air that cannot be mistaken and everything in nature metaphorically 'pricks up its ears' and takes note.

During this tide, the majority of hibernating animals emerge after their long rest, begin to search for or reunite with mates and turn their minds to the propagation of their species. The woods and fields begin to resound with the songs of the male birds calling to the female, the sight of bright plumage and colourful, furry displays as one sex calls to the other and mock or serious battles take place to determine who is fit enough to pass on their genes to the next generation. Nesting materials are sought and new homes built or old ones repaired, dens and setts are 'spring cleaned' and old bedding exchanged for new. Many of the larger mammals, which mated in the previous Autumn, will now begin to give birth to their young and the early birds will lay their first clutch of eggs, to take advantage of the new insect life that is just emerging from its Winter dormancy. The lambing season will begin in some areas and continue through much of this tide, in days past bringing a welcome new and fresh source of protein in the form of milk and meat.

It is also now that we start to see the first, real flush of new plant life. Slowly at first, heralded by the early Snowdrops, Catkins and green shoots of Bluebells peeping through the decay of last year's leaf litter, the slow trickle becomes a rush and riot of early colour. Many wild, herbaceous plants that are native to our woodlands need to flower, be pollinated and set seed quickly, before the burgeoning canopy of leaves above blocks out most of the available Sunlight. Our woodlands are therefore a celebration of colour and perfume in Spring, a delight to all the senses. Later in this tide, most of the trees will have put forth new shoots and leaves, many of which have medicinal and/or magical properties. Otherwise they are good to eat or brew from and will spread a gentle shade with their canopy from the slowly-strengthening Sun. Many of the smaller, earlier flowers that have so delighted us will already be fading and we will not see them again until the beginning of the next Spring Tide. However, these give way to the full, Summer flowers and herbs that follow after.

In this vein, the great Powers in and of the Land begin to stir now too. Although they have not fully slept through the Winter Tide, their energies have receded from us, to let us find our own way in the dark and to obtain some much-needed respite from their labours of the year just passed. Now their energies begin to be felt once more, as they put forth their senses in the green shoots and burgeoning Life all around us. Their Winter sojourn in the Underworld is nearly at an end and they make ready to walk the Land in preparation for the work of the Summer to come. The Powers never truly leave us, but they recede and give us a chance to act on our own; now they are beginning to return in full force and invite us to work in tandem with them once again.

As the planet spins, tilts and moves further from the Sun, new constellations and star systems begin to become visible and have an influence in our night skies. No longer the dark, deep Mysteries of the Winter months, but gradually brighter and fresher influences come to bear. We say farewell to the Wild Hunt and the fierce, warrior enthusiasm of Aries bursts through, initiating the swirl of changing energies at the Vernal Equinox and all the conflicting feelings that come with it. This sets the stage for the manifestation of the life-giving energies at Roodmas and the culmination of the Spring Tide.

On the domestic front, there is also a stirring to be felt, the gradual 'wake-up and stretch' that we all feel as the increasing length and light of the days begins to take hold. The changing of the clocks to British Summer Time at the end of March gives a big jolt to the system – artificially timed as it is – and impetus to new projects. There is the urge to cast out the old and renew and refresh that which remains, just as in the animal and plant kingdoms, to purify and cleanse and prepare for all the new tasks that lie ahead. Plans will be laid that will culminate, hopefully, in a fruitful harvest later in the year and the seeds of that future harvest are now sown.

All in all, the Spring Tide brings with it a sense of hope and optimism that was sometimes lacking and hard to see in the darker days. It is now time to focus less on our scrying bowls and divination tools for a while and get back to a more physical approach to Life's Mysteries with some good old hands-on spadework!

February

⁂ ✳ ⁂

The Sun rises around 07:42 a.m. and sets around 04:46 p.m. at the beginning of the month.

The image for February – known as the Whirling Month – is the following:

> *Cloathed in a dark Skie-colour, carrying in his right hand the Sign Pisces.*

Times & Tides
Around the beginning of February (or maybe even earlier), we see the manifestation of the energies that were released at the Winter Solstice on the inner realms, namely those of cleansing, purification and new birth. This earthing of

inner tides does not take place on a set date, although it is often named "Candlemas" by those who follow a Natural Craft and sometimes also "The Quickening" and placed on either the 1st or the 2nd of the month. It will vary in date from year to year and from place to place; hence in one year this process may already have occurred in East Anglia, while those in Yorkshire may still be waiting for it to happen. The signs of the beginning of Spring that are accepted by individuals will also differ. Some may wait for the first Snowdrops to blossom, some will celebrate at the New Moon around the end of January or the beginning of February, some may wait for the first lambing to begin, whilst still others may wait for a combination of these things, or others. All, however, will be aware of a certain feeling in the atmosphere, a certain shift in the 'sense' of things that will tell them, along with the other signs, that Spring has arrived. In a Natural Craft setting, this feeling is not dependent on a calendar date, but will be reflected in the signs that the individual sees around them, combined with their own, inner awareness. Thus, this feeling may occur as late as the middle of February depending on the year, but will reflect an actual reality, rather than what is 'supposed to' happen.

As far as Natural Craft is concerned, it is the energy tides of the year itself that are acknowledged and celebrated, whenever they occur. This is done with full knowledge and awareness of what is being done and why, anything else is cultural accretion and 'window-dressing'. As an example, in an area where there is no Sheep farming there would be no celebration of the lambing season, as it is irrelevant to the local conditions, and the symbolism would pertain to other local traditions and folkways, if any. The whole focus of this festival is to honour and mark the ending of the Winter Tide and the springing forth of new life, as evidenced in the emerging greenery and quickening lifetide all around, in whatever way is locally appropriate. Ceremonies of purification are generally performed by Crafters, using salt and water, to symbolically cleanse the 'atmosphere' and refresh the area, ready for another year's round. Fires may also be lit to honour the new life in the Land and bad habits, thoughts and actions that may have accumulated during the Winter may be symbolically cast into the flames. The fires also signify the blossoming and nurturing of one's own inner illumination and the awakening of the inner senses and powers within the individual, after the dormancy and rest of Winter. Personal Oaths and Vows may be renewed and/or new ones taken on for the year. It is now time to become more active again and set aside the time of contemplation and passivity. We salute also the Dark Lord as he leads the Wild Hunt out on its last ride of Winter, before returning to the Hollow Hills, to await the opening of the gates at All Hallows once more.

A personal ritual practice for this time of year may be conducted as follows. As far as possible, find a natural source of flowing water (a stream or spring would be ideal), or failing that, a cauldron or large pan of spring water/rain water will suffice. Before setting out, write out on a piece of paper those things which you find negative or counterproductive about yourself, and all the magical cobwebs that you have accumulated over the dark tide that you now wish to be rid of. Put this to one side and take a hot bath or shower, keeping the idea of cleansing and purification in mind all the while (you can add a little natural salt to your bath as well if you like, along with some of the purificatory herbs discussed herein). Dry yourself and put on clean clothing, take your piece of paper and a lighted, white candle and go to your working site, which you have prepared earlier. Place the candle down by the source of water, making sure it does not go out and, by its light, recite clearly those things that you wish to be rid of, bearing in mind that it may take some considerable effort on your part to achieve this. When you are ready, touch the paper to the candle flame and let it burn completely to ashes, which you must then cast into the running water or cauldron. Dip your fingers into the water now and make an 'X' on your forehead, saying such words as:

Thus I cleanse and purify my inner and outer being that I may waken afresh and kindle the flame anew.

Now sit before the candle for some time, contemplating the enlivening that is taking place all around and within you and the cleansing that has taken place – really feel it. Take the flame into you that you may be quickened and illuminated by its light and prepared for the fresh tasks of this new tide. Spend as much time as you wish over this. When you are ready, rise and blow out the flame, remembering that, as an image of your essential spirituality and divine spark, it is eternally kindled within. If you have used a cauldron, overturn it now to let the ashes and water flow away, then just turn your back and walk away into the Spring Tide.

This is a deceptively simple rite, but relies on two essentials to be really effective: the Crafter must sincerely wish to partake of the incoming tide of purificatory energies and must at the same time be able to contact them effectively. When and if these two things are accomplished, this simple rite is decidedly powerful.

Some practitioners link this festival with the Church celebration of Candlemas on the 2nd of the month, using some of the same symbolism as the "Purification of the Virgin Mary", whose 'date' this is, considering it to be but another facet of the same commemoration. The Church festival does not appear to have taken over any pre-existing Northern European pagan festival, notwithstanding the fact that the 1st of the month is also St. Brigit's Day, maybe adopted/taken over from Brighid/Brigantia, one of the Old Powers of Light and Fire. However, it was readily welcomed by the 'locals' and the symbolism adapted to their own conditions and thoughts of the ending of Winter. The fact that there may have been at one time an acknowledgement of this period in prehistory is borne out by recent discoveries of passage graves in some of the outlying Scottish islands. There are 'openings' above the doorways, similar to those at Newgrange and Maeshowe, but these newly-discovered sites let in the light at the end of October and the beginning of February, which is not thought to be coincidental and may indicate certain observances at those times.

Following on from this stirring of the fires of life within the Land, it is only natural that people in general will begin to feel more 'alive' and on the 14th of the month comes that annual celebration of love and romance, known as St. Valentine's Day. No one appears to know the origin of this celebration, as the first mention of this date specifically records the pairing of birds; only later was it applied to humans. However, from the Middle Ages onwards it was known and celebrated by both rich and poor alike. There are two St. Valentines known to have existed; both were Romans who died in the 3rd century with no connection to amorousness, except that they died on the eve of Lupercalia, (February 15th) which was a Roman festival of purification and fertility. This festival died out after the Fall of the Empire, but the date remained in common memory and some of its attributes came to be applied to this early Spring festival of love. Originally people were chosen by lots to be Valentines, or it was the first person that you encountered on that day; later, people chose their own. The giving of gifts preceded by centuries the sending of cards and sometimes these were very rich and expensive. Children also expected to be involved and often went a-begging on Valentine's Morn for their own 'favours'. Eventually the Valentine's Card that we all know was developed during the Victorian era and, despite a brief period of disfavour in the early 20th century, has been with us ever since. These cards were often quite elaborate affairs, being handmade with feathers, silk, lace and other frills; sometimes a lad would carve his sweetheart a token of his affection and these were known as "country swains" or "wooden valentines" and were often cherished as keepsakes and passed on as family heirlooms. Sometimes they were created deliberately as magical love charms, designed with the intention of attracting and keeping the object of desire. Although this was – and still is – a common practice, I wouldn't advise the forcing of someone into doing something as serious as falling in love against their will – much better doing it because they want to!

Towards the end of the month there occurs an annual festival that everyone seems to enjoy, whether of a spiritual/religious frame of mind or not, and that is Shrove Tuesday – "Pancake Day". Because of the dating of Easter (which I shall discuss later), this celebration that marks the last day before the beginning of Lent, is very much a moveable feast and does not have a set date, so it can occur anywhere from the middle to the end of the month. Shrove Tuesday was anciently known as "Fastern's E'en" and otherwise as "Guttit Tuesday", "Bannock Night" or "Doughnut Day". It was the day on which all the rich foods had to be finished up and the larder emptied, as they would not keep during the 40-day fast of Lent when they were forbidden. Hence, across the country, the custom of making various types of pancakes, cakes and scones, with various traditions attached to them can be found. These cakes may have their ultimate origin in the cakes made by our Anglo-Saxon forebears, as February was known to them as "Solmonath" or "Flat Cakes' Month". According to the monk, the Venerable Bede, they would make small cakes in honour of their deities and the return of the light of the Sun after the dark Winter. After the Reformation, the strictures on what could and could not be eaten were generally disregarded, but the custom of making these cakes was so deeply imbedded in tradition that it continues to this day. As at other times of year, small tokens for divinatory purposes would be placed inside some of the cakes and one's fortune determined by what was found.

Some cakes were known as the "Dumb Cake", as they had to be made in absolute silence. Parts of these would then be placed under the pillow at night to induce prophetic dreams of one's future (this is somewhat reminiscent of the "Dumb Supper", held in silence, to evoke the shade of a deceased loved one).

The next day began Lent proper. Ash Wednesday, as it has come to be called, marked the beginning of the Mediaeval fast of 40 days, stemming from the Anglo-Saxon term "lenten" or "lenct", referring to both "Spring" and the actual fast. The word appears to mean "lengthening", referring to the increased daylight that became more noticeable at this time of year, and to the feeling of joy that it imparts. It did not become shortened to "Lent" until the 13th century and did not mean only the feast itself until the 17th century. The "ash" of Ash Wednesday refers to the blessed ashes of burnt "palm crosses" or equivalent, that were mixed with holy water and smeared on the heads of penitents in church on this day. This was done the better to confess their sins and seek absolution before they began the holy fast. Most of the meaning and import of these actions – and indeed the fast of Lent itself – were done away with by the successive reformations of the Tudor and Stuart periods. Only very recently has some semblance of meaning returned to these practices in some traditions. To a follower of Natural Religion, dual-faith or not, this is a period of internal cleansing and introspection. Just as the Winter has been banished and cast away with the Candlemas rites, so now must the same cleansing take place within the individual. This is a very personal and private matter and the individual would perform whatever forms of cleansing and purification that they deemed appropriate. Having said this, there is no sense in which this is done as an act of atonement or confession, Natural Craft not accepting 'sin' in this sense. It is an act of personal exploration, the better to understand oneself in an attempt to move forward in and deepen one's personal spirituality.

At the end of the month, once in every four years, occurs the "leap day, that extra day that keeps our current calendar aligned with the solar year. That the Earth takes slightly more than 365 days to orbit the Sun (or the other way round, as it was seen in ancient cultures), was already well-known to the Romans, whose leap day fell on February 24th which was the day after the end of their old year. By 1752, when Britain adopted the reformed, Gregorian calendar, we were 11 days adrift from 'actual' time, so these 11 days were dropped from the calendar in that year and a 'correct' leap day added in on February 29th every fourth year. In terms of a seasonal flow of energies however, this actually makes no difference at all to a Natural Practitioner, as they do not go by calendar dates. It is how, what and when the natural rhythms react and happen that really matters. Having said that, tradition states that on this one day in every four years, a woman may ask a man to marry her and woe betide him if he refuses as a fine will have to be paid. The smallest and simplest fine is traditionally a kiss, but in the past it could have been a pound (in money), a pair of lace gloves, or even a silk evening gown – so, gentlemen, beware!

Flora

Surely one of the most obvious harbingers of Spring in the plant kingdom must be the Snowdrop (*Galanthus nivalis*). Commonly known variously as "Candlemas Bells", "February Fair Maid", "Mary's Tapers", "Snow Piercer" and "Dingle Dangle", this plant holds an ambiguous place in native flora, as no one is quite sure if it is indeed native. It is first mentioned as growing wild in the 1770s, in Gloucestershire and Worcestershire, yet there is a reference to it as a garden plant in 1664. However, in the first edition of Gerard's *Herball* published in 1597, there is an illustration and full and unmistakeable description of it, but under the name of "Bulbous Violet". The common names of "Candlemas Bells" and "Mary's Tapers" would seem to indicate quite an early date for it, as the Catholic feast of Candlemas was mostly abolished in the Reformation and it is frequently and plentifully to be found growing in the grounds of ruined monasteries and abbeys. The Catholic Church accepts it as a recognised symbol of Candlemas and it is also an emblem of the Virgin Mary. It is often used to decorate the altar at this time, therefore it would seem to have been named at an early date in this country. However the question of its origins and age may be resolved, it is unquestionably one of the prime symbols of this time of year and will obviously remain so. It is a hardy plant, often pushing its way up through the frozen ground and covering of snow in the harshest of conditions, its brilliant, gleaming white petals shining out in the surrounding gloom. It reproduces mainly by bulb division, rather than setting seed, because of the time of year. However, it is known to produce seedlings when plants are growing close together and it is a warm February, allowing the insects to emerge and pollinate it. The best time to propagate it in the garden is now, by splitting clumps when still in flower and redistributing them around. It spreads very slowly across a hillside and is one of the main indicators of an ancient woodland, if appearing in any quantity. Conversely, it spreads rapidly along stream and river banks, the water carrying the bulbs downstream to colonise other areas. Consistent with its ambiguous origins is its status in folklore and usage. It is seen as a symbol of virginity and purity in the "Language of Flowers" and also as an emblem of death, being one of the flowers it is unlucky to bring indoors. This notwithstanding, it has been used for centuries in the purificatory incenses used at this time of year and also in love sachets in folk magic for Valentine's Day, the dried and crushed flower heads being mainly used in this fashion. It has little if any scent, but a vase of it on a bright windowsill at this time of year can do wonders to lift the spirits and conjure Springtime into the home.

Although some people associate the Rowan tree

(*Sorbus aucuparia*) with this time of year, it is normally still dormant now and showing neither bud nor leaf, let alone flower or fruit. A more appropriate tree to look at is the Hazel (*Corylus avellana*), some of whose folk names are "Halse", "Hezzel", "Ranger", "Woodnut" and of course "Lambs' Tails", referring to the dangling catkins, the male pollinating organ. These obviously-named features can come out as early as late December, but are generally seen in all their golden-powdered glory in February, doing their job of fertilising the tiny, red female organs, which grow on the same branches, ready to provide the bountiful harvest of rich, oily nuts in the Autumn. At least two Hazel trees growing nearby are needed for fertilisation and the production of the nuts, as the female buds usually ripen later than the male catkins of the same tree and hence need pollen from a different source. Walking through a Hazel copse at this time of the year, one is liable to come out shimmering from a dusting of golden powder, after ducking beneath all the dangling tails above! (The Alder catkins are also producing an abundance of pollen at this time, so if it is a mixed woodland you may come out looking more like a golden statue.) The Hazel was one of the first trees, shortly behind the Birch, to recolonise the British Isles after the last Ice Age and has been of great benefit to mankind ever since. The shells of the nuts, in particular, have been excavated in great quantities from Neolithic communities' midden heaps. Strictly speaking it is a shrub and not a tree, rarely growing to 30 feet in height. It can grow as a single-trunked plant, but if browsed or damaged by animals it will quickly send up new shoots which, if left, give the tree a much more shrub-like appearance. These shoots become the straight shafts that are "coppiced" (cut down at the base of the trunk to leave a "stool" from which new shoots will grow) and put to so many uses in woodcraft. Because of their rare ability in the tree world of lending themselves to being both split lengthways and twisted or bent at sharp angles, they are ideal for the framework of fences and wicker-work walls. Until very recently, most common houses were built of wattle and daub, which was based on the Hazel hurdle, which had remained unchanged for centuries. The beautiful, straight shafts of Hazel also lend themselves well to the making of magical wands and staffs, particularly so as it is seen as a symbol of wisdom and knowledge, conferring Otherworldly power on the bearer. Most water divining rods were – and still are – made from Hazel, forked or not, and it is definitely a property of this magical wood, treated in certain ways, that aids the "Water Witch" and not just a learnt technique. The bark, leaves and fruit of the tree all have various medicinal uses, including the treatment of varicose veins, circulatory disorders, menstrual complications, arthritis, piles and wounds that are slow to heal themselves. Hazel oil is an excellent base for making soap and Culpepper prescribed the nuts, sprinkled with pepper, for drawing "*rheum from the head.*" An incense made from the leaves or twigs may be used for most magical purposes, as it strengthens the magical Will and aids focus and concentration and it was/ is one of the nine sacred woods used for kindling magical fires. The nuts make good fertility charms but go easy – they are very effective, so don't use too many!

At the base of these trees at this time of the year, the bright green shoots and stems of Dog's Mercury (*Mercurialis perennis*) are to be found pushing through the leaf litter. Known also as "Dog's Cole" and "Boggard Posy", this member of the Spurge family is a common woodland plant with foliage very similar in type to the true Mercurys (Chenopodium), but very different in nature. Its name "Dog" means "false" or "bad" and refers to the fact that it is highly-poisonous to both animals and humans, though its different colouring and habitat should make it easy to distinguish from the true Mercurys. The symptoms of the poisoning, should it inadvertently be taken internally, consist of vomiting, pain, gastric and kidney inflammation and reddening of the cheeks and jaw in severe cases. It can kill the old and the very young, but healthy, mature adults will usually recover or suffer little. It grows in dense, leafy colonies in ancient woodland and tends to shade out more light-needy plants, even young Ash seedlings, but can spread rapidly given the chance and right conditions. It spreads by underground rhizomes that form 'clones' of the original and some are becoming almost evergreens in their ability to retain their leaves long into the Winter. It is an herbaceous, perennial plant and male and female specimens tend to form separate colonies, distant from each other and rarely producing seed, just like the Snowdrop. Although poisonous if taken internally, the old herbals advocate it for a variety of uses if applied externally (be careful though!!!). Washes can be made from the leaves for warts, sore eyes (!) jaundice and 'women's diseases' and a lotion can also be made for antiseptic, external dressings. The leaves and stems, bruised and steeped in water, give forth a glorious, fine blue colour, similar to indigo, but although permanent it is not fast, and will fade. It is one of the first green, leafy plants to show its head above ground in the year, so for this reason alone perhaps, it should be welcomed as another harbinger of Spring.

Seasonal Skies

Looking almost directly North in the night sky, slightly towards the left, one of the main circumpolar constellations is very evident, that of Cassiopeia, the seated Queen. She is one of the oldest known and recognised of our constellations, the Iron Age peoples naming her Llys Don, the "Court or Palace of the primal Ancestress", and Spenser even referred to her in his poem "The Faerie Queen". She is immediately recognisable as the celestial 'W' or celestial 'M', depending on the time of year (M, sort of on its side at the moment), because of the shape made by her stars and is easily found by most people. Her brightest star is named Schedar and means "Breast", her secondary being called Caph, which is from the Arabic name for the constellation, meaning "Hand", which she waves towards Perseus. Her Classical story refers to her overweening pride and vanity for which she was cast into the heavens as punishment and ended up in a somewhat 'lewd' and unbecoming position for a Lady, being seated askance on her throne or couch. In native tradition, she is much more revered and venerated and is seen as the Great Celestial Queen, the Lady and counterpart to the Lord of Ursa Major. She is the keeper and dispenser to the deserving of the inner Mysteries of the feminine side of the Craft, along with Her daughter Andromeda, who I shall look at in a later chapter. It is by her stellar energies that one may progress in knowledge of the Fates and Wyrd of the World. Through petitioning her a Natural Practitioner may gain great benefit and insight into the hidden side of Nature. By her continual turning around the central point of the heavens, she is an exemplar of the hidden tides and rhythms of the inner realms, and directs us to look inwards to our own spiritual and natural energy flows. She is the Great Mother of the Skies and Divine Ancestress of the magical kin, and it is to her we look for inspiration in our inner work and personal progress.

Later in the month, the Sun passes into the 12th and 'last' sign of the zodiac, that of Pisces. Known to our Anglo-Saxon forebears as "Fixas", this constellation can be seen low down on the Western horizon at this time of year. Generally depicted as two fishes tied together by their tails with a cord, the names for this constellation in ancient cultures seem to refer only to one fish, not two. They imply a female water deity with the head and upper parts of a woman and the body and tail of a fish. This was later changed into Aphrodite/Venus, rescuing her son Eros/Cupid from the monster Typhon in Classical cultures, by jumping into the water and transforming into a pair of fishes, in which form they escaped. Although often considered to harbour the 'dregs' of the energies of the zodiac, being the last sign before the fresh energy of Aries comes to the fore, the energies of this constellation would rather seem to relate to gentleness and kindness. After the rush and deluge of the cleansing and purificatory energies of Aquarius, the quieter healing balm of Pisces comes after and soothes what can often be a rough passage from Winter into Spring. It is a constellation little considered in native lore, but more work with it on an individual basis may bring some remarkable internal discoveries, especially at this most 'awakening' time of year.

The weather in February is still remarkably unsettled – despite all the old rhymes and methods of prediction – and this month can often be one of the coldest. Burst pipes and ice skating both come to mind here! It is often a damp month as well, not necessarily because of rainfall, although we often get enough of that. The returning Sun is not yet strong enough, or the days long enough, for there to be sufficient evaporation to dry anything out. The month begins with the following rhyme for the 2nd:

> *If Candlemas be fair and bright,*
> *Winter will have another flight.*
> *But if Candlemas Day be clouds and rain,*
> *Winter is gone and will not come again.*

Which just goes to show the two-faced nature of this month – try it and see.

It is traditional for the livestock farmer to still have half his straw and half his hay left at Candlemas time. Although February has been reached, Winter may still stretch a few fingers out and the new Spring growths may not yet be depended upon to feed the animals. Conversely, "*A dry Lent means a fertile year*". Predictions were made for the bean harvest at this time too, as there would only be a good yield if there was an early, warm and dry Spring – always something to be desired! As far as general prognostications go, the old saws say:

'*February fill dyke, black or white. If it be white, it's the better to like.*' This meant that whether it rained or whether it snowed this month, the ditches would usually be filled to overflowing, but if they were iced over, the weather later in the year would be fine and fair.

'February makes a bridge and March breaks it'. This refers to bridges, or surfaces, of ice which will form readily on even the largest bodies of water, but will generally be thawed and gone by the time March arrives.

For gardeners, there is the following advice for this month: *'At the waning of the February Moon, sow onions and leeks. Sow parsley at February Full Moon.'*

From the Mediaeval period comes this: *'In February the farmer shall make ready his garden grounds to sow and set therein all manner of herbes. He shall repair the hedges of his garden. He shall buy Bees, he shall clean their hives very carefully and kill their kings.'*

And to end this section of weather lore on a nicely up-beat note for this month:

'As the days lengthen, so the cold strengthens.' You can never say our ancestors weren't always optimistic now, can you (even if they were right)!

Fauna

One of the things that jumps to most people's minds when they think of Spring is lambs and it is from February onwards that the lambing season takes place, sometimes for several months, depending on when the ewes were mated. Sheep were never originally native, British animals, but have been here for at least 5,000 years, so that makes them pretty native in my book. Domestic Sheep derive from a Eurasian breed called Ovis orientalis, but the representative of our oldest-surviving 'native' breed is the Soay Sheep (Ovis aries). It is so called because it hails from the island of that name, near St. Kilda in The Hebrides, and may be of Viking origin. It is now making a bit of a comeback and is farmed throughout Britain, despite its originally unwelcoming description from the 16th century: they are *"so wild that they cannot be taken with a snare; their hair is long ... neither like the wool of a sheep or a goat ... with horns longer and thicker than those of an ox"*.

This may be a slight exaggeration, especially today, but they are a very tough and self-sufficient breed that has given rise to many of our better-known domestic breeds. Around now the new generation of lambs is being born and, in the past, this would have been of great benefit to our forebears. Throughout the Winter they would have survived on dried and preserved food, with very little if any fresh produce at all. The arrival of the lambing season meant the first fresh milk in months from the nursing ewes, and also a welcome bit of fresh meat from the stillborn offspring and the docked tails. The tails in particular were considered a great delicacy and were made into nourishing soups and stews to stave off the cold. They were included as part of a shepherd's wages up until very recently, when modern, factory farming arrived and destroyed the more traditional methods. The milk could be used as it was, or made into cream, butter and cheese which no one would have tasted since last Summer. There was no way of keeping dairy produce fresh during the Winter, certainly in the poorer households at least. Whilst the warm wool from the mothers may have kept everyone secure during the bitter days of Winter, it was the new lambs that provided a much-needed boost of protein to many needy people well into the 20th century and we tend to forget this today.

It is also around now that the Frogs (*Rana spp.*) and Toads (*Bufo spp.*) who have been burrowed underground in suspended animation during the Winter will begin to emerge and seek mates to breed, although Toads tend to mate and breed slightly later than Frogs. Scientifically there is no real difference between the two and indeed folklore tends to lump the two together, even using the same names for each. The most common of which are "Jack/Natterjack" (although Natterjack is also the name of a designated species, which is now protected as it is rare and endangered) and "Paddock/Puttock". Frogs tend to have a smoother, damper skin and spend more time in and around water, jumping rather than walking/crawling around. Toads have a drier, warty skin and only tend to enter water during the mating season and preferring to walk or crawl as a means of locomotion. There are only two or three native species of each in these Isles, all the rest being introduced fairly recently, including the African Clawed Toad, the Edible Frog and the American Bullfrog. Both Frogs and Toads need water to breed, as the eggs (spawn) must be kept moist and the young need to hatch in water, being purely aquatic at this stage in their development. Frogs lay large masses of frothy spawn, whilst Toads lay long, double strings of single eggs. Both hatch out into tadpoles, which gradually metamorphose from black, tailed blobs, into miniature editions of their parents. As already mentioned, traditional lore draws little distinction between the two animals and the charms, remedies, magic and uses prescribed for one are frequently found for use with the other. They have been used for everything from cough and cold cures (hold a live Frog/Toad in your mouth and you will be cured), cancer cures (rub the skin of a live Toad over the affected area and cover it with a plaster of houseleeks), sore throats (hang a Frog, or parts thereof, in a linen bag around the neck), to weather prediction (a bright, healthy skin foretells fine weather, a dull one rain). Their magical uses are legion also, from the well-known procurement of the "Toad Bone", to the use of thorn-pierced hearts as protective charms buried around the home. Most of these charms and folk uses inflict mild to severe harm on the animals, even torture and death in a lot of cases, and are not to be advised these days. However, the study of the reasoning and energy behind these practices should be examined for the enhanced knowledge of the Natural Crafter. As water is seen as a liminal space and point of contact with the Spirits and Powers, and as Frogs and Toads are amphibians, equally at home in water or on dry land, they hold a very important position in British magical lore. They are held as representatives of the Otherworld and Underworldly Powers, possessing access to them through their underwater passageways.

If you keep a keen eye out, you may see a bright flash whilst walking through the woodlands about now. This will probably be the Green Woodpecker (*Picus viridis*), which is becoming more active during this month. It has one of the longest collections of folk names in these Isles, of which some of the more common are "Ecall/Eccle", "Hecco", "Heffalk", "Kazek", "Nickle", "Rain Hen", "Snapper", "Sprite", "Whittle", "Yaffle" and "Yuckle". This indicates that it has long had a place in folk tradition and indeed, much lore has built up around it. It is one of the three native, resident Woodpeckers, the other two being the Greater Spotted and Lesser Spotted varieties, with the Wryneck being a Summer visitor. It is very common throughout most of the country, but is absent from the North of Scotland, Eire and the Isle of Man, which consequently have little lore relating to it. The typical drumming sound that is associated with the Green Woodpecker is not actually the bird making holes in the wood for food. It is a form of communication with others of its species, for which its skull is specially adapted for the heavy vibrations it produces. It finds food by sticking its exceedingly long and sticky tongue into holes and crevices in the wood and dragging out the insects, bugs and grubs that adhere to it. The tongue is often longer than the bird itself and is kept wrapped behind the brain at the back of the skull, when not in use. Some of its folk names refer to laughing, because of the supposed sound of its call, and others refer to rain, as it was both supposed to foretell and bring on wet weather by its actions and habits. When seen up close it has striking colours: yellow-green back and wings, contrasting with a red cap and a long dark beak in the males; the females are less colourful. However, the bird is mostly seen as a bright flash at the corner of the eye, as it moves from tree to tree, and was commonly thought to be leading people on into deeper woodland. It therefore has an association with Greenwood initiation and as the revealer of knowledge and information. They are closely associated with the Oak tree, where they find much food, which has led to a great reverence for them in folk culture and it is postulated that there may once have been a "Green Woodpecker cult" in Neolithic times. Despite this possibility, they have also long been considered as pests, because of the damage they do to trees when digging out nesting holes. This is not necessarily for the holes themselves, although this can be damaging in itself, but because of a wood-destroying fungus which they then admit to the tree by breaking the bark – they are even a problem with telephone poles and the like. Once settled into the nests, both males and females incubate the eggs and guard the young and feed them by regurgitation of food, rather than presenting them with whole insects. One last thing – beware of plucking wild peonies during the daylight hours, or the Green Woodpecker will come and pluck out your eyes!

Hearth & Home

If keeping to the old system of not taking the Yuletide decorations down until Candlemas, then they all need to be cleaned out now, or there will be a death in the family – apparently! The old rhyme for this time goes as follows:

> *Down with the Rosemarys and Bays*
> *Down with the Mistletoe;*
> *Instead of Holly now upraise*
> *The greener Box for show.*
> *The Holly hitherto did sway,*
> *Let Box now domineer*
> *Until the dancing Easter day,*
> *Or Easter Eve appear.*

Box, it would appear, was the one plant that was still acceptable.

Keeping a clean and tidy house is not just a matter of physical hygiene and etiquette; there are sound magical principles behind this. In any house or building there is a flow of energy – indeed, this can be said of any space or area – and as long as the energy is kept flowing, all will be well and good. However, if we liken this flow to a stream or river, we can see that occasionally the flow slows down, gets obstructed or blocked or even becomes stagnant, in which case this can cause problems. One of the prime causes of so-called hauntings or other 'paranormal' activity in a building is a build-up of stagnant – not 'evil' – energy. Just like in a river, the energy is blocked, has nowhere to go and hence stagnates, becomes foetid, and starts to give off noxious 'fumes'. This affects the balance of the energies in a place and hence causes problems. This is not so bad in a warehouse or barn perhaps, but is not so desirable in a home where people are living. This stagnation then affects the inhabitants – by affecting their own energies – and all sorts of problems can arise. So, at this time of the year, when we are concerned with cleansing and purification, it is traditional for the Natural Crafter to have a thorough, ritual spring cleaning of the home.

Initially, ensure that there is a free flow of energy around the home. This means removing blockages such as clutter in stairwells, obscured doorways or corridors, blocked or stuck windows, piles of unwashed clothing/ crockery etc. left lying around. You don't have to be obsessive about tidying up, but make sure there is a free flow for energies to pass around. (Of course, by this I am not saying that energy cannot flow through, as opposed to around, objects, purely that it impedes the flow in certain ways and can make it less 'harmonious'.) Secondly, have a thorough cleanse of the house; dust and vacuum more intensely than you normally would, wash the windows and frames and all curtains and bed linen and mop down all non-carpeted floors and doorsteps. Next, having conscientiously performed the above, you can do one of two things (or both if you feel like it). Take a bowl of warm water and dissolve into it a teaspoon of natural salt (Maldon salt is best) at the time of the waning moon. Sprinkle this with intention all around your home and leave overnight. In the morning have a good sweep and empty the dirt outside somewhere, preferably in a natural place not on your property. The salt effectively absorbs any stale or negative (to you) vibrations and you can safely get rid of them elsewhere. Alternatively, make up a spray bottle of suitable essential oils diluted in a spring-water base and spray these around the home. I would suggest oils such as lavender, juniper, angelica, sage, cedar, pine or eucalyptus, either singly or in combination.

Should you feel that all your previous cleansing has not done the job properly, that there is a long-standing energy problem that your cleaning has not solved or an actual spirit presence that won't go away, there is another procedure that can be used and that is Suffumigation or Incense Burning. The field of incense making and blending is vast so I will mention only a few points that are relevant here. In this instance, the incense is essentially acting as a stronger version of, or a step up from, the salt and water. It needs to be compounded of ingredients that will both banish any negativity and also replace it with a better atmosphere. Different people will have their own favourite ingredients, but I will suggest some here and you may add or subtract when making your own, as long as you bear in mind the purpose and understand the ingredients.

Frankincense: Any good incense should have at least one good gum or resin as a base on which to mix all the other ingredients. It should be a keynote for the incense and 'describe' what you are trying to do. Frankincense is linked to the Sun and has been used for thousands of years to bring blessings and healing. It clears and banishes 'darkness' and replaces it with fresher energies.

Myrrh: Sacred to the dark powers of death and the waning Moon, this resin is ideal for banishing any unwanted energies that are around. Used as a preservative in times gone by, it acts as a complement to the powers of the Sun in this mix.

Bay: A solar herb as we have already seen, this plant brings the blessings of cleansing and healing and combines well with Frankincense.

Juniper: Astringent and antiseptic, the berries of this plant crushed in the mix act to cleanse any foul energies in the area.

Mugwort and Wormwood: Both from the Artemisia family, these plants were often used as strewing herbs to rid the house of pests and vermin, and internally to rid the system of worms and parasites. They can act the same on a magical level. (There is more on these particular plants in a later chapter.)

Dragon's Blood: One of the most powerful and protective of ingredients, a pinch or two of this bright red, powdered resin adds strength to any mix it is added to.

Essential oils: Once all the dry ingredients have been combined, you may mix a few drops of one or more essential oils into any incense blend at the end for added impact and cohesion. In this case I would suggest Basil and Black Pepper.

All the ingredients should be mixed well together and burnt on charcoal. Take the burner throughout the home, paying particular attention to places where you feel there is a special problem. Suitable prayers and invocations may be made whilst doing this.

Once you have finished all this, it is nice to gather all the family/friends/associates around for a good meal, full of light and laughter. Ensure that there are plenty of white candles all around and maybe some vases of Snowdrops and Lambs' Tails, as well as any other seasonal flowers or plants that may already be out. Serve a meal rich in butter, milk or cream (hang the diets!) washed down with some home-made parsnip wine. This is a traditional, robust wine that utilises a root vegetable widely available at this season and you may use this same recipe for other root vegetables, such as swede, turnip, etc.

Ingredients:
    4lb parsnips
    8 pints water
    2½ lb sugar
    juice of 2 lemons
    8oz raisins, chopped
    1 tsp white wine yeast

Method:
Scrub, top and tail, chop and boil the parsnips in the water, without peeling them. Do not boil too long or this will make the wine cloudy. Strain the water onto the sugar, lemon juice and raisins and stir thoroughly. Cool to blood temperature and add the yeast. Cover and leave for 10 days. Strain into a demijohn and seal with an airlock, then transfer into a fresh one when it has finished bubbling (about three months). After another three months, transfer into bottles and leave for a further six months before drinking. Obviously, this wine needs preparing a year in advance, so get cracking now and you'll have plenty in time for next year's festivities.

March

✻✿❈✿❈✻

The Sun rises at approximately 6:48 a.m. and sets at around 5:38 p.m. at the beginning of this month.

March – the Month of Winds – is traditionally imaged thus:

> *Is drawn in Tawny, with a fierce aspect, a Helmet upon his head, and leaning on a Spade, and a Basket of Garden Seeds in his left Hand, and in his Right hand the Sign of Aries: and Winged*

Seasonal Skies
It is often said that:

> *If March comes in like a Lion,*
> *It goes out like a Lamb.*

If it comes in like a Lamb,
It goes out like a Lion.

This invariably proves to be true and March is often a very mixed month, weather-wise, still harking back to Winter but also exhibiting very Spring-like weather. Although fully stationed within the Spring Tide, it is a bit of an 'in-between' month, displaying everything from howling gales to balmy, sunny days and shirt-sleeve weather. The first three days of March are 'allocated' to three separate saints: St. David on the 1st, St. Chad on the 2nd, and St. Winnal on the 3rd and I will speak more of these later, but here they lend themselves to some interesting weather and farming lore. *"First comes David, next comes Chad, then comes Winnal, roaring mad"* is a country expression referring to the weather on these days. These three days are sometimes called the "Blind Days" and are considered to be unlucky and no sowing should be done, especially peas or beans as they will come to nothing. However, it is also said *"Sow peas and beans on David's and Chad's, be the weather good or bad"*, which seems a direct contradiction. Another old saying has it that the last three days of the month are called Blind Days and no seeds should be planted.

The weather is often windy and stormy at this time, particularly around the Equinox, and some traditions say that these three days have been borrowed from April. This may all appear to be very confusing, but this only goes to show the variation in traditions around the country and the need for the Natural Crafter to be aware of their own place on the Land. The further South you are in the country the more likely it is that the weather will be better earlier; likewise, the further North you are, the weather is likely to get better later, hence the discrepancy in the traditions.

However it works out in actuality – and each year, regardless of climate change, will be different – March is traditionally the month when the sowing of the cereal crops starts, the Sun's rays now being strong enough to warm the soil sufficiently. (This is unless they have been sown the previous Autumn to get a head start, when the crop is then called "Winter Wheat".) There is a very old method of testing whether the ground is ready for planting or not, which was widely used before the modern methods of farming became the norm. The landowner would take himself off into the fields, being careful first to make sure he was not being observed, and drop his trousers and underwear. He would sit himself down on the soil and if his cheeks did not take cold, then the soil was warm enough for the seed. I am reliably informed that this practice still takes place, though few would admit to it in this day and age!

Although warm enough for planting, this month can still hold a few surprises and there is another old saw that goes *"As many mists in March as there are frosts in May"*. This shows the close connection in the country mind between Spring and Summer and the uncertainty in anything to do with the weather. It is interesting that the majority of the weather lore for this month revolves around the beginning and the end – showing the in-between nature of the month again – except where it concerns the Vernal Equinox, but I shall come to that anon. Suffice it to say here, beware of late-budding and late-flowering Blackthorn trees as it betokens the dreaded "Blackthorn Winter", a renewal of bad weather just when it seems that all is well. Finally, don't forget that the last Sunday in March is when the clocks are put forward one hour, for British Summer Time. This is an entirely artificial construct which takes us away from natural time and causes much confusion until all are adjusted. It was instigated during the First World War, so that there would be more light in the evenings for work to continue later in the munitions factories. It was intended as a temporary measure but was never repealed, so for more than half the year we are at least an hour adrift from 'real' time. When timing any important rite or activity make sure you adjust from the hours given in a diary, calendar or ephemeris! Alternatively, use your inner sense to tell you when the timing is right.

Looking almost directly North, just below the Pole Star, the constellation of Cepheus is prominent this month. Like Cassiopeia, with whom it shares a link in Classical myth and which it faces, Cepheus is also a circumpolar constellation, although not so bright. It is imaged as the husband of Cassiopeia and father of Andromeda, who sailed with Jason and the Argonauts on the quest for the Golden Fleece – a fitting image for this month – and was placed in the night sky in his own right for his actions. The constellation looks a little like a child's drawing of a house, being a square with a fifth point above it for a sloping roof, or of a church with a squat steeple. The name of the star which makes the 'point' of the steeple or roof, Errai, means "Shepherd" and in approximately 2,500 years' time, because of the phenomenon of precession, will become our Pole Star. The image of Cepheus is invariably that of a king with outstretched arms, supposedly in supplication to the higher Powers for favours. However, there is another possible explanation; in British tradition, he is sometimes thought of as a blacksmith and linked with Wayland's Smithy, in which case he may be offering up his work, or requesting payment for it. His is not an exceptionally powerful energy and indeed many people dismiss him as unimportant in comparison with other more obvious constellations. However, he projects a measure of care and pride in work done and his energies are well worth cultivating for those of a workmanlike nature, or those involved in craftwork of a manual kind.

Around the 20th of the month, the Sun appears to pass into the constellation of Aries, the sign of the Ram, announcing the Vernal Equinox. Called simply "Ramm" in Anglo-Saxon and later "Ariete" in Middle English, this has always been a constellation denoting power, energy and confidence. The Ram of the sign is traditionally the Ram of the Golden Fleece that Jason and his Argonauts sought in the Classical – and highly enjoyable – ancient Greek tale. The Ram had originally rescued the young Prince Phrixus from his jealous stepmother Ino and taken him to safety to Colchis, whereupon Phrixus promptly sacrificed it on an altar in gratitude to the Powers; some gratitude to the Ram! In Britain, it was also seen as the Biblical Abraham's Ram that was caught in the thicket (also a highly-meaningful symbol in Traditional Craft) and, too, as St. Peter, the first bishop of the early Church, with the Ram's head as his mitre. It has also been seen in a more pious light as the Lamb sacrificed on Calvary for a sinful humanity at the start of the Christian era. Aries is seen as the first sign of the zodiac and has a connection with the planet Mars and all the fiery and martial energy that goes with it; however it need not be viewed in such a bloody light as it generally is. Although it very much represents a certain headstrong attitude, with care this can be overcome and Aries can give the Practitioner that drive to conquer, against all odds. Just because it represents the energy that starts all projects and aspirations, that doesn't necessarily mean that that energy need fade and die away.

Fauna
It is about now that one of Britain's native and traditionally muchloved animals begins to make itself known and that is the Brown Hare (*Lepus europaeus*). It has one of the longest list of folk names of any native animal, among which are "Aunt Sarah", "Old Sally", "Bandy", "Cuttie", "Donnie", "Malkin/Mawkin", "Puss", "Jack" and "Wintail". Native to these Isles since at least the Iron Age, if not well before, it is much larger than the later, imported Rabbit, having longer ears and back legs and is a much faster runner. As well as a huge list of common names, it also has a vast body of lore surrounding it which, sadly, is being ignored in favour of the more popular Rabbit. For a fuller appreciation of this lore than I can give here, I would direct the interested reader to the excellent Leaping Hare by George Ewart Evans and David Thomson (see Bibliography). The name "Hare" is Old English, the female being called a "doe" and the male a

"buck", often with the appellation "Jack" added. The young are known as "leverets" and will be found nestled in the "form", a kind of scrape in open ground. The Hare, unlike the Rabbit, does not burrow and prefers wide open country and fields as its natural habitat. Tradition has it that the Hare can change sex, as there are no male Hares, and the female must fertilise herself. This is plainly incorrect as can be seen in the seasonal activity that gives rise to the expression "Mad March Hare". This striking boxing display, to be seen in many fields around about now, is usually a buck and a doe 'courting', only the doe is not yet receptive to the buck's advances and is firmly discouraging his suit! The jumping, punching, running, turning and leaping is a marvellous thing to watch and shows to good effect the agility of this much-hunted animal. It is not always caught at the end of the chase however, as it is exceedingly canny and will disguise its tracks and scent in numerous ways to confuse and lose its pursuers. The Hare is very closely linked to the Witch in traditional lore – like the cat, with whom it shares many folk names – and is often said to be one, either in disguise or shape-changed, in which case, any injury inflicted on the Hare is later mirrored on the Witch and marks her out as such. In folklore, a white Hare (albinos are quite common) was given special attention, as it was thought to bring bad luck, or was possibly the returning soul of a loved one who had died tragically. Whereas a black Hare (equally as common) was thought to bring good luck and was the origin of the fast-fading custom of saying "Hares, Hares" at the beginning of the month. Like many other customs surrounding the Hare, this has now been taken over by its introduced cousin and it is now more common to hear the cry of "*White Rabbits, White Rabbits, White Rabbits*" early on the morning of a new month. A pregnant woman must take especial care not to let a Hare cross her path, or it was believed that she would give birth to a child with a facial fissure in the midline of the upper lip, commonly called a "Hare lip" after the animal that had crossed her. To prevent this, she must immediately rip her petticoat upon seeing the Hare. She may also, in revenge, turn the offending creature into the traditional dish of "Jugged Hare", or keep one of its preserved paws about her as a charm against cramp, rheumatism or wind. Alternatively, if her child is fretting, she may feed it a posset of Hare's brains to soothe it! Although considered a sacred and prophetic animal by our Iron Age ancestors, the Hare has since suffered much in the popular imagination!

Also emerging into the public gaze around now is the Hedgehog (*Erinaceus europaeus*) which is waking from its Winter hibernation. Like the Hare, the Hedgehog has a wealth of folk or common names, among them "Butterbump", "Erchin/Urchin", "Furzehog", "Hedgepig", "Hirchen", "Nertchard", "Perpynt", "Rock" and "Vuzpeg". The modern word "Hedgehog" dates from 1450 and has replaced the earlier Middle English "Hurcheon", from the French "Herichon". This became debased into "Urchin" in English, both for the animal and the child, as an urchin was popularly supposed to be a mischievous Elf in disguise. The name also continued to be used for the Sea Urchin, because of its resemblance to the animal, and it was once called the "Sea Hedgehog". The Hedgepig is one of three British mammals to truly hibernate (the others being the Dormouse and the Bat), but it may become active for short periods over the Winter, when the weather is milder. It does not make its own burrow but may use that of a Rabbit; otherwise it stays above ground in a pile of wood, leaves and other secure vegetation. It emerges around now as its main foods such as slugs, snails, frogs and other small creatures are also emerging, and it is not averse to robbing a few ground-nests of their eggs either. It is a voracious feeder and may consume up to 30 slugs and snails in a single night, making it much loved by the modern gardener. It can be found over most of the British Isles, having been introduced into Eire around 1700, but is rare where Badgers are found as they tend to feed on the same prey, Badgers even occasionally consuming Hedgehogs. The well-known prickly back usually carries around 6,000 spines and these are gradually renewed over a period of 18 months. The spines on the newborn young are quite soft, but gradually stiffen as they get older. The Hedgehog is notoriously flea-ridden and performs an act called "self-anointing", possibly to rid itself of its pests. It produces a frothy saliva which it then proceeds to lick all over its body, even rolling over onto its back to reach its underside. This procedure may also deter other predators, such as Foxes and large birds of prey. There is no truth in the old tradition that the animal carries fruit on its back, stuck to its spines after rolling on them, as it rarely touches fruit, much preferring meat. However, there is some truth to the other tale of Hedgehogs suckling from cows and stealing their milk. Although they obviously cannot reach the udders (even with the little ladders that they are supposed to have obtained from somewhere), they have been observed licking the milk from the ends of the teats when the Cow is lying down – strange but true! Like the Hare, Hedgehogs have also been linked with Witches, either as familiars or themselves shape-shifted, but the most common thing said about them is how good they are to eat. Hedgehog is the famed Romany dish of "Hotchy-Witchy" and is prepared by killing and gutting the animal, stuffing it with herbs, then encasing it in wet clay. It is then placed in the embers of the fire and left to bake until the clay cracks, whereupon it is peeled off and the prickly skin comes with it. The meat is supposed to be superb to eat and the fat was also used for medicinal purposes, right up until very recently, if not currently. The dripping, or oil, was used to cure earache and deafness and also as a remedy for epilepsy, fits, lunacy and other irrational behaviour.

A vocal addition to the garden population at this time is the Blackbird (*Turdus merula*). A member of the Thrush family, it is one of the commonest British breeding birds, but for all that has not acquired very many regional or folk names, among which are "Amsel", "Blackie", "Colly/Colley", "Merle", "Ouzel" and "Woofell". It is also surprising that of all the number of black British birds (notably the Crow family) this one alone should become known as the Blackbird. This appellation has come down to us in the old name "Colly" or "Colley", which originates in the meaning of "coal-black or sooty" and is well-preserved in the "Four Colly Birds" of the popular "Twelve Days of Christmas" song. Having said this, albino or part-albino birds are common, or at least not rare, and it is only the male that has the beautiful, glossy black feathers and bright, yellow beak, the female being a much duller brown and mottled. This is the time when, in common with many other songbirds, the Blackbird begins to court and mate. The male has a beautifully fluid voice and is one of the leading lights of the dawn and dusk choruses, although its alarm call is very harsh and strident – that's the point though! It was a fairly elusive bird until quite recently, much preferring woodlands and thickets in which to nest but, with the increase in the popularity of gardening in recent decades, it has become much closer to and bolder with humankind. In fact, the hen birds can become most annoying to gardeners as I know to my cost; for the last few years I have had my hanging baskets destroyed every time I make them up, by one persistent little female. She doesn't even use the material she happily pulls out – plants, moss, soil, seedlings – and strews over the garden, seemingly doing it just for the fun of it! In partial revenge, therefore, it is good to note that their flesh has been used for centuries for medicinal purposes in folk medicine, being considered good for ills such as consumption, colic, dysentery and freckles. Blackbirds have long been served at table too, being baked into puddings and pies, as evidenced in the old nursery rhyme "Sing a Song of Sixpence", with its "four and twenty Blackbirds baked in a pie". However, this is thought more to have a political origin, as the bird has been used as a symbol for 'factions' on more than one occasion. It was a Jacobite symbol in Scotland, where Charles II was called the "Black Boy" when young, apparently due to his swarthy complexion.

Flora

As the Spring Tide advances and the energies in the Land quicken apace, plants and flowers seem to appear overnight, as if by magic. Many plants that were dormant now begin to wake up and poke their heads above the ground and give a welcome boost to flagging energies. Daffodils are probably the most commonly thought of at this time of year; then there are the Primroses and Cowslips – both sadly endangered in their natural, wild varieties, so never pick them without permission – Crocuses, Wood Anemones and early Violets, all of which add a touch of magic and beauty to the countryside. But it is a less-favoured couple of plants that I would like to look at first, before going on to a much more obvious one.

The Stinging Nettle (*Urtica dioica*) is usually viewed as a weed and a damn nuisance by most people, but it is a plant very much worthy of consideration. Called variously "Devil's Plaything", "Hokey Pokey" and "Jinny Nettle", it has been used by humans for millennia in one form or another. It is similar in makeup to the Flax plant, from which the cloth called "linen" is obtained. The Nettle can be used in a very similar way, making a thread from the stem, which is then woven into a cloth of a like texture. In fact, the common name "Nettle" comes from an old word meaning "to twist", referring to the making of thread from the fibres. The thread has also long been used for string and rope and even a fishing line can be twisted from the tough fibres. A flint arrowhead has recently been discovered in Britain, bound to the remains of its shaft by Nettle fibres. As a food it has an equally long and distinguished history, having been used by both our Iron Age forebears and the Romans, who made a kind of soup or broth containing oatmeal, out of the leaves. It was used as a subsistence food during the Irish potato famine and during the First and Second World Wars in Britain, as it contains many of the nutrients necessary for good health. A delicious and healthy soup can still be served up today as a seasonal starter to a meal or, with the addition of some potatoes and herbs, as a hearty main course. Treat it as a leafy vegetable like spinach, chop it up, boil lightly for a few minutes, purée and there you have it. Medicinally, Nettles are highly-favoured, having a great many uses in both folk and modern herbal medicine. They contain high levels of vitamins (including Vitamin C), serotonin, histamine, acetylcholine and also large quantities of minerals (including iron, calcium and silica). They are an excellent blood tonic, diuretic, circulatory stimulant, expectorant and antiseptic. They can be used to counteract anaemia, eliminate uric acid from the body (great for gout sufferers), remineralise the body, relieve the swellings and pains of arthritis, detoxify the blood and can help expel gravel stones. They are excellent when used as a tonic at this time of year, to get over any lingering effects of the Winter. The Romans, and later sufferers, used to beat themselves with the whole plant to relieve the pain of aching joints and arthritis and this has been shown to be highly effective – if not somewhat painful – and has led to the treatment of these conditions with other forms of 'sting', notably Bee venom. It would appear to be the histamine content in both that does the work. This is the best time of year to start picking Nettles, either to use fresh or to store, as after June, due to chemical actions, the plant becomes toxic and should not be used until it has a second 'flush' in Autumn. Pick only the fresh, green tops and use straightaway, or store and dry in paper bags in a warm, dark place. Magically speaking, the Nettle is associated with the planet Mars and can be used for acts of energy, drive, passion and perhaps revenge; this is a prime time for these works as the energies of the Vernal Equinox will soon be available and the star sign of Aries – soon to be dominant – is also associated with the "Red Planet".

Usually growing providentially alongside the Nettle plant, you will find another that is generally thought of as a weed and a nuisance and that is Cleavers (*Galium aparine*). Also known as "Clivvers", "Goosegrass", "Goose Weed",

"Sticky Willy/William", "Bobby Buttons", "Herriff", "Cleggy Maggies" and "Robin-run-the-hedge", this plant also has a venerable and useful history. As some of its folk names suggest, it has long been used as feed for Geese and Chickens, and also as a vegetable for humans; prepare as above for Nettles. Its main common names, however, come from the fact that it is covered all over with small spines, like hooked bristles (although these soften when cooked!) which will catch onto any even slightly-roughened surface and stay there. They were therefore a favourite with children in their games and cursed by adults. It is a rambling, vine-like annual plant, which produces many small round fruits, which also stick to everything. These fruits, however, do have another use, as when dried they were employed in days gone by to top lacemakers' pins, to stop them pricking their fingers. As with Nettles, Cleavers can be used to make a relatively low-alcohol, refreshing beer, either on its own or with the stinging plant, with which it is better, but it is primarily used for its medicinal purposes and always has been. Its main use is in the drainage of the lymphatic system and as a detoxifier to the whole bodily system, reducing enlarged lymph nodes (especially in the throat and neck) and other swellings such as cysts and boils. It has been used to help in cases of obesity as a cleanser and diuretic, for dry-skin disorders such as psoriasis, and for urinary disorders where it soothes the bladder and eases painful urination. In a wash or lotion form it can be used topically for freckles, and also for flaky and itching scalps in cases of dandruff. Used by itself, or in conjunction with Nettles, it can ease the symptoms of arthritis, fever and jaundice. A poultice can be made for external application on sore swellings and an infusion for internal use. Taken together with Nettle as a tincture or infusion (see next paragraph) it is a sovereign tonic for all that ails you at this time of year.

Before going on to our next plant, I would like to take a moment to look at Infusions in a little more detail. I have discussed Tinctures previously and their usage in herbal medicine, but at this time of year there is no need to use dried and preserved plants. Fresh growth is all around us with the burgeoning of the Spring Tide and the plant matter can be used fresh and directly. An infusion is basically what has become known as a "tea", but was in use for thousands of years before the Tea plant proper (*Camellia sinensis*) was known in the West. However, a proper infusion is prepared a bit more carefully and exactly than your normal 'cuppa'. For medicinal purposes, the usual dosage is one ounce of the dried herb to one pint of water, or one heaped teaspoon of the dried herb to one cup of water. Always use freshly-drawn water, not some which has been sitting around in the kettle for half a day or more, and bring it to a rapid boil, then pour it directly over the herb or herbs. Leave for at least 10 minutes (flowers and leaves) or 15 minutes (stalks and thicker pieces) to infuse. This is longer than you would normally brew a cup of tea, but you need to extract more of the active ingredients for a medicinal infusion. Strain the liquid and take the prescribed dose, usually one cup at a time. If using fresh herbs/plants, and that is the better idea at this time of year, use two large handfuls per pint of water, infuse and keep the rest of the infusion for later (the general rule is twice as much fresh herb as dried, by weight). It's a bit fiddly using fresh plant matter for just one cup, so make up a pint, and strain and drink the remainder cool later on. Always use a glazed, ceramic pot or cup to infuse the plant in, never metal, as this may react chemically with some plants and destroy the active ingredients. A glass vessel is also fine to use, as it will not react negatively with the plants either.

The Broom plant (*Cytisus scoparius*) begins to flower from around the middle of March onwards, in a glorious golden-yellow display that can be quite dazzling in bright sunshine. The Old English term "Brom" was applied to many coarse shrubs, including Gorse and Heather which were also used for sweeping, but over time came to settle on this plant alone, because of its more common usage. The long, thornless, whippy stems were ideal for bundling together to clean an area and are still used today for sweeping leaves and other garden litter. The plant's alternative Latin name – *Planta genista* – became the basis for the name of the Plantagenet line of kings, who adopted it as their badge and emblem and who were also rumoured to be secret adherents and leaders of the Old Faith. It is a common plant of sandy heathland and open woodland throughout Britain and is one of the nine Faerie Herbs. A cologne can be made from its blossoms which is said to inspire affection in those that come within range of its scent and the smell of its flowers is said to calm wild horses and rabid dogs – although I wouldn't advise trying it alone! It is a strong lymph tonic, mildly diuretic, and has long been used in the treatment of dropsy (fluid retention around the heart). It is useful in the treatment of gout and sciatica, but should be used with caution, due to one of its main active ingredients, an alkaloid called sparteine sulphate. In large doses this can cause excitation and hallucination, as it has the properties of both increasing the power of the heart and slowing it down by reducing the frequency of the heartbeat. (For this reason, it is one of the plants often found listed as an ingredient in historical Witches' "Flying Ointments".) It should therefore only be used by a qualified, medical herbalist. However, in small quantities it is perfectly harmless and the green tips of flowering branches have long been used, in bud or fully open, fresh or pickled, as an ingredient in salads. It is a plant of Spring and jollity, often used to decorate country weddings when tied with gaily coloured ribbons, and acts as a good luck charm. Popular folklore sometimes gives it a sinister slant though, according to the old rhyme:

If you sweep the house with blossomed Broom in May
You will sweep the head of the household away.

But as Broom is essentially a plant of the Spring Tide and May is the beginning of the Summer Tide, as long as you don't use it then, you'll be fine – do all your sweeping in Spring!

Hearth & Home

Talking of sweeping in Spring and brooms in general leads me on to consider the broom itself. In folklore, the broom, or "besom", is usually associated with the traditional picture of the Witch and there are very good reasons for this. The besom itself contains various aspects of symbolism that are not necessarily readily apparent to the 'non-initiated'. It is well known that the brush of the besom can be a veiled reference to the "bush", the female pubic hair. It is less well known that one end of the handle in a traditional besom is often carved into a phallic shape and is concealed inside the brush-end. This would only be in the case of a besom used for magical purposes of course, and not just for sweeping the house. The traditional besom is commonly made from three kinds of plant: the handle of Ash wood, the brush of Birch twigs, and they are bound together with Willow withies. There are quite a few regional variations on this, including the Broom plant itself for the brush, but these are the norm. The Ash is used to represent the World Tree in most Western mythologies and stands for the upright pole around which the rest of the world, or worlds, are centred, hence giving stability and a 'core' for the magical use of the besom. The Birch represents cleansing and purification and is also reckoned as a 'female' tree, hence balancing the pronounced masculinity of the Ash. The Willow binding represents the powers of the Moon, flight, and the Otherworld and the energy that ties all things together and connects them. Together they are a symbol of the "Hedge", the boundary between our world and the Otherworld and the original name of the Witch, "Hedge Rider", is taken from this tool. It is thus an ideal instrument to be used for 'flight', whether that be actual or metaphorical. In common lore, a broom is used to indicate various situations when left by, near or over a doorway. If it is thought that a wife has been away from home longer than is considered proper, then a broom may appear over the doorway, stuck in the chimney or in the window, as if to advertise for a new housekeeper and thus chastise the absentee wife. If the man himself has put out the broom, then it is the husband inviting his friends around for a 'get-together', the broom acting the same as the symbol of a bush, which was also the old sign of an inn. If the husband is away and the broom appears outside the door with the brush upwards, then it is a sign that the wife is willing to dally, but if the brush is downwards, then suitors are warned to stay away. It is said that to sweep all the dust out of the house with a broom when cleaning, or at least over the threshold, is ill advised, as all the luck of the house is being swept away. And in my home county of Suffolk, to stand the broom up in a corner after the room has been swept is to cause strangers to visit the home unexpectedly. "Strangers" in this case probably means uninvited guests of the worst kind i.e. thieves and cut-throats – still not unknown in this day and age.

However, folkloric warnings apart, a broom is meant for cleaning and as this is the tide of cleansing and purification, it would be well to do a little magical 'sanitising', just before the time of the Vernal Equinox towards the end of the month. Although the energies involved in the Equinox are mainly confined to the astral realms, and do not earth or manifest generally until the beginning of the Summer Tide, for the Practitioner of Natural Craft it is well to take advantage of the magical tides as well as the earthly ones. I will focus on the Equinox itself in greater detail later on, but for now it can be seen as a time of great change and the turning from one type of energy to another on the inner planes. Domestically, this is an excellent time to have a good cleanout of all that you wish to leave behind and give everything a good 'spit and polish'. The Practitioner would normally have had a good, magical purification in February, to commence the current tide, but now it is still worthwhile having a second cleanse, the better to 'ride the current' so to speak. If you do not already possess one, make yourself a traditional besom out of the woods listed above, or those that are traditionally sacred in your area.

If you find it difficult obtaining or making the traditional besom, try just a small, hand version – maybe a bundle of Broom sprays tied together with some natural twine. You may feel like sprinkling some more of the salt and water mix already mentioned around the house before sweeping, or using salt alone. Or maybe some of the Mediaeval "strewing herbs" that traditionally cleansed the house of negativity and vermin: things like Mugwort or Wormwood could be used. In keeping with traditional lore, do not sweep the dust – real or metaphorical – out of the doorway, but into a pile in the centre of the room. Once there, collect it up with a dustpan and brush, or similar, and empty it out into the garden or compost bin. Whispering a few words of intent while you are doing it doesn't go amiss either.

The fourth Sunday in Lent is Mothering Sunday (or Mid-Lent Sunday) in Britain, which is very different to the modern, commercial, "Mother's Day" (held on a completely different date in the United States). Some say it goes back to a pre-Reformation custom of visiting the Mother Church or Cathedral of the diocese to make offerings at this time, or perhaps it refers back to an even earlier, pre-Christian custom of making Spring offerings. Alternatively, it began at a time when young people and children lived away from home, in service or training for a craft, and returned at this time to visit their homes and, in particular, their Mothers. They would bring gifts of food, clothing and flowers and a great reunion would be had by all the family. Richard Simmons wrote of this in 1644, saying: "*Every Mid-lent Sunday is a great day at Worcester, when all the children and god-children meet at the head and cheife of the family and have a feast. They call it the Mothering-day.*" However and whenever it began, it is a long-standing custom, which honours both the home and the local sacred place and, most importantly, the "head and chief" of the family, the Matriarch. This custom is especially kept up in Natural Craft families as it is part of the natural order of things, and it would be unthinkable to omit this occasion from the natural calendar of observances. There is one item that would always be brought to the table, or made especially for this feast, and this is mentioned in Robert Herrick's poem *Ceremonie in Glocester* of 1648:

I'le to thee a Simnell bring
'Gainst thou go'st a mothering,
So that, when she blesseth thee,
Half that blessing thou'lt give me.

"Simnel cake" is a traditional 'dish' for this occasion and the name probably derives from the Latin "simila", meaning "a fine flour". However, there are various other theories, including a rather amusing one deriving from a warring couple named Simon and Nelly. In brief, they could not decide whether the cake should be boiled or baked, it partaking of the nature of both. They finally came to an agreement and the cake was named for them both thereafter. However it came to be, it is a fine dish and worthy of being cooked in honour of the Mothers at this time of year, so I will give a traditional recipe in full, hailing from my home county of Suffolk.

Ingredients:
6oz butter
6oz caster sugar
3 large eggs & 1 egg white
8oz plain flour
pinch of salt
½ level tsp ground cinnamon
½ level tsp ground nutmeg
4oz glacé cherries, quartered
12oz mixed dried fruit
finely grated rind of 1 lemon
1lb almond paste
milk if necessary
icing sugar for rolling

Method:

Grease a 7-inch round cake tin, line with greaseproof paper and grease the paper. Cream the butter and sugar until fluffy. Lightly whisk the whole eggs and gradually beat into the creamed ingredients. Sift the flour, salt and spices over the surface and fold into the mixture. Add all the fruit and the lemon rind, folding together to give a smooth, dropping consistency. If too firm, add a little milk. Divide the almond paste in half. Lightly dust a surface with a little icing sugar and roll out one half to make a 6½-inch circle. Spoon half the cake mixture into the prepared tin, place the round of almond paste on the top and cover with the remaining cake mixture. Press down gently with the back of a spoon to smooth and level the surface. Bake in the oven at 150⁰ C for 2½ hours. Cool in the tin for one hour. Divide the remaining almond paste into two. Roll out one half to a 7½-inch circle and make the rest into 11 small balls. Lightly beat the egg white and brush over the top of the cake. Place the circle on top, crimp the edges and, with a little of the egg white, fix the balls around the top edge of the cake. Brush the almond paste with the remaining egg white and place under a hot grill for one to two mins, until the paste is well-browned. Tie a ribbon round the cake for decoration before serving.

This is a fine thing to present to one's Mother on this special day and don't forget to leave at least a few crumbs for the House Spirits as well!

Times & Tides

As already mentioned, the first three days of March are dedicated to three separate saints: David, Chad and Winnal, in that order.

St. David's Day on March 1st commemorates the patron saint of Wales, when the wearing of Daffodils by the faithful is undertaken. This is a late tradition, being introduced only in the early 20th century. The more traditional plant to wear is the Leek, which has been associated with the saint and Wales since at least the early Mediaeval period and refers back to a famous Welsh victory over the Saxons. David was born in the Kingdom of Ceredigion around the year 500 CE (estimates range from 462 to 512 CE) and died on 1st March 589 CE. His mother was Non or Nonna, later St. Non, who may have been a nun who had been violated, but there are traces of an "Earth Mother" type of deity in her story. It is therefore unclear as to exactly what David's origins are, although his father is said to have been the king, or a local kinglet. He was educated in the monastic system by St. Paulinus of Wales and in later life he went on to found many monasteries himself, before becoming Archbishop of Wales. His monastic rule was quite harsh: monks had to pull the plough themselves without draught animals; to drink only water; to eat only bread with salt and herbs; and to spend the evenings in prayer, reading and writing. No personal possessions were allowed. He gave a famous speech before his death, part of which was *"Do the little things in life"* (*"Gwnewch y pethau bychain mewn bywyd"*), which is today a very well-known phrase in Welsh. He is very much associated with rivers, springs and wells and would spend much time standing up to his waist in a freezing torrent, in meditation. His veneration is of course mainly centred in Wales, but a curious custom came to be observed on the March 1st all over England and elsewhere, which may or may not be associated with him. It was believed that on this day all doors and windows had to be kept shut to keep the fleas out: *"If from fleas you would be free, on 1st March let your windows closed be"* or *"The Devil shakes a bag of fleas at everybody's door on 1st March."* This is a curious tradition, with little or no discernable reason for it!

March 2nd is dedicated to the 7th-century Anglo-Saxon Bishop of both Mercia and Northumbria, St. Chad. Although an Anglo-Saxon, his name is actually derived from the British tongue of the time (similar to Welsh) being originally "Ceadda" and meaning something like "Battle". It is also the name of an Iron Age deity associated with springs, brooks and streams, which were highly venerated by the folk of the time as entrances to the Otherworld and crossing places between the worlds – as they still are. It is appropriate to make a pilgrimage to draw water from a sacred well or spring and, in keeping with the tide of cleansing and purification; if necessary take the time to clear the watercourse of any debris that has accumulated during the Winter. It is also appropriate to leave a coin bearing the portrait of a head in offering to the Spirit of the Waters at this time. The head was an object of great veneration and importance to our forebears and was often deposited in water in just such a manner. There is little to connect the two, St. Chad and Ceadda the deity, but it is curious that the saint is also associated with water (although more in a purificatory manner) and that they share a feast day. At this time in March the weather is often exceedingly 'wet', and a feature of all the saints at the beginning of the month is their link with water. The historical saint was born around 634 CE and died on March 2nd 672 CE, spending most of his life in the political and ecclesiastical turmoil and manoeuvring of this period. Apart from being part of the initial trio of saints in March, St. Chad is most commonly-known for beans – St. Chad's Day is traditionally considered the most propitious day to sow broad beans in England!

St. Winnal's Day, March 3rd, is known for its storms, hence the "roaring mad" of the rhyme at the beginning of this chapter. Winnal is an obscure Celtic Christian saint and very little is known about him, but he does appear to be the patron of tides and weather. In this he, unsurprisingly, shares his day with Aegir, a Norse/Germanic sea deity. Both he and his Christian counterpart control the sea's tides and weather. This day is associated with storms, as evinced in the East Anglian proverb "There is always a tempest on St. Winnal's Day". St. Winnal is known by many different versions of his name, including "Winaloe", "Winnold" and "Guenolé", but precise details of his life and actions are exceedingly elusive; the best thing to do on this day is to stay indoors and maybe do a bit of spring cleaning!

✤ 151 ✤

St. Patrick's Day is March 17th and he is remembered as the patron saint of Ireland or Eire. The dates for Patrick's life are contentious, but it can be said that he was active in the late 5th century and that March 17th was the day on which he died. Stolen as a youth from the West coast of Britain, he spent some five or six years as a slave, working as a herdsman in the North of Ireland. He eventually escaped and came back to Britain where he 'took the cloth' and returned to Ireland some years later to begin his mission. There are many fanciful tales about St. Patrick: how he banished all the snakes from Ireland (there weren't any there to start with); how he usurped the place of the King and his Druids to light the Bealtainne Fires on Teamhair (Tara) Hill (he would have been immediately executed at that time); how he preached using the Seamróg (Shamrock) as a model of the Trinity (the plant had long been held as sacred before his arrival); and many others – but actual facts are hard to come by. What is known is that he was rabidly Christian and would brook no argument from the folk of the Elder Faith. He caused many of the sacred groves of the time and place to be cut down and desecrated many shrines, having churches built on top of the ruins. This day is a chance for the individual Crafter to remember the things that have been lost to over-zealous missionaries, and to reflect on the contribution that the Irish have made to the body of Natural Craft lore. There have been many emigrations from the Emerald Isle to the mainland of Britain and elsewhere over the centuries, and those emigrants have brought much of their native lore with them to enrich that already existing, not the least the large body of Faerie lore and practice that has become joined to the native practice.

The Spring Equinox, or more correctly Vernal Equinox, occurs around the 19th/20th/21st of the month each year. Due to the elliptical orbit of the Earth and its somewhat flattened shape at the poles, it is not a set day each year – this is the same with the other Equinox and the two

Solstices — but varies by a day or two. The Equinox is not a day of group festivity or celebration in Natural Craft, as it is an occasion of great magical energy and hence is utilized by the individual Practitioner for their own personal uses, normally with solitary rites. A great deal has been written about this Equinox by many modern writers, much of which is of dubious provenance and some just downright inaccurate. Until recently, this time of year was never called "Ostara" or "Eostre" by any of our forebears and was not associated with Hares, Rabbits or eggs. This is a modern pagan accretion, compiled over the last 50 years or so. In Chapter 15 of his work *On Chronology*, written in the early 8th century, the monk Bede provides us with the only ancient and historical reference in British literature to the name "Eostre" in giving the Anglo-Saxon name for the month of April, which is "Eosturmonath". The name for March, in which the Equinox of course occurs, he gives as "Hrethmonath", referring to the deity "Hretha" whose name means "Glory". It is probable, but not certain, that "Eostre" is the origin of our word "Easter", which I will discuss in the next chapter, but the name has no connection with March or the Vernal Equinox at all. "Ostara" on the other hand — which is often given as an alternate name for the Vernal Equinox — is possibly a German Saxon female deity, who may be related to the name "Eostre", which name is associated with the Dawn and the East. She is a 'reconstructed' goddess, being given form by the folklorist Jakob Grimm. He believed from his researches that a goddess of this name and type must exist, as he seemed to have found evidence for her in the course of his work. However, no actual name was forthcoming, so he extrapolated the name from linguistic sources available to him. (Unfortunately, he was in error and the actual, literal, translation of the name he gave means something like "The festivals held in Springtime".) She has no connection in history with the Equinox either, nor with Hares or eggs. Neither of these putative feminine Powers is linked with any animal, historically, and neither is connected to any specific events, such as Equinoxes.

In the outward, physical world, the Vernal Equinox is the time when the Sun rises exactly in the East and takes 12 hours to cross the sky, crossing the celestial equator moving Northward and setting exactly in the West. Due to the refraction of light at the horizons for an observer, it never actually appears to be exactly 12 hours, but astronomically speaking, it is so. From that point onwards the hours of daylight will be longer than the hours of darkness, until the Autumnal Equinox occurs in September and the reverse will be true. On the inner planes, or the astral, it is a bit more of a turbulent story. The great energy tides that drive the inner realities are about to change over, from those that have flowed and been the dominant influence, magically speaking, for the last three months to those that will now take over from them. Imagine if you will, two streams of force or energy meeting and at their junction, a hurricane, spinning round and round, with the eye of the storm at its centre and all around it whirling chaos. Or perhaps the confluence of two powerful rivers, that create a great maelstrom or whirlpool at their convergence; on the one side is the outgoing stream of energy, on the other the incoming stream that will determine the type of the new energy tide. It is a time of immense change on the inner planes, as the presiding energies shift from those of cleansing and purification released at the Winter Solstice to those of fresh life, growth and passion which will now take precedence. Natural energies are in great disarray for a few days – possibly up to a week – either side of the Equinox, and most people find that their links with the Otherworld(s) will be disrupted during this period and need to be re-established after this time. However, at the point of the Equinox itself, the very day and hour of it, there is a relatively short period of great stillness and peace – the eye of the storm – which may be utilized for true magical purposes. March is the planting time, when we sow seeds to come to fruition later in the year, and this is exactly how a Practitioner of Natural Craft would utilize the tides and energies of the inner realms at this time. It is not a time of celebration or feasting, but of serious magical work. At this point the energies of new life, passion and growth are being released and it is a prime time to use these energies for our own purposes; almost like hitching a ride on their backs, if you like. By performing our magics now and, metaphorically and actually, casting our seed-desires into the eye of the storm, they can take root in the inner world. They then come to fruition in the physical world later in the year, around harvest time or the Autumnal Equinox, when the next, great inner turmoil takes place. This is a very powerful time for setting events into motion that need time to gestate and develop, and hence too valuable to be spent in feasting and making merry.

How the individual performs their magics will vary greatly from one to another. Some may simply 'tune in' and mentally cast their desire into the melting pot. Another would perform a full-scale ceremony, calling on their Powers and Spirits for aid in bringing about their desires. Another may perform a simple candle spell, inscribing their wish on a fresh candle, empowering it and leaving it to burn out by itself. Or yet another may work with the natural energies of the plants and animals around them. Each will have their own favoured method, but the essential point is that they will use the seasonal, tidal energies to work with in actuality, not to put some emphasis on it that it does not and never did have. Try standing in the eye of the storm yourself at this time of year. Feel the energies around you, the howling hurricane, and then just state your desire, cast it off into the maelstrom to be empowered and enlivened by the natural tide of the year – and await manifestation at the time of harvest.

Coming shortly after the Equinox, March 25th is commonly called Lady Day, but is more correctly termed the "Feast of the Annunciation". It is the day when the

Archangel Gabriel announced to the Virgin Mary that she was to bear a child of immaculate conception – appropriately enough nine months before Christ Mass. It can be seen as another form of setting seed in this month. From the 12th century until 1752 when the calendar changed, this day was also the start of the New and Legal Year. Rents were due, tenancies were reviewed, commenced or terminated and a new season was formally begun. It is said that a good sunrise on Lady Day brings a blessing on the whole year and an offering of a nice bunch of Daffodils to all the ladies, of whatever connotation, would not go amiss.

Finally, at the end of the month, on the 31st there is the Feast of Luna which was originally brought to Britain by the Romans, but has remained popular with Natural Practitioners ever since. It is a festival that celebrates the Powers of the Moon in its feminine manifestation and, whatever the phase of the Moon at this time of the year, it is the day to partake of those particular energies, and to honour and celebrate them.

April

❃✣❃

At the beginning of April, the Sun rises at approximately 5:38 a.m. and sets at roughly 6:31 p.m.

Known variously in traditional lore as the Month of Primroses, the Grass Month, the Pussy Willow or Rainbow Month, April is imaged thus:

> *Young Man in Green, with a Garland of Mirtle, and Hawthorn Buds: Winged; in one hand Primroses and Violets, in the other hand the Sign Taurus.*

Times & Tides
The month of April begins with a smile, as the first day is known as All Fools' Day, or April Fool's Day, when various

types and kinds of practical jokes are traditionally played on all and sundry. This is not an overly long-standing tradition – the first mention in writing being only from 1686, although it was probably observed for a period before then – but it has become a firm favourite and has continued with great dedication up until the present day. *The English Dialect Dictionary* states that it is said to have originated from allowing insane persons to be at large on that day, while sane folks found sport in sending them on ridiculous errands. This may seem unnecessarily cruel in these days of political correctness, but it is likely to have some truth in it, yesteryear not being known for its sensitivity. These days, various types of hoaxes are normally played on an individual, with the media also now keenly taking part each year; remember the famous 'spaghetti trees' and recently the 'flying penguins'? As with many traditional customs, there is a time limit and anyone trying to play a joke on someone after 12 noon is liable to be taunted with the rhyme:

> *April Fool is gone and past,*
> *You're the biggest fool at last.*

The tradition would appear to have originated in either France or Germany and became transferred to these Isles in the 17th century, where it quickly became very popular, being considered 'universal' by the 18th century. Strangely enough for a day of laughter and frivolity, it was considered ill-omened to start a new project or enterprise on this day.

It is very appropriate that April 1st is also known as the feast day of Loki, one of the most enigmatic and ambiguous of the Germanic Powers. He has been 'labelled' as an embodiment of the element of fire, and this has raised much contention and debate. This is allegedly based on a misunderstanding of the term "logi", meaning "fire" in Old Norse and that actually refers to a completely separate entity. In fact, both Logi and Loki appear as 'combatants' in one old myth, so they presumably cannot be one and the same. However, from the traceable and remaining folk customs of Scandinavia, it would seem that Loki was indeed connected to fire. He is remembered and honoured as a guardian of both the hearth and forge fires and is given offerings and offered prayers as such. It also seems that he had a very important role in the religious and sacrificial rites involving fire in Norse times, because of this connection. In addition to this, Loki is also seen as the essence of trickery and patron of thieves – well supported by his mythology – and it is therefore fitting that his feast day should be celebrated now. He is still venerated by some paths of Traditional Craft today and it is known that a Traditional coven in the North of the county of Norfolk still holds him as one of their patron deities. In a nearby district, he was named in a healing charm against the ague, or malarial fever, used in the Fenland district of England right up until the 19th century. A horseshoe had to be nailed up using the left hand, whilst reciting:

Father, Son and Holy Ghost,
Nail the Devil to the post,
Thrice I smit with Holy Crook,
With this mell I thrice do knock,
One for God, one for Wod and one for Lok.

("Smit" in the above is smite or hit, a "mell" is a hammer, "Wod" is Woden and "Lok" is obviously Loki.)

The 14th of the month sees the festival of Sommarsblot being celebrated by those with a Norse or Anglo-Saxon cultural background. It is the feast of the opening of the waterways, the ocean roads of trade and voyaging so important to a seafaring people, that also ushers in the Summer season of exploration and adventuring. By this time of the year, the Equinoctial gales should have passed and the weather be settled enough for the trading ships to put to sea for another year's business and enterprise.

Of course, these days with the huge intercontinental sea freighters that can ride out any storm, there is no need to wait for a fair season, but those who keep up the old traditions still spill a drop of wine or mead in libation to those Powers that govern wind and tide and usher in the fairer weather at this time.

It is around now that the Christian festival of the Death and Resurrection of Jesus is held, namely that of Easter. The dating of this festival has always caused much controversy and not a little confusion, even up to the present day. The Crucifixion of the historical Jesus is fixed in the Gospels as occurring at the Jewish festival of Passover. "Pesach" is the proper Hebrew name, from which most European languages, except English and German, derive their term for the feast. But from as early as the 4th century, different parts of the Roman Empire were celebrating Easter on different dates and it was not until the 8th century that the reckoning became fixed across the whole of Western Europe. The method that was finally used to calculate the date of Easter Day was settled as being the first Sunday after the first Full Moon after the Vernal Equinox, and this is still the method of calculation used today. From this it can be seen that Easter can fall anywhere from the end of March until almost the end of April. However, it is most usually found towards the beginning of this month and is a seasonal or tidal festival in the true sense of the term.

As mentioned in the last chapter, much has been said on the naming of this festival in the English (and German) language, in that "Easter" is unique in these two languages in Europe in not deriving from the Hebrew term Pesach. As also mentioned, it is usually stated that it derives from the term given by Bede for the month of April in the Anglo-Saxon calendar – Eosturmonath – and relates to a deity of the same name whose rites were held then. As this is the only reference we have in the whole of the ancient literature that we possess, it is obviously open to debate as to whether he was accurate in his descriptions or not. The word "Eastre" does signify the season of Spring and is also associated with deities representing the dawn, the East and new beginnings in other related languages and cultures, so it is always possible that he was equally correct. However, we have no other evidence that there was a European Spring festival at this time other than the customs and folkloric remains that are still practised at Eastertide. So, in truth, the question is still open to debate. Be that as it may, the name is now firmly established and has been for many centuries, along with the practices that go with it.

Good Friday begins the festival proper in most people's minds and many practices are traditionally associated with it, not necessarily connected with what the festival is actually meant to be commemorating! For example, it is supposed to be the time when the vegetable garden is prepared and potatoes and peas should be planted and parsley sown, as the Devil was supposed not to have any power over crops planted on this day. It is more likely that this is a remnant of the old Moon lore, in that it would be near to Full Moon – if not actually on it – and a good time to plant things and ensure that they would thrive. Washing linen, particularly clothes, was said to bring extreme bad luck on this day, even death, and anything hung out to dry would be spotted with blood when brought in. For such a gloomy-seeming day – bearing in mind what was supposed to have happened – it was a traditional day for playing many different types of games. In particular, skipping and marbles, and in many areas an annual Hare Hunt would take place, either on this day or on Easter Sunday itself. Many animals were slaughtered at this time, but it was not customary to then eat them apparently, for there is little mention in the literature of this being done. But perhaps the thing that is most often associated with Good Friday is the wonderful, spiced and aromatic Hot Cross Bun. Any bread, buns or biscuits baked on this day were supposed to be especially fortuitous and bring good luck, but the "Crossed Buns", as they were originally called, were the most fortunate of all. The origin of this bun is lost in the mists of time, but small cakes like these and bearing an equal-armed cross are reputed to have been made in honour of Diana, Queen of Heaven, during the Roman period. It is unlikely that this tradition would have survived such a lengthy passage of time and it is more probable that they began as imitations of the consecrated Communion Host, elevated with especial reverence at Mass on this day. The custom continued amongst the laity after the Reformation and from the 18th century, street vendors in London could be heard singing:

> *Hot Cross Buns! Hot Cross Buns!*
> *Give them to your daughters, give them to your sons!*
> *One a penny, two a penny, Hot Cross Buns.*

And so, the name by which they are now known was born. I give a traditional Suffolk recipe for making these delicious breakfast rolls later in the chapter and I advise you to at least try making them yourself – they are so much better than shop-bought ones. Traditionally these had great healing powers and would be hung up in the home to act as a protective charm, only being replaced when the next year's buns were ready to replace them. Gratings of the dried bun would be placed on wounds, and also taken on long road or sea journeys to safeguard the traveller. (Incidentally, a note on usage here. In keeping with the custom of 'borrowing' items/dates etc. from different religions, why not use Hot Cross Buns in your ritual meal at the Vernal Equinox? The symbolism of the equal-armed cross lends itself perfectly to the time of year, it is certainly a time-honoured and traditional food and who knows its actual origins? Play around with the recipe, make some of your own substitutions, use local ingredients and you will soon have your own 'traditional' fare for your rites.)

Easter Sunday, Easter Day itself, is the another important focus of this festival in the natural flow of things and many customs attached themselves to this time as well. It was traditional, nay essential, for new clothes to be purchased and worn at this time, particularly gloves, which were often given as a gift from tenant farmers to their Lords the day beforehand. This was the beginning of the Summer fashion season and it was considered great bad luck if you could not afford even one new piece of clothing. Birds would drop on you or dogs attack you at least! It was also widely held that the Sun dances for joy at dawn on Easter Day and it was traditional (and still is in some families) for people to rise early and watch the Sun come up and receive the blessing of these first rays of light. It was said to spin and jump and even rock to and fro, but that if you could not see this then you were not sufficiently devout or that the Devil was deliberately obscuring your view. If indeed there were pre-Christian Spring rites held at this time of year, then the name given by Bede, that of Eostre, referring to the East and dawn would be particularly appropriate for this custom and may even be a vague memory of it.

The other, main custom of this day is of course the giving and receiving of eggs, these days mostly made of chocolate. Although there are some tales from the European continent linking the Hare with the laying of the Easter egg (which were taken to America by European immigrants and exported back again in the guise of the Easter Bunny), the origin of the custom probably lies in a far more prosaic explanation. Eggs were one of the foods that were forbidden during the Lenten fast and, as they were so abundant at this time of year, would have been the ideal thing to break that fast with as soon as it was over on this day. That the egg was also taken as a sign of new life, Spring and Resurrection would also be most appropriate, whatever your religious affiliations. They were often called "Pace", "Peace" or "Paste" eggs, all names deriving from the Mediaeval Latin term "Pasche" for Easter, itself descended from Pesach. These eggs were often decorated in various ways – which I shall speak more of later – and used in a variety of manners. Children would go from house to house on Easter Morn, begging for eggs to celebrate the death of "Jack O' Lent" and this custom was called "Pace Egging". They were used in a game similar to conkers (hard-boiled of course) where the ends of two eggs would be tapped together by two opponents and the winner was the one who first cracked the shell of the other, keeping the losing egg in forfeit. In some places, even up to the present day, boiled eggs were rolled down hills or down to beaches, and a fine feast was had at the bottom with the cracked eggs, again breaking the fast. A more common game was for parents to hide eggs around the house and garden for the children to hunt and find, a small prize being given to the child who collected the most.

The reader may be wondering by now why, in a book on Natural Craft or Religion, I have spent so much time on the main Christian feast of the year and what relevance it has to a natural belief. A good question. Apart from demonstrating part of the rhythm of the year – and Easter is timed to the natural tides after all, however Christian it may be – it also has an underlying meaning to those who practice the Craft. The late Magister of the Clan of Tubal Cain, Robert Cochrane, once wrote that Good Friday was an especially good day for practising the Craft. Now, apart from being the day on which I was born and a Full Moon that year to boot, what could he have meant? The point is that Easter demonstrates a vital concept in the thinking of Natural Craft or Religion as well as Christianity, and that is the theme of Death and Resurrection. In many esoteric belief systems – and the Craft is very developed in this area – the concept of 'dying to oneself' and being reborn in a new form is very strong, and Easter very succinctly demonstrates this to people of more than one theology. The historical Jesus has always been honoured by Craft Practitioners, respected for his original teachings and considered to be an avatar of divine illumination and insight. His descent into "Hell", his overcoming of his mortal side and condition, and his Resurrection into a perfected state is a goal and an example which many Crafters aim to follow. Some of the deeper aspects of Craft lore deal with the death of the mortal part of the individual and the realisation of the divine, or the crossing of the bridge of death whilst still alive and returning with the knowledge of the Otherworld. Many of our native myths and legends deal with the descent of the hero or heroine into the Underworld, the conquering of some entity or the achievement of some task, and a return with a new and fresh understanding of Life and their part/role in it. Odin's sacrifice of himself unto himself, by hanging on the World Tree and discovering the runes, comes to mind here. I would like the reader to consider this aspect of Easter, rather than just dismissing it as an imposed Christian festival and just enjoying the chocolate and the days off work. The symbolism of Easter is a valid and integral part of Natural Craft and Tradition and, whether it is clothed in Christian disguise or not (as are many of our native Mysteries) is worthy of great attention and consideration.

April 23rd is known as St. George's Day and he is honoured as the patron saint of England. His story is rather obscure and, like other national saints, he never set foot in the country. He is said to have come from either Greece or Turkey (Cappadocia) originally and to have been a soldier in the Roman army, having converted to Christianity early in life and subsequently being martyred for his faith during the Roman persecutions. His story, along with the legend of his dragon-slaying activities, was brought back to England by the early Crusaders and his feast day was subsequently established as a public holiday in 1222. He did not, however, become the patron saint until the 15th century, ousting the much milder St. Edward the Confessor (who himself had replaced the original patron, St. Edmund). He enjoyed huge popularity throughout the Mediaeval period, but his cult was severely damaged during the Reformation, when the adoration of the saints was abolished, and never truly recovered after this. His legend of slaying the dragon has resonances with many native themes, not least the annual battle between the light and the dark halves of the year, Winter and Summer, death and rebirth, good and evil and, on a deeper level in keeping with the theme of this month, that of overcoming the lower personality and being reborn into higher knowledge. He can be seen as similar in nature to many of the native solar deities and it is fitting that his Day should be celebrated at this 'resurgent' time of year. He has been lacking in favour in recent decades, but is now seen as a rallying figure, both for pride in English nationalism – in a beneficial sense – and also as a symbol of the native Mysteries that are once again making a bid for wider attention.

This day is also held 'sacred' to another English hero, William Shakespeare – the "Bard" – and is supposed to be the date on which he was born, and also died. This is debatable due to the calendar changes and lack of reliable records and the only thing we know for certain is that he was baptised on April 26th and died on April 23rd. That notwithstanding, he is revered on a level at least equal to that of St. George, if not higher. He has given not only England, but the world, literature which is truly sublime and worthy of praise. He also knew his Craft as well, as there are many clues and references within his writings to things that would mean little if they were not read in this light. The 23rd is also the traditional day for picking wild Dandelion flowers, either to make infusions for medicinal purposes or for brewing into a delicious wine. This is the day when the 'weed's' properties are meant to be at their peak and full use should be made of them.

A couple of days later on the 25th is St. Mark's Day, which is traditionally a day for all kinds of divination, particularly those kinds relating to marriage, sickness and death – but not necessarily in that order! St. Mark the Evangelist, who lived in the 1st century, is traditionally believed to be the author of the second gospel in the New Testament and a companion of St. Peter. He is reputed to be the first Pope of Alexandria and hence the founder of Christianity in Africa. His symbol is the Lion and he is the patron of both Barristers and of the city of Venice. However, the divinatory practices performed on the Eve of his festival are of much more relevance here. It was traditional to wait in the local churchyard, before midnight, and you would see the Shades of those who would die in the coming year. The manner they appeared in would indicate the nature of their deaths and the earlier they arrived, the sooner in the year they would die. The Shades were said to pass into the church and spend the night inside and a murmuring noise could be heard inside all the while they were there. This practice has – nearly – died out, hastened by the fact that not a few people have seen their own Shade enter the church and have perished within the year themselves. A happier tradition on this date was to perform divinations for love and to find your true mate. A traditional rite would be for a woman to run around a haystack nine times at midnight, holding a ring in her hand. She must call out, "Here's the sheath, but where's the knife?" as she ran and an image of her lover would appear before she went to bed. Alternatively, a woman could pick 12 leaves of Sage, whilst the clock was chiming midnight and, equally, a vision of her true love would appear.

The very end of the month, on the night of the April 30th (St. Walburga's Night/Walpurgisnacht), is traditionally the time for celebrating the start of Summer and May Eve. I will however discuss this in the next chapter, as the festival of "Roodmas", although customarily also known as May Eve/Day, does not necessarily fall on the 1st of that month. As it is a natural and seasonal festival, occurring in its own time and tide, it cannot be fixed to a calendrical date and will be discussed with that consideration in mind.

Hearth & Home

Making your own bread and cakes is an enjoyable experience and can also be filled with magic if the right focus and concentration is applied. For those of a Natural Craft persuasion, making seasonal fare is a normal thing to do, either for enjoyment of the season, or for a special ritual occasion and, as promised, I here give a recipe for home-made Hot Cross Buns that is tried and tested – delicious too! You will need:

Ingredients:

    1lb strong flour
    1 tsp salt
    2oz butter
    1 egg
    ½ pint milk
    1oz fresh yeast (or ½ oz dried yeast)
    1oz sugar or honey
    1½ oz chopped peel
    2oz sultanas
    1 tsp powdered cinnamon

Method:

Add the yeast and sugar/honey to the warmed milk and set aside for about five mins. to become frothy, then add the melted butter and egg. Warm the flour and sieve with the salt. Put the yeast mixture into a mixing bowl along with the warmed, dry ingredients and add the fruits and spices. Mix to form a soft dough and then beat well until the mixtures detaches from the sides of the bowl. Cover with a cloth and leave the bowl in a warm place to prove (rise). When the mixture has doubled in size, knead it and shape it into bun-sized pieces. Cover tightly with greased paper to stop a skin forming on the buns and leave to prove for a further 15-20 minutes. Lay two small strips of pastry in a cross-shape on the top of each bun and brush over the top with either a little milk and sugar or egg to glaze it. Place in a pre-heated oven and bake at 200°C for about 15-20 minutes, or until golden brown. Cut in half, spread liberally with real butter and eat whilst still warm. Heaven! (If you can, try to keep at least one to hang up in the kitchen as a charm and a heal-all, but everybody will understand if the temptation to eat them all is just too much!)

Another enjoyable task that can be performed in the kitchen at this time is to make your own decorated Eggs for the Easter celebrations. As mentioned above, most people have mass-produced, factory-made chocolate eggs these days; how much more personal and meaningful to create your own using fresh-laid real eggs and natural plant materials. This is highly traditional and would have been the only method of obtaining something special in years gone by for many ordinary folk, chocolate being an expensive and luxury item until relatively recently. The simplest method is just to dye the egg a single colour, by hard-boiling it with various materials. Onion skins will give a dark yellow or golden-brown tone, Gorse blossoms give a light yellow, Spinach or Grass give green and Crocus petals produce a yellow-red colour. Once dyed, you can then scratch away certain portions of the shell with the tip of a knife to produce patterns, symbols or inscriptions. Alternatively, you can boil the egg for a short time to heat the shell, take it out of the water, then draw designs on the warmed outside with a wax candle, let it cool and then return it to the pot with your choice of plant material. The wax will stop that area of the shell from being dyed and produce the desired pattern or symbol. Another, admittedly trickier method, is to wrap the eggs individually with leaves, petals or grasses to create more intricate designs. Collect the leaves/petals of your choice and carefully wrap them round the egg, then secure them in place by covering them with scraps of coloured cloth that will release their (natural) dyes also. Tie them in place with string or thread. Alternatively, omit the cloth and tie the plants in place with thread, using plant material in the water for colouring. Boil as normal, remove from the water and leave to dry, then unwrap and see what magical designs have been produced. There are as many different variations on these methods as your mind can conceive, but it should be said that if you intend to eat your creations later on, don't use plants or dyes that are liable to poison or harm you in any other way or your celebrations may come to a premature end!

To accompany your eggs, why not make a salad from the fresh, wild greenery that is now available in most areas? You could use some blanched, drained and cooled Nettle leaves and/or Cleavers, as mentioned in the previous chapter, for their delicious taste and nutritious, health-giving properties; the fresh green buds of the Elder tree (ask permission of the tree first before picking – you have been warned!); the slightly nutty-tasting new leaves of the Hawthorn, or the leaves of wild Watercress that is at its best around this time. If you know where and what to look for, this excellent salad vegetable can be found growing in streams and rivers and is ideal at this time of year for its rich taste and high iron content, especially good for those that suffer from anaemia during the Winter and Spring months. If you are picking it yourself, do make sure that the water is clean and unpolluted and away from sheep; their droppings can contain liver flukes which will attach themselves to plant material and can be ingested. If you are unsure, purchase some from a local market and enjoy it with an untroubled mind. If you have any eggs or greenery left, chop them all up and use them for sandwich fillings when you go out to enjoy the Spring air.

Flora
Throughout April, more and more plants begin to show leaf and unfurl their buds and one of the most well-known is the Pussy Willow, particularly associated with the Eastertide decorations in churches. The Willow family (*Salix spp.*), also known colloquially as the "Sally Tree" and the "Sallow", contains various species, but all are treated

much the same in folklore and use. All species are water-loving and will normally be found growing on banks by rivers or streams, or in boggy, well-watered areas. The Pussy Willow is the Goat or Grey Willow, both species of which have silver-grey male catkin buds, which burst into golden-yellow fluffy balls in late March and April. Other varieties are known for making excellent cricket bats (*Salix alba*) and for basket making and weaving (the Osier, *Salix viminalis*). Because of its love of damp and watery places, Willow bark has for centuries been used as a treatment for the ague. This is a name for fevers resulting from malaria, and also the aches and pains associated with arthritis and other joint pains, along with the headaches that can accompany them. The bark contains high quantities of salicylic acid (as does Meadowsweet – *Filipendula ulmaria*), another damp-loving plant) which was 'discovered' by the pharmaceutical industry and synthesized into our modern Aspirin. Unfortunately, isolating an active ingredient in a plant and synthesizing only that substance can lead to unseen side effects, such as irritation in the lining of the stomach in this case, and it is far better to take the original plant matter with all its balancing 'safeguards'. Willows have been used by lovers for ages in many different ways, both to procure love and to ensure that 'love' may be consummated. This love spell comes from East Anglia and is of unknown age, but has been passed down so there may be some use to it!

Take a green willow switch and firmly tie a knot in the middle. As you do, say these words: "This knot I tie, this knot I knit, for my true love, who I know not yet."

Plant the switch in the ground in some secret place and, as it grows, so your love is sure to come.

Willows are notorious for 'striking' whenever a branch or twig from one is placed in damp earth, so this spell should work well!

Another recipe, this time for an aphrodisiac, states to

steep Willow seeds strongly(?) in fresh spring water and drink before the act of love. However, a man that does so will have no sons and only barren daughters. This last may link the Willow with the darker, more sterile side of the Moon Powers (it is considered sacred to the Moon) and explains its association with loss and remorse in folklore. This has been made famous by the band "Steeleye Span", amongst others, in the song "All Around my Hat", where a maiden is bemoaning the loss of her lover. A Willow wand, although most useful for works of healing, inspiration and love, can also be used for baleful magic as well. In some paths of Traditional Craft, a branch of Willow that is shaded and has never seen the light of the Sun, is cut, dried, then rubbed with bone dust, the whole time concentrating on the maleficia intended. The whole thing is then burnt whilst stating the intent and the ashes cast in the direction of the person or people concerned. This magic is rare and I would not advise attempting it, as all works of harm will eventually exact a price.

On a much lighter note, it is from early April that one of our best known and loved wild plants comes into flower, namely the Bluebell (*Hyacinthoides non-scripta*) and the blooms can last until at least the middle of May in a good year. Variously known as "Culverkeys", "Auld Man's Bells" and "Jacinth", this is a truly native British woodland plant and a truly spectacular experience when the flowers are seen as a whole carpet across the floor of an ancient wooded grove. Nowadays it is under threat from the cultivated Spanish Bluebell (*Hyacinthoides hispanica*) which has escaped from gardens and is cross-breeding with the native plant; it is more vigorous in growth and it is estimated that within 20 years the population of British Bluebells may be entirely hybrids if it is not contained, even within native ancient woodland. The native flower has a stalk that rises up and then curves over, with the pendulous, blue bell-flowers dangling down. The Spanish import stands straight up and has 'bells' sticking out at all angles all around the stem.

However, the native Bluebell is truly a sight to see on a sunny Spring day, amidst the dappled shade of budding woodland, and probably rivals the Rose in popularity as England's national flower. In native lore the Bluebell seems to have been under the protection of the Old Powers in male form – hence the folk name "Auld Man's Bells" – and it was said to be unlucky to pick them and bring them into the house, as they were a plant of the wild outdoors. (It is now also illegal to pick – let alone dig up – wild Bluebells as they are a protected species.) Medicinally they have few uses, although the bulbs – poisonous if eaten raw – can be dried and powdered and used as a diuretic and styptic in very small amounts. The herbalist Gerard says of them in 1597, *"The roote is bulbus, full of a slimy glewish juice, which will serve to set feathers upon arrows in steed of glew, or to paste books with: whereof is made the best starch, next unto that of wake robin rootes"*. ("Wake Robin" is the "Cuckoo Pint", see below). The root actually contains no starch at all, but a substance called "inulin", which acts as a sticky substitute. The juice of the Bluebell has also been used to cure snake bites in the past and this should be applied to the wound, not taken internally.

The plant to use if you really want to starch those Mediaeval ruffs and collars is the wild Arum Lily, "Lords and Ladies" (*Arum maculatum*). This is the only British member of the Arum Lily family and has a wealth of colloquial names, numbering among them "Cuckoo Pint", "Starchwort", "Wake Robin", "Ramp", "Jack-in-the-Pulpit", "Pintle", "Willy Lily" and "Snake's Meat". The large, green spear or halberd-shaped leaves begin to appear earlier in the year, sometimes mottled with black or purple spots. The flowers begin to show around the middle to end of April and the beginning of May, contained in a pale-green sheath, called a spathe. These are upright, reddish spikes, which later give way to a club-like stems which hold the berries on the end. These are green at first, later turning red to purple. Most of the plant is highly acrid and poisonous if taken internally, and will bring a burning sensation to the hands if the juice makes contact externally. However, the tuber roots once baked are edible, high in starch and very nutritious. The starch in the roots was used for all those ruffs in the Elizabethan Age but was very hard on the hands. Gerard says, "*The most pure and white starch is made of the rootes of the Cuckoopint, but most hurtful for the hands of the laundresse that have the handling of it; for it chappeth, blistereth, and maketh the hands rough and rugged and withal smarting*". However, the starch from the powdered root was popular as a cosmetic for the skin and was known as "Cyprus Powder" and it was also used to remove freckles from hands and face. The name Lords and Ladies is supposedly derived from the usage of the starch for the clothing of the aristocracy – and there is no doubt that it was – but there is an alternative story here too. The plant flowers around the time of the Mayday festival, Roodmas, the main stem looking like nothing so much as an erect penis (from which it gets its name Pintle – a penis) suggesting the erotic rites around this time of year. The pollen of the flowers also gives off a faint light at dusk giving them other appellations, namely "Faerie Lamps" and "Shiners". Now, the Faere Folk are also known as the Shining Ones and the Lords and Ladies, and they are also very active at this time of year (see next chapter). So, this all combines to suggest that this plant was either once honoured at the old rites for Roodmas, or was perhaps a natural timer for their commencement and shed some light to show the way to the revels. It is surely worth considering!

Seasonal Skies

April is known as a month of sunshine and showers and it almost always lives up to its reputation, despite the change in the global climate. It can be pouring down with rain one minute and bright with sunshine the next;in fact, they often occur at the same time and produce that wonderful celestial phenomenon of a full-coloured rainbow. As a special occurrence, it is often worth taking note of the weather at Easter, as this lends a certain importance to any prognostications for later in the year; *"Easter in snow, Christmas in mud, Christmas in snow, Easter in Mud"* is one such saying and *"If it rains on Easter Day, there shall be good grass but very bad hay"* is another. This means that hay-time will be wet and that means a wet June. Showers are traditionally at their worst on the last Saturday of the month: *"Thunder in April, floods in May"*. However, *"When April blows his horn (thunders), 'tis good for hay and corn"*, which means that we shall have a fine Summer for crop-growing. Conversely, *"A cold April yields a full barn"*! As the precursor to the Summer Tide, April has both the best and the worst of the seasons both before and after it, so you should really be ready for anything at this time of the year.

Around the 22nd-23rd of the month there occurs the Lyrid meteor shower, logically enough appearing to originate in the region of the constellation of Lyra, low on the Northern horizon. In actual fact, these meteors are part of the dust tail of the Thatcher comet, lit up by falling into our atmosphere as the Earth passes in its wake. They are of middling brightness and pinpoint the position of Vega, the main star of Lyra, with precision. Vega was the Pole Star about 14,000 years ago and is a brilliant star, about three times the size of our own Sun.

Just below Lyra and now beginning to rise from below the horizon facing North, around the middle to the end of April for the Summer months in the Northern hemisphere, is the notable constellation of Cygnus the Swan. The name of this constellation originates in the Greek, but may have meant something else to begin with. Alternative titles are translated as either "Bird" or more specifically "Hen". Weight is added to this alternative name when you realise that the term for the brightest star in Cygnus, Deneb, originally came from the Arabic "Al Dhanab al Dajajah", which translates as "the Tail of the Hen". Be that as it may, "the Swan" is now the official name and it is associated with the Classical myth of Queen Leda, who mated with Zeus in this ornithological form. Leda gave birth to two eggs and when they hatched, one egg contained the twins Castor and Polydeuces (Pollux). The other produced that Helen, so beloved of the Trojan Prince Paris, that two countries went to war over their infatuation. The actual shape of the constellation is that of a cross (the Swan appearing upside down) which is known as the Northern Cross, and is one of the main sights of the Northern hemisphere during the Summer months. In days past it was a great aid in navigation, before reliable compasses and other directional aids were developed. Native mythology has it though that the shape is actually a Goose. Coincidentally the constellation rises – and appears to be flying along the Milky Way and away from the Pole Star into the North – just when the migrant Goose population is getting ready to return home to more Arctic climes after its Winter sojourn in our Isles. Tradition suggests that the Goose is acting as a Psychopomp (Soul Leader/Guide), and taking all the heathen spirits that have died during the Winter and Spring months, and that still remain in "Middle Earth", back to their original home "beyond the North wind", there to remain with the Old Powers until it is time for them to move on. That the Goose flies along the Milky Way is extremely significant, in that it has always been seen as the "divine highway" in British lore and is used by both the Powers and discarnate spirits to travel in their ways between the worlds. Hitching an astral ride on the back of the Goose's flight at this time of the year could well prove to be an interesting experience – but be careful you do not travel too far with this stellar avian, or you may discover realms you were not intended to – yet!

The Sun appears to enter the constellation of Taurus the Bull about the 20th of the month and this is one of the earliest and most noted of all constellations, marking the Vernal Equinox during the period from approximately 4000-2000 BCE. It was during this period that ancient astronomers appeared to be most active and this constellation begins the year in all ancient zodiacs preserved down to this time. The general depiction of this constellation is of the forepart of a long-horned Bull, facing East, positioned just to the North-West of Orion. Its main star Aldebaran (Arabic – "The Follower") is seen as the red eye of the Bull and is close to a small cluster of stars – The Hyades – that mark the Bull's face. A larger cluster of stars – The Pleiades – mark the Bull's back and shoulder blade. The two clusters of stars are both known as the daughters of Atlas in Classical mythology, but each have long been marked in their own right, particularly The Pleiades often known as the Seven Sisters, although there are possibly up to nine of them. As for Taurus itself, native lore refers to it as "the Ox", much used before plough-horses to till the land for the Spring planting, although it would be a bit late to start if left until late April. Rather, the energies referred to would be those of the lusty Bull and be called upon to strengthen the individual for the coming May Day revels. The Bull is also a very much- neglected form of the Horned Lord in native Witch lore and close attention to the energies, mythology and symbolism of this form would richly reward the Crafter, particularly at this time, the threshold of the Summer months.

Fauna

April is the month that is associated with the return of the Cuckoo (*Cuculus canorus*) to these shores, and various parts of the country have their traditional feast or fayre days on the customary 'day' that it is said to arrive. The Cuckoo can return as early as the 6th or 7th of the month, rarely as late as the 26th, which is the date of the latest fayre held in its honour. There is often a tradition that tells of an old woman who comes to the fayre and lets the Cuckoo out of her bag, basket or apron, and in many places divinations are made depending on where you are standing when you first hear the Cuckoo call that year and what your fortune will be because of it. Workmen traditionally downed tools on hearing the first Cuckoo of the year and would go off to spend the rest of the day drinking beer or ale in celebration. This was commonly called "Wetting the Cuckoo" or "Cuckoo-Foot-Ale" and was very popular amongst the men – obviously less so with the bosses! Most of the colloquial names for the Cuckoo are variations on the term "Gowk" ("Geck", "Gog", "Gok") which is Norse in origin and linked to the word "fool". The bird is generally considered to be quite stupid in British folklore and is often linked with the April Fool early in the month. The term "Cuckoo" is from the Latin "Cuculus", which properly applied means "adulterer", although it has strangely come to mean a "cuckold" and applied to the aggrieved husband instead. All this refers to the supposed promiscuous behaviour of the bird (even to naming a plant "Cuckoo Pint" because of its phallic symbolism) and its well-known preponderance for laying its eggs in other birds' nests. (Not to be sexist about it, the term "Cuckoo's Nest" is sometimes used to refer to women's genitals in English folksong!) The Cuckoo eggs are frequently larger than the host's (although this never seems to bother them) and never terribly well-disguised, although some effort is usually made. Once the interloper is hatched, it generally ousts any remaining eggs, or indeed other chicks, from the nest so that it retains the undivided attention of the poor foster parents, who now have to rear their giant fosterling. The parent bird(s) play no more part in rearing the young once the egg is laid and are free to begin fattening themselves up again on the abundant insect life, in preparation for their return journey to Africa in the Autumn. There are many rhymes about the arrival and departure of the Cuckoo, one of the best-known being:

In April come he will,
In May he sings all day,
In June he changes tune,

In July he prepares to fly,
In August go he must.

This is sometimes capped by extra lines that state:

If he stays until September,
'Tis as much as the oldest man can remember.

Which neatly describes the actions of the bird during its Summer visit. In many places in Britain there are old stories of people attempting to capture and keep Cuckoos, in the belief that they could capture eternal Spring, as symbolised by the bird. Needless to say, this never happened and the bird always managed to escape, stupid as it was supposed to be. This is quite an ancient belief and there are many places around the country named "Cuckoo Pen" after this practice. They would seem to be ritual enclosures where annual rites for the arrival of Spring may once have been held, although there is no hard evidence for this. Nevertheless, as a symbol of brighter, warmer weather and good times to come, the arrival of the first Cuckoo of Spring has always been keenly sought and awaited.

Another visitor to these shores, whose arrival is eagerly awaited and looked for at this time of year, is the Swallow (*Hirundo rustica*). Although "One Swallow does not a Summer make" (it is April after all), this beautiful and graceful bird is indeed a welcome sight as it flits overhead and wheels and turns in its never-ending quest for insects in flight. Traditionally, the higher they fly, the better the weather will be. The word "Swallow" is ancient in provenance, traceable back at least to Middle English and probably originates earlier in a term for a "cleft stick", referring to the bird's forked tail. The colloquial terms for this bird – "Barn Swallow", "Chimney Swallow", "House Swallow" and others – generally refer to its preponderance for nesting on or near the dwellings of humans, rarely on natural structures, and reinforces its close affinity with mankind. Indeed, it is generally seen as great good fortune in traditional lore to have a family nesting anywhere about your dwelling, and you remove the nest and inhabitants at great peril to your life and fortune! The Swallow builds an open, cup-shaped nest of mud, lined with feathers, which is usually attached to rafters underneath the roofs of houses and barns. Mated pairs remain together for life, usually returning to the same nest sites, year after year, to raise their young. Although it is generally considered to be great good fortune if Swallows nest on your house, if they flock in large numbers around it, it means that someone inside will die and their spirit will leave with the birds. If one falls down your chimney that also portends a death, but if one flies under your arm, then the arm will be paralysed. In Eire, the Swallow is one of the Devil's birds. In Scotland, it is believed to have a drop of the Devil's blood under its tongue, like the Magpie, and hence has long been persecuted because of it. However, it has also been credited with great talismanic powers, being able to find a stone that can bring sight to the blind, and also able to bring fire in times of need. Swallows were also reputed to hibernate or fly to the Moon in Autumn, or to lay themselves up in holes or caverns during the Winter and only emerge in the Spring. They have been used in folk medicine for various reasons and here is a rather gruesome recipe from a Still Room book of 1692, describing how to make "Swallow Water":

> *Take 40 or 50 Swallows when they are ready to fly, bruise them to pieces in a mortar, feathers and all together, you should put them alive into the mortar. Add to them one ounce of castorum in powder, put all these in a still with white wine vinegar. Distill it as any other water … You may give two or three spoonfuls at a time.*

This distillation was said to be

...very good for the passion of the heart, for the passion of the mother, for the falling sickness, for sudden sounding fitts ... for the dead palsie, for apoplexies, lethargies and any other distemper of the head. It comforteth the brains ...

Now that the Sun has begun to warm the soil once more, we begin to see renewed activity in that small, furry animal that incites so much loathing and anger in both the gardener and the greenkeeper, namely the common Mole (*Talpa europaea*). Considering it is such a small animal (approximately five to six inches long) and is so very rarely seen, the Mole causes an inordinate amount of grief to a lot of people throughout mainland Britain, although it is naturally absent from Eire. Its main alternate name "Moldwarp" (including over 60 variations on this around the country) is Middle English, from Old English meaning "Earth Mover". It probably provides the Late Middle English term "Mole" and is a very apt description, considering that that is almost its entire occupation. The molehills (also known as "tumps") that can now be seen dotting beautifully-kept lawns with increasing frequency are the spoil heaps from the Moles' excavated tunnels, made with their large, spade-like forefeet as they search for food. They eat almost exclusively earthworms, but will also take slugs, centipedes, millipedes and insect larvae. They can burrow up to a metre deep and construct elaborate networks of tunnels, which contain sleeping chambers lined with grass and moss, and sometimes larger mounds are built over nesting sites. These mounds, called "fortresses", can act as 'caches' where the Moles store worms in times of shortage or hardship and can contain several hundred individual worms at a time. The Mole bites off the head, twists the body into a knot and leaves it in the cache. If the worm is not needed, the head regrows and the worm escapes! Many, many methods have been used to get rid of these small, furry creatures in the past, from garlic stuffed down the holes, to moth balls, from slug pellets to various forms of vibration or gassing, but nothing seems to work and the only way of truly getting rid of them is trapping. This was once big business and trappers could earn (relatively) large sums of money from selling the skins to tailors' shops in the larger towns. This was one of the reasons for the popularity of "moleskin" trousers and waistcoats at one time, as the material was so readily available. Nowadays things are more regulated and the fur has fallen out of favour, although it is beautifully soft and smooth and can come in a variety of natural colours, including white and orange! Despite popular opinion the Mole is not blind, although its eyesight is not good, and although it has no external ears to speak of it is not deaf either. It does have extra organs in its snout that are extremely delicate and sensitive and are able to detect minute changes in humidity, temperature and atmospheric pressure. Despite being so sensitive, it is not true that a blow to the nose will kill a Mole instantly. Moles never seem to have been eaten by humans, probably due to the fact that their flesh goes rancid very rapidly after death, but they are taken by Foxes, Herons and Buzzards. This hasn't stopped them being used in folk remedies however, as a male Mole, skinned, dried in the oven and powdered was considered until very recently in the Fenland district to be a sure cure for the ague (malarial fever and similar complaints). Dried Moles' feet were also often carried in the pocket to ward off the effects of cramp and rheumatism – the forefeet for the arms and the hind feet for the legs – and if the feet were cut off a living animal they cured the toothache too! Dripping the blood from a freshly-killed Mole onto warts was said to cure them, and if the blood came from the nose of a living Mole and was dripped onto a lump of sugar and eaten, then it would control fits and seizures. Needless to say, these latter remedies are not advised today on "Molitarian" grounds, or they may decide to encircle your house with their tumps, which is a sure sign that someone inside is about to die. "Mole Country" is a dialect and extant Craft term in East Anglia that refers to the Underworld!

With this chapter, we come to the close of the Spring Tide and turn our faces to the tide and things of Summer. Already we may have seen the signs that announce its arrival, indeed it may already have manifested with a vengeance, as it is apt to do more and more these days. Having swept away the cobwebs, cleansed and purified on all levels, it is now time to take full advantage of the rush of new energies and get on with the activities that require the exuberance of the Summer Tide.

THE SUMMER TIDE

꜡꜡ꙁ ✤ ꙁ꜡꜡

From around the beginning of May onwards, the tides of Life really start to increase in intensity and energy. You would have to be stone-dead if you could not feel the pulse and throb of the rhythms of Life as they increase in tempo all around. It is during this tide that Nature really puts forth all her efforts to reproduce herself and a corresponding urge is felt in most forms of animal, plant and human life. The gentle, light and cautious energies of Springtime are swept away in a great rush and surge of passion as the height of the year is reached in the longest days. After this they gradually begin to wane with great reluctance towards harvest time and the more mature energies of Autumn. This is the period when it is imperative to be mostly outdoors, working with the rush of energy all around and taking part in the tides of growth and expansion. It is time to lend our energies to those of the Great Powers that let us, as they stride through the Land bestowing their gifts of increase and vitality about them. Practising a Natural Craft is not all hard work – and the Powers would not expect it to be – there is fun and merriment at the heart of it too and this ought never to be forgotten.

From May onwards, most of the trees come into full leaf and the gentle shafts of light lancing through the lightest of green leaves gradually give way to more shadowy and shadier groves as the leaf-cover reaches its maximum. The early Spring flowers and plants that covered the woodland floor have now seeded and begin to die back as their light source is cut off. Hardier plants that prefer a shadier habitat, such as Ferns and Foxgloves, begin to appear in the woods and more Sun-loving plants like Buttercups and Cow Parsley begin to blossom in the fields and meadows. The hedgerows become rich with the warm aromas of May blossom and Elderflower. Wild Roses and Woodbines begin to twist and entwine their way up and around any available stem before bursting open in great drifts of colour and Summer scents.

Birds and animals that have already mated will soon begin to hatch their first clutches, or later, give birth to litters of furry young. These are then ready to take advantage of the growing abundance of insect, plant and animal nourishment available. Life lives from Life, so any new young that are around will inevitably become prey to others higher up the species ladder. However, there will still be time to rear another brood or litter before the Summer is over and, hopefully, this time, bring them to full growth and see them on their way in the Autumn. The increased plant life now gives a welcome boost to those pollen-loving insects like Bees and Butterflies and the longer, warmer days give a chance for Mayflies, Dragonflies and other short-lived beauties to emerge, mate and fade way.

It is time to turn our backs now on the 'darker' and maybe more 'ponderous' influence of the Winter and Spring stellar energies in the North. Time to turn our faces to the South, the realm of the Summer stars and the brighter, more intense energies that they bring. The constellation of Boötes is now rising high during this period and the Dog Star, Sirius, will soon usher-in the period of Summer madness and the hours of daylight will reach their peak with the presence of Cancer making itself felt. The nights will not be so long during which to observe and make use of these energies in our nocturnal rites, but they will be warmer and we will feel more alive and all the better to take greater advantage of them in our working.

On a more human level, it is time to start collecting and preparing all the fresh, new supplies that are becoming available to the Natural Crafter. The trees and the shrubs are putting out new leaves, many of which have magical and/or medicinal properties. These can be collected, dried and stored for later, or can be brewed into fine wines and liqueurs to be enjoyed at this time next year. They serve to remind us how good these things can be and prompt us to collect some more. It is during the Summer months also that most herbs become available, so the Crafter will be out and about collecting those that are most available, precious or rare and carefully preserving them for use in simples, potions, incenses, charms, powders and other magically-useful creations.

May

✳ ✢✿✱ ✤ ✱✿✢✱ ✳

At the beginning of this month, the Sun rises roughly at 4:34 a.m. and sets at approximately 7:21 p.m.

May, evocatively known as the Flower Month, may be imaged thus:

> *With a Sweet and lovely Countenance, clad in a Robe of white and Green, embroidered with several Flowers, upon his Head a garland of all manner of Roses; on the one hand a Nightingale, in the other a Lute. His sign must be Gemini.*

Times & Tides

The festival known in Natural and Traditional Craft either as Roodmas or May Day, like all the great festivals of the year, is a moveable feast. It can occur anywhere from around the middle of April to the middle of May, depending on various signs. The Church feast of Roodmas proper occurs on May 3rd but the name has long been used by Crafters to denote the festival that marks the beginning of the Summer Tide of energies and all they entail. Although generally fixed these days in modern practice to either May Eve or May Day, the traditional timing of this festival was always linked to the flowering of the Hawthorn tree, once certain signs and energies had been seen and experienced. Obviously, this would mean that people in different parts of the country would be celebrating at different times. This is only as it should be in a natural system that is not tied to an artificial calendar that has changed many times. Even the main indicator, that of the blossoming of the Hawthorn or May tree, is surrounded by provisos. I remember one year seeing the first blossoms onApril 6th, but the weather was still quite cold and no other signs of Summer were apparent, so celebrating was delayed until the other signs were apparent. In other years the May has not been out until the middle of the month it is named for, but that was equally all right, as by then the other signs were also apparent and the timing was appropriate. These are things to be taken into consideration when attempting to tune into the natural flow of energies in the Land and Sky, rather than following a book-led system. The Catholic Church has dedicated this month to the Virgin Mary and it is equally true that those of the Elder Faith see this month as the beginning of the time of the Summer Queen in all Her glory.

The coming of the month of May has for many centuries denoted the start of Summer in traditional practice and lore, whatever else 'official' timings may have said. In many pre-Christian or non-Christian calendars, only two seasons were recognised – Summer and Winter – and May marked the beginning of the Summer season. The old Saxon name for this month was "Thrimilci" or "Trimilchi", referring to the fact that the cows needed to be milked more often, due to the increased lushness and abundance of the fresh, new grass on which they fed. Butter, cheese and milk were also then much more abundant and offerings were made in gratitude to the Spirits of the Land in the form of the Faere Folk and their like. It has also been traditional for many centuries for folk to take the Day (or more than one) off work and celebrate the coming of the better times, with games, dancing, singing and feasting. Many of these gatherings were known as "Ales" or "Wakes", after the old term for "watching" i.e. waiting up on the Eve of the festival, all night, for the Sun to rise the next day. These took place throughout the month of May, not just at the beginning. The one thing that was considered essential to have in many places, as the centre and focus of the celebrations, was the Maypole. This varied greatly in height and decoration from place to place, but was always keenly contested, villages often mounting expeditions to steal their neighbours' poles if they could not get their own, or they thought the other was better. The poles themselves were made of various different types of tree, most often being either Birch or Ash. They were often taken from the local woods without the permission of the owner, though most Lords condoned and supported the practice, even donating considerable sums for the entertainment. Until very recently, there was never any suggestion that the Maypole was a phallic symbol; that is an 'invention' by Victorian folklorists seeking to backdate every traditional pastime to an idyllic, pagan Golden Age, usually with a 'fertility' theme. They were simply a focal point for the festivities and dancing of the May feasting. There is a possibility that the Maypole originally served some geomantic function, perhaps in collecting or distributing the energies aroused by the dancing, or enhancing the energy in the fields, but this is now ignored. Nor were these poles decked with ribbons that the dancers wound round them in their dancing – another Victorian addition. However, they were often covered in greenery and garlands, with maybe an image of a golden ball or the May Queen at the top. Fashions changed over the centuries and what was common in one era was unknown, or suppressed, in another. The May Fairs could be exceedingly rowdy and bawdy affairs and frequently incurred the displeasure of evangelising reformists during the Reformation and later. They were banned altogether during the Interregnum in England – although they were restored with great joy by the populace after the Restoration – and entirely after this period in Scotland.

Speaking of Scotland, it is only in the Highlands and Islands here, and in certain places in Ireland and a few isolated locations in Wales, that the famous Beltane or May Fires were lit. This was not a common practice at all in most of the British Isles and seems not even to have been a common Gaelic or "Celtic" practice either. It was confined only to those places where a certain type of animal husbandry was practised, and not universally even in those regions. The famous "Druid" Fires were lit in only a few places – the cattle being driven through in a magical and 'homoeopathic' practice of banishing the evils of Winter and blessing them for the Summer. These lingered until the 19th Century in only a few very scattered places in the Scottish Highlands and Welsh valleys. Various rites were still carried out until fairly recently to bless and protect both the flocks and herds, and also people at this time of year, but they were never common or widespread, even in Gaelic farming areas.

So, in Natural Craft terms, what exactly are we celebrating here, on a deeper level than 'just' the beginning of Summer? Well, in truth, not a lot more, but understanding the true meaning of this time is essential to celebrate it fully. The Roodmas festivities are the acknowledgement of the manifestation of those energies released on different levels at the Vernal Equinox i.e. energy, passion and growth, and their release into/onto our material world. Natural and Traditional Craft has never been a fertility religion per se, except in the widest possible sense of the word. However, it does acknowledge these energies in the Land and the People and there is absolutely nothing wrong in celebrating these things when they happen. When the whole world around you is bursting with Life and Energy, there is no point in sitting back all po-faced and miserable. Get out, enjoy and live and if that means disappearing into the woods with a favourite partner overnight, then so be it! Life is for living and the great Powers that move through the Land and Sky are the essence and personification of that and would not want us to cut ourselves off from the wellsprings of that very Life that gives them – and us – existence.

Of course, having said this, there is a deeper or more esoteric side to all this as well. Traditionally at this time, the Hollow Hills where dwell the Faere Folk, the Lordly Ones, are opened and they ride out, across the Land. They bring the new tides of energy with them as they pass into different territories and realms for a new season. In fact, these 'shifts' occur at each of the cross-quarter days and it can be said that, in this particular context, the Faere Folk themselves embody the earthing of the energies released at the Solstices and Equinoxes. Their 'riding forth' manifests these energies on the physical plane. The Crafter will be aware of this and will make use of the energies released at this time for his or her own purposes. These energies are often depicted as fires or lines of fire/serpents/dragons within the Land, particularly at this time of year – one of the three "Spirit Nights" in the natural calendar. It is possible to partake of these energies and 'ride' them at certain times and places, and to gain a greater insight into the inner workings of the Land and the Spirits and Beings that indwell it. We then also gain a greater understanding of our own energies and our connections with others not unlike ourselves. Personally, I remember one year being in the right place at the right time and seeing what is known as the "Faerie Rade" pass by. It was an awesome sight and feeling, and one I shall remember for many a year. I shall not attempt to describe it – I can't – but the sight of these

Left: 1. November; First Frosts

Below: 1a. Ancestral Remembrance

2a. The Orb

2. December; Light Returns

3. January; Winter Bites

3a. Early Pilewort

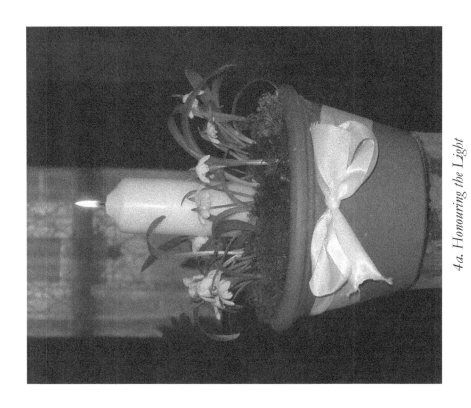

4a. Honouring the Light

4. February; Spring Struggles

5a. Blackbird

5. March; Shade and Light

Above: 6. April; Bluebell Glades

Left: 6a. Hot Crossed Buns

Left: 7. May; Herald of Summer

Below: 7a. Heady scent of Mayblossom

Above: 8. June; bursting with life

Left: 8a. Wild Dog Rose

9a. Summer's Bounty Preserved

9. July; Haysele

Left: 10. August; Harvest Ready

Below: 10a. Lammas Loaf

11. September; Light and Shade

11a. Illuminated Web

Above: 12. October; Mists and Mellowness

Left: 12a. The Eternal Return

great Beings as they travelled by, neither acknowledging nor ignoring me, and the feel of the energies as they passed, was a great honour and a joy to have experienced. It is for just this type of experience that Crafters adhere to their practices and traditions.

If you wish to try experiencing something of the essential energies at this time of year, I would suggest adding this simple practice to whatever rites you perform around now, or even as a separate practice in itself. (The 4th of the month is sometimes known as Faerie Day, so you may wish to work then, but a note of caution though; despite popular opinion these days, the Good Folk are not particularly interested in us and can be quite hostile at times. Be careful in your dealings with them, do not anger or upset them and always give thanks for any favours done you.) When you feel that the time is right and you feel the stirring of the Summer energies in the Land – and the Hawthorn has put forth its creamy blossoms – prepare your ritual space in your accustomed manner, in a place that is wild and secluded (obviously having first obtained the permission of the local Guardians). At the centre of your space, light a small fire in a safe container (a small cauldron maybe, or a ring of stones in a depression in the ground) and call on the Powers and Spirits that you work with to be with you. Tread the Mill around the fire, focusing on the flames and what they symbolise at this time and attempting to become one with the energies that are around you. When you have reached an appropriate state, stop pacing and take up a bowl of bread and milk and dedicate it to the Powers in the Land and the Faere Folk. Then pour it out on the ground beside the fire, letting it sink fully into the earth. Sit down and begin to gaze into the flames and you will see what you will see. If you are lucky enough to make a direct, energetic link with the Fire in the Land – really feel it pulsing in your veins – then let yourself be pulled along with it and see where it will take you. After whatever experience you receive, on your return you should ensure that you 'ground' any energies that you have raised or encountered. As this is May, well, I'll leave the most appropriate method to your own imagination. If you are able and it is safe enough to do so, stay the night, falling asleep a little way apart from the fire – safely banked – and see what dreams may come. If this is not possible, clear all away carefully and retire for the night, but always take especial note of your dreams in the morning. If you are lucky and blessed you may be honoured with something quite extraordinary.

As stated above, although the May Day festival is often termed Roodmas, the correct date for this Church festival is May 3rd and actually celebrates the "Finding of the True Cross" by St. Helena. She was the mother of the Roman Emperor Constantine, who finally made Christianity the official religion of the Empire. "Roodmas" comes from the Old English "Rood", meaning a "Rod", "Staff" or "Cross" and "Mas", a "Mass", and this term was adopted by Crafters to describe the rites at this time. The Rood or Staff implies the Crafters' Stang and all the symbolism that goes with it, which is very appropriate for this time of year. It may also have some connection with the Maypole – so much a feature of celebrations at this time of year – as being the Rood around which the celebrations took place. Meditation upon this subject will produce added insights into the inner meaning of this festival.

On the seventh Sunday after Easter comes the Church festival of Pentecost – again, a seasonal moveable feast. This was when the gift of the Holy Spirit descended upon the Disciples, but it is so much better-known in Britain by the name of "Whitsun". No one can say exactly what the term means, but the favourite has it that it refers to the white robes worn by babes being baptised on this day. It was a favourite day in the year to have this done – hence "White Sunday". For many, if not most people though, this was an excuse to continue the May festivities that had gone on nearly uninterrupted for most of the month, with a little bit more 'respectability' added. "Church Ales" or "Church Wakes" were now celebrated and, of course, this carried on to the Monday when it was made a Bank Holiday. It is now renamed erroneously as the Spring Bank Holiday and placed at the end of the month. Many of the traditions, such as Morris Dancing, Mumming, Garlanding and Parading that were traditional on May Day also attached themselves to Whitsun and were celebrated with gusto, as they still are in many areas today.

At the end of the month, on the 29th, is Oak Apple Day, or Royal Apple Day. It commemorates the day in 1660, when Charles II reclaimed his throne by his formal entrance into London. It was also his birthday and so was proclaimed a day of thanksgiving. It was traditional right up until very recently to wear an Oak leaf or Oak Apple to show your allegiance to the Crown and the Day, and anyone not doing so was liable to be punched, kicked or whipped with Nettles. This gave it the alternative name of "Nettle Day" in some areas. The reason for the adoption of the Oak on this day is because in 1651 the King had hidden in the now-famous Boscobel Oak when he fled for his life after the execution of his father, and so honoured the tree for giving him sanctuary. Traditional May festivities were celebrated throughout the Day and many toasts were given to the Crown in celebration of all the pastimes banned under the Puritan rule. The honouring of the Oak at this time, however, masks older rites that were traditionally held at this time in honour of the tree and for the beginning of the Summer. The Oak (see below) is an initiatory and Gateway Tree which comes into leaf at this time of year, signalling and heralding a great time of change in the energies of the Land. To spend some time under, or in, the branches of a mature Oak at this time can be a truly revelatory experience and may unfurl some deeper meanings to this time of the year.

Flora

As already mentioned, the tree most associated with this month is the Hawthorn (*Crataegus spp.*) and after which it is sometimes named i.e. the May. There are two main species in Britain: Common Hawthorn (*Crataegus monogyna*) and Woodland Hawthorn (*Crataegus laevigata*). The lore surrounding this tree is vast and it is known as one of the most magical of our native species. It has been given names such as "May", "White May", "Whitethorn", "Quickthorn", "Bread and Cheese"; and "Awes", "Azzies", "Agars", "Boojuns" and "Hoppety-Haws" for the fruits. The pinkish-white blossoms signal the start of the Summer season and under their heady scent many a "Greenwood Marriage" has taken place. The association with sexuality and the Hawthorn is ancient and, as well as referring to the time of year, also has to do with the scent of the blossoms, as it is the female sexual scent which is given out. The Queen of Summer is also the Lady of Venery and governs the revels at this time of year; the Church may have its Virgin, but the Craft has its (all) Woman. However, the scent of the blossoms is not to the liking of all and it may be this which began the taboo on taking them indoors (although this seldom bothers Crafters). One of the main constituents of the scent is triethylamine, which is also the chemical that corpses give off when they start to putrefy. In the past, when the deceased were laid out in the home before burial, this would have been a well-known smell, particularly during the Great Plague. To deliberately bring it into the home at a time full of life and rejoicing may well have seemed ill-omened and therefore banned. Another reason is that, before the Reformation, most people made up "Mary Altars" in the home in honour of the Virgin during this month. They were generally decked with May blossom, as this tree is sacred to the Female Powers in all their guises. After the Reformation, it would have been a **dead** giveaway to have this plant in the house at this time, disclosing your allegiance to the suppressed religion. The fruits, or haws, can also be strung together to form a rosary – which can be used by Catholics and Crafters alike, albeit for probably different reasons – and would also incriminate any house in which it was found. However, it was fine to use the blossoms for outdoor decorations; houses, barns, Maypoles, even adults and children, could all be found decked with May garlands at this time of year and think themselves the more blessed for it. The Hawthorn is also one of the prime Faerie Trees and is famed throughout the British Isles for this association. Many people will not uproot a Hawthorn for fear of angering the Faere Folk and many is the tale of disaster told if this has actually been done. The Hawthorn is often linked with the Oak and the Ash and, together, these trees are known as the Faerie Triad. Wherever they are found growing together is seen as a haunt of the Lordly Ones and a gateway to other worlds. The Hawthorn itself has often been used as a hedging plant, most specifically since the enclosures of the 18th and 19th centuries, but was known and used long before this for this purpose. The Anglo-Saxons referred to the Witch as a "Haegetesse", usually translated as "Hedge Rider", which indeed is its meaning, but the "Hedge" component "Haege" also refers to the "Hagthorn" or Hawthorn. It denotes the fact that it was seen not just as an ordinary boundary marker for this world, but also as a liminal boundary between this world and the next. The Witch was the Rider of the Hedge between the two worlds, who brought back knowledge, wisdom and power and could make Otherworldly things happen. Magically, Hawthorn leaves could be chewed with intention to aid focus and Otherworldly contacts at sacred sites. Whereas the thorns from the tree, equally as sharp as those from the Blackthorn, could be used to pierce poppets for love magic and healing. Carrying the thorns in a pouch around the neck was thought to bring luck when hunting, and a rosary of haws could be used for meditative purposes or to count the number of chants used in a spell. The blossoms made into a wine (easy on the amount of blossom!) could be used to toast the Lady of Love at the May rites and a wand made of the white, peeled wood could be used to control malevolent spirits and cast enchantments. Medicinally it is mostly used in treating cardiac conditions. The leaves, flowers and particularly the fruits have the ability to strengthen the heart function and lower or heighten the blood pressure. If the pressure is too low it will raise it, if too high it will lower it. It strengthens the heart muscle and increases blood flow through the heart without raising the beat or pressure. It is used to lower cholesterol levels and can help in cases of angina, over-exertion or mental tension, is mildly diuretic, can ease an alcoholic heart and is used to sustain the heart under stress or sustained physical pressure. Altogether a very useful plant to have around when celebrating in the Greenwood!

The other major tree to feature at this time is the Oak (*Quercus spp.*) which is usually known simply by its own name. There are two major species in Britain: the Common, Pedunculate or English Oak, (*Quercus robur*) and the Sessile Oak (*Quercus pwoodetraea*). The Common variety has an obviously gnarled bark, leaves with deeper lobes or indentations that are practically stalkless, but acorns on long stalks. The Sessile Oak has a much smoother bark, less-indented leaves set on long stalks and acorns that are practically stalkless. The Common Oak is more widespread and accounts for the majority of Oak woodlands in the British Isles. It is about now that the Oak comes into leaf, a soft, almost luminous light green in colour, that gradually darkens over a week or so. This tree can also put out a second growth of leaves around early August which is known as the "Lammas flush" because of the timing. The leaves, picked now and used fresh, make a superb wine that may be drunk at any time, but is particularly useful when celebrating rites for or in the Greenwood. The Oak is a very long-lived tree and can grow to be 800 years old or more, especially if it is pollarded (cropped for its branches periodically, at head height). It houses the greatest number of living species in its leaves, bark, branches, trunk and roots of any British tree and because it lets in quite a lot of light through its canopy, many other plants receive enough energy to grow beneath it. It is probably the best known and well-recognised of all British trees and has long been a symbol of strength, tenacity and endurance. Oaks were

anciently used as gathering places, beneath which to hold
meetings, courts and parliaments, and later to preach the
words of the new religion, hence becoming known as
"Gospel Oaks". Its wood has long been used for many
purposes, notably for building the frames of houses and
ships and is especially useful in the fact that it can be used
when still green. It has fine, closed-grained timber and so
is especially good as a long, slow-burning fuel. It produces
a concentrated heat which lends itself ideally to smithing
and the like, although there is a taboo on using it in many
magical fires, depending on time of year and location. Some
people say the Yule Log should be of Oak, others find
that to be anathema. In Wales, the May Fires were lit from
the friction of Oak on Oak, whereas in England this was
taboo. The wood is also used to magically stake or ground
energies and to form strong barriers around the working
area. The fruit of the Oak, the acorn, although very bitter
to humans, has been useful in times of famine. Ground
down into a flour it can be used in its place to make bread
and can also be drunk as a type of coffee substitute. From
Saxon times onwards, the common folk drove their pigs
into the Oak woods in Autumn to fatten them up on the
fallen acorns and these "pannage rights" still exist today
in the New Forest. The other 'fruit' of the Oak, the gall,
which is actually a by-product of parasitic larvae living on
the tree, was once much used by monks and other literate
people as the basis for ink. The galls were dried, ground
down to a powder and mixed with a weak solution of gum
arabic and perhaps some soot, and made the only available
writing medium in times gone by. Unfortunately, it was not
terribly fast and either ran or faded fairly quickly, but it
was all they had! As the Hawthorn blooms and represents
the Female Powers in and of the Land at this time, the
leafing of the Oak shows the Masculine Powers at work.
It heralds the arrival of the Summer King, whether He be
known as Jack-in-the-Green, the Green Man or simply the
Oak Lord. As one of the Faerie Trees, the Oak is a tree to

be wary of, as the old rhyme goes: *"Turn your coats, for faerie folks live in old Oaks"*.

And yet it is a tree of great magical and mystical benefit also. As stated above, it is a Gateway Tree, a doorway to other realms and will let those that know how, pass from this realm to Others, with the blessing and protection of the Beings that inhabit and guard it. Finding a place where two Oaks grow next to each other can be particularly efficacious, as walking between them with intent can literally be like walking through a doorway into another world. The experiences given by Oaks can be strongly initiatory and their magic and lore is at the heart of the native British Mysteries. On a more earthly level, Oaks have been used medicinally for centuries, mainly due to the strong astringent and antiseptic properties of their bark. This should be collected at this time of year, from younger trees, as later in the year it becomes harder to remove, and trying may damage the tree. It is the inner bark that is used and this can be made into teas, tinctures or ointments for various purposes, or dried and powdered and taken as snuff. Oak is mainly used for varicose veins, diarrhoea, mouth and external ulcers, haemorrhoids and dysentery. As a snuff, it was used very effectively against the early stages of consumption, and tanners – who used Oak infusions to tan hides – were known never to suffer from this disease.

The Comfrey plant (*Symphytum officionale*) is in full flower at this time and can be seen at the edge of many a secluded wood, ditch or leafy waterway. Known variously as "Knitbone", "Bruisewort", "Boneset", "Ass Ear", "Pigweed", "Gum Plant" and "Yullac" or "Yalluc", it grows to about three or four feet high. It has spear-shaped, mid-green hairy leaves and pale cream or purplish flowers, which hang in bell-like clusters on the top of tall stems. The English name is thought to stem from the Latin "confervere", which means to "grow together", hence its common and folk attributions. Its main use is in the healing of wounds – as its common names suggest – and in this it is supreme, exceeding even many modern medicines in its efficacy. It is mainly the leaves and roots that are used, usually externally. Comfrey contains alkaloids that may be toxic to the liver if taken in large amounts over a longer period, although eating a leaf or taking a cup of tea occasionally is perfectly safe. Comfrey contains a chemical called "allantoin" which promotes the growth of connective tissue in human and animal flesh. The plant is usually used in cases of broken bones, sprains, bruises, ulcers (internal and external) and abrasions. The root was once scraped to form a pulpy mass and applied to arms or legs with broken bones, in the same manner as plaster is today. The mass set hard and the active ingredients promoted rapid and effective healing, knitting the bones back together again. The leaves would be used as a poultice in a similar way, or rubbed on minor wounds to effect the healing. Today the plant is usually made into a cream, oil or ointment and applied, although never on a deep wound. Comfrey heals from the skin surface downwards and, if the wound is not clean, can trap harmful matter in the wound, hence leading to abscesses or festering. It is also a useful plant in other ways as it can be fed to livestock in times of shortage of other feed. It is a rich source of the vitamin B12 and is high in protein, estimated to contain the same percentage as soya beans and 10% more than cheese. It also makes an excellent manure for the garden. Its taproot can grow up to 10 feet deep and draws up nutrients from the soil that other plants cannot access. Used in this manner it is either deliberately grown on a plot of land and then just dug in, or the leaves are picked and placed in a container and covered with water and left to rot away. The result is a horrible, stinking infusion, but once the leaves have been filtered out and the liquid sprayed over the garden, it is worth its weight in gold. The leaves can be put on the compost heap or more added and topped up with water for another 'brew'. Magically speaking, Comfrey has always been used as a protective plant. It can be carried on the person in a charm bag, particularly when travelling, or used in an incense or suffumigation to smoke the traveller before setting out. This can be performed over pets and objects too if you wish to protect them or make sure they come back to you. Consecrating a protective talisman in Comfrey smoke would ensure the success of this charm.

Hearth & Home

As mentioned above, one of the most traditional practices during May was to bring in from the woods the blossoming boughs of the Hawthorn tree. It was used to decorate the home, usually outside but sometimes also indoors, especially by the Natural Crafter. As well as all its other connotations and attributes, Hawthorn has always been considered a powerfully protective tree and was used as such, particularly at this time of year. This may be due to its close association with the Faerie Folk – perhaps in a propitiatory manner – but also because of its use and association with the Powers of Life that are in full flow during this month. Many people, as well as decorating their homes with "the May", would also take small slivers or twigs of the wood and tie them into crosses using red thread (as is also traditionally done with Rowan wood, which was also used at this time of year). These would then be placed at strategic locations around the home, those deemed most likely to attack or intrusion, such as the kitchen, dairy or nursery, or those places seen as liminal entrances to the Otherworld, like windows and doors, or fireplaces and chimneys. This would be accompanied by whispered charms or prayers to whatever Powers were honoured in the home, and the charms that had been placed the previous year would be taken down and replaced with the new ones. This is a similar practice to the Wardings performed at All Hallows at the beginning of the dark time of year. However now, rather than the focus being on protection against malefic powers (although that is included), it is more a supplication to the Powers that Be to bless the hearth and home and keep it whole and hearty. Some householders – especially in the Gaelic-speaking areas – would put out all the fires in the house at this time, clean the hearths, lay fresh fuel and light new fires. This is signalling and honouring the start of a fresh tide of energy and acknowledging the beginning of Summer at last. If you wish to follow these traditions, I offer the following as something that may be done during this month, to benefit the home and all who live in it. It is drawn from traditional sources, but has been adapted to cope with modern situations – as all good traditional material is!

Obtain four sprigs of flowering Hawthorn, or make four equal-armed crosses tied with red thread from slips of Hawthorn wood – all obtained with the tree's permission of course. Stand at the hearth of the house, or its focal/central point, and light a pure beeswax candle, saying the following:

> *Upon this house now I do pray,*
> *All hostility, deceit and illusion be far away.*
> *Upon this house now I do call,*
> *Health, Wealth and Blessing for one and all.*

Repeat three times.

Place the candle in the 'hearth' and kindle some Comfrey incense in a burner (use the dried stalks and leaves, well-chopped). Once it is alight, address the resident house spirits and Powers with the following:

> *Spirits of this House and Hearth,*
> *Blessings on you now I lay;*
> *Be welcome, happy, quick to mirth,*
> *If in this dwelling you will stay.*

Take up your Hawthorn charms and pass them through the incense smoke, saying:

> *I call Blessings upon this House, from the North and the South, from the East and the West. From the Heights and the Depths, may every Direction bring Blessings and Protection upon this House.*

❖ 203 ❖

Now, taking your incense with you, go to place a sprig/cross at an Eastern window/place in the house, saying:

> *I place this May/Cross in honour of the newly-risen Sun of the Summer. May it Bless and Protect this House.*

Cense the place well.
Go now to place a sprig/cross at a Southern window/place in the house, saying:

> *I place this May/Cross in honour of the Mid-day Sun of Summer. May Luck and Fortune abound here.*

Cense the place.
Go now to place a sprig/cross at a Western window/place in the house, saying:

> *I place this May/Cross in honour of the Evening Sun of Summer. May no evil pass this way.*

Cense well.
Finally, go to place a sprig/cross at a Northern window/ place, saying the following:

> *I place this May/Cross in honour of the Midnight Sun of Summer. May darkness never descend upon this house.*

Cense once again.
Finally, return to the 'hearth' with the incense and place it beside the candle, leaving both to burn out completely. An offering to the House Spirits of a small bowl of cream should also be left out, but never mentioned for fear of scaring them away.

A bowl or dish of fresh cream was also the prize in bygone days, for the first maid to bring her mistress a bunch of Mayflowers early on May Morn. The maid would no doubt have been up early to collect the dew, traditionally either from an Oak or the Hawthorn tree and to bathe her face in it. It is said that those that follow this practice would be the most beautiful and have a 'creamy' and fresh complexion for the rest of their lives. It was/is a customary practice at the Summer Solstice too – but you would need to get up even earlier for that! Having washed the face and brought in the May, thoughts would then turn to making and placing the Garlands that were – and in places still are – so much a feature of May festivities. The fresh, green flowering boughs of Hawthorn would be carefully wound together over a wooden or metal hoop, together with other seasonal greenery, flowers and brightly-coloured ribbons into a circular garland. Sometimes two or more of these would be joined at right angles to form a kind of cage, in which would be suspended more bunches of flowers, gilded balls, or highly-dressed female effigies or dolls. These latter were often said to represent "the Queen", but it was uncertain which queen was meant by this. It could have referred to the Queen of the May, to the Virgin Mary in pre-Reformation times (or even after), or some other Power that should not be named for fear of invoking Her displeasure. The garlands were usually then hoisted onto or suspended from tall poles and taken around the local district with songs and cries for money or other gifts from all they passed. Many would call at the local 'big house' in expectation of largesse and then wend their way happily either home at the end of the day, or to further merriment on the village green for one of the Ales or Wakes, there to dance or watch the ancient "Morris" played out. The garlands would then either be hung up on the outside of the house or barn, left at the local holy well or shrine, or taken back to the Greenwood and returned to the tree that gave the branches for its making. This practice is still continued in many districts in Britain today and many Natural Crafters take part, honouring older Powers than are apparent to the casual onlooker. If there is no tradition of this practice in your area or family, you may like to "invive" (invent/revive) one and create a garland each year, leaving it and a gift for the Powers at a local holy place, or your own house/hearth shrine. It is a simple act, but can bring much joy and attract a lot of the fresh energy that is so prevalent now to the home and family members.

I would like to finish this section by giving a recipe that utilises the abundant life force at this time of year: Beech Leaf Noyau. Best known for its delicious and fortifying nuts, the Beech (*Fagus sylvatica*) also produces a wonderful-tasting liqueur from its leaves. Traditionally regarded as a tree of knowledge and learning, the word "Beech" comes from the same root that gives us the word "book". The best time to pick the leaves for this brew is in late April and early May when they have just unfurled and are still an almost translucent, light green. Once they turn darker they are too bitter for making this drink. You will need the following:

Ingredients:
   fresh Beech leaves
   sugar
   water
   gin
   dash of brandy

Method:
Pack a large, screw-top glass jar about nine-tenths full of fresh, clean leaves and pour over the gin, pressing the leaves down to make sure they are all covered. Screw on the top and leave to steep for two weeks. Strain off the now-brilliant green gin and compost the leaves. To every pint of gin, add 12 ounces of sugar, dissolved in half a pint of boiling water and just a dash of brandy. Stir well to mix all the ingredients and bottle when cool. You will now have a thickish, sweet liqueur, fairly mild and slightly oily, somewhat like Sake in taste, but pretty devastating in effect!

Fauna

There are many fascinating creatures to look out for this month, but one of the most interesting is the Adder (*Vipera berus*), the only native poisonous snake to be found in Britain (excluding Ireland of course, as St. Patrick expelled all the snakes!). Also known as the "Ether", "Hog-worm" and "Viper", the Adder was originally the "Nadder", coming from the Old English "naedre", meaning "a snake or creeping thing". The "n" was lost in Middle English and hence the Adder was born. It is not a big snake, the females growing to about two feet in length, males shorter, although larger specimens have been known. I have certainly been startled by at least one that was three feet long, but they are quite stout and are identifiable by their remarkable patterning. Generally light in colour (although there are black varieties and females tend to be darker than males), they have the distinctive zigzag-shaped or lightning pattern down the length of their backs that is unmistakeable. They kill their prey with a poison which is a nerve toxin, being able to kill a lizard from one bite in about a minute. It is generally non-fatal to humans, except rarely to the very old, young or ill in health. Of the roughly 90 people who are bitten each year, no one has died of the bite in the past 20 years. It is a fallacy that if one is bitten you should cut the wound and suck out the poison (this would enter your blood stream more easily and probably infect the wound as well). Nor should you apply a tourniquet, as this is a very dangerous thing to do, affecting the blood flow in the rest of the body also. Get to hospital as quickly as possible and get treated; only in very rare cases is antivenin applied, as most people recover by themselves. In traditional lore, there is a link between Adders and trees, particularly the Ash and the Hazel, in that the snake was supposed to be afraid of them and avoid them. Striking an Adder with an Ash or Hazel wand was supposed to kill it instantly. If you are foolish enough to try this, it is demonstrably false! Adders are actually very shy creatures and will try to get away if at all possible if disturbed by humans, only attacking as a last resort in self-defence. The Adder has long played a part in traditional medicine and magic, being much sought after for its distinctive skin. Although it moults each year after coming out of hibernation around March, as do most snakes, the cast skin is brittle and transparent and does not bear the magical zigzag pattern; hence it is the actual skin of the animal that is required. This has been and still is used in many different ways. Medicinally, the dried and preserved skin can be wrapped around the afflicted part of the body to alleviate the symptoms, or even cure the complaint totally. This was particularly used for rheumatism, headaches, thorn pricks and wounds. Otherwise the skin could be powdered and added to drinks or soups, which were supposed to be good for various internal complaints or skin diseases. If the patient could be held still enough, even a live Adder was allowed to slide over him or her and 'lick' the skin with its flickering tongue. This was because the snake was supposed to live on various magical and medicinal herbs and grasses, the effects of which were concentrated in its saliva and passed to the patient. Magically speaking, the dried skin has been used in various forms of divination, and as garters or hat bands which denote membership or rank in the Elder Faith. As an animal close to the Land, it has always had the 'ear' of the chthonic Powers and is sacred to them, hence being consulted when major decisions are to be made. Eating the flesh of the snake will convey the power to understand the speech of all animals. It is emblematic of the power that flows through the Land, denoted by its markings, and also of the lightning Powers that live in the sky. Both of these can be called upon and worked with by using the Adder. The most magical thing about this animal though is its "dance", which, with luck, may be seen at this time of year. Two or more males meet and rear up to half their height, come together in an entwined embrace and seem to sway backwards and forwards to an unknown rhythm, as if dancing; it is a most curious and eldritch sight. Actually, what they are doing is competing for an available female, the one trying to force the other to the ground and out of the competition by the force of its body. This may be the origin of the famous description by the Roman writer Pliny, of the nest of serpents entwined together, rearing up, who produce the magical Serpent's -Egg from their combined saliva and cast it aloft. Either way, it is a rare sight and one not to be disturbed if chanced upon.

Once thought to fly to the Moon or hibernate in caves, hollow trees or the mud at the bottom of ponds when it was not present in Winter, the Nightingale (Luscinia megarhynchos) is one of the most famous and beloved of our Summer-visiting birds. Surprising then that it seems to have only one folk name, "Barley Bird", which is given it in East Anglia and nowhere else, as it is said to arrive when the Barley is being sown. Nightingale comes directly from the Old English "Nihtegale", meaning "singer of the night" and, whilst unchanged through the centuries, is not strictly true, as it does indeed sing during the day as well, if less so. It is a rather nondescript, medium-sized brown bird with a reddish rump and tail, that more than makes up for its appearance with its wonderfully musical voice. Mainly living in deciduous woodland, coppice and dense undergrowth, they are a slightly later arrival on our shores than the larger and more nefarious Cuckoo, although they are often linked in folklore. They are now in great decline, having disappeared entirely from Wales and appearing mainly in East and South-Eastern England, although there have been attempts to reintroduce them to the rest of Britain. May is the time when its song begins to be heard again and its liquid notes trill into the still night air, undisturbed by the revellers out late at night, intent on bringing home the May, or something slightly more earthy. Maybe because of the fact that they are so loved for their song, most folklore concerning Nightingales revolves around that, although quite a bit refers to its arrival on our shores in late Spring, alongside the Cuckoo, and that it is only found where Cowslips are plentiful or Hops are grown.

They are said to have talismanic powers – protective that is – but are sometimes considered to be birds of decidedly ill-omen. In Shropshire it was said that death follows closely on their singing. The flesh of this bird has sometimes been used medicinally, being considered beneficial for cases of consumption, cachexia or 'evil dispositions' of the body. The gall of the Nightingale was used as a treatment for disorders of the eye. Surprisingly for such a well-loved bird, it has no place in heraldry, nor is it used in place-names around the country. The best thing to do during this month is to get out into the Wildwoods at night, with a bottle of Oakleaf wine, lie beneath the boughs of the Hawthorn watching the silvery stars and listen to the sound of the Nightingale as it sings the song of Summer.

Whilst lying there, you may be sure that you will not be attacked by, but may hear the high clicking notes of, any one of the 14 types of Bat that are native to these Isles. The family name for these furry, aerial creatures is Chiroptera, but each type has its own genus and species designation, too many to go into in detail here. Suffice it to say that they tend to be indistinguishable in folklore; a Bat is a Bat. This word comes from 1575 and replaced the Middle English "Bakke", which was Scandinavian in origin. Common names for them are legion and include "Airy Mouse", "Backe/Backie", "Flickermouse/Flittermouse" and "Raamis/Raird/Ramsh/ Rare" and many variations on these. They are the only mammals that have evolved to actually fly – as opposed to glide – and have especially adapted 'finger bones' to support the thin flight membranes that form their 'wings'. Contrary to popular opinion they are not blind but it is not known to what extent they use their functioning eyes, relying almost entirely on their hearing for echolocation. They have developed this function to a remarkable degree, each species having a different 'call-sign'. They each emit many numbers of 'clicks' in rapid succession, which may number in the hundreds per second, and pick up the echoes with their specially enlarged ears. It is also a fallacy that

Bats become trapped in long hair, many experiments having proved that they easily avoid humans in their way and that, if deliberately placed in hair, they escape quite easily without getting entangled. They are one of the few British mammals to truly hibernate (although they may emerge during warmer periods), preferring to spend the Winter months in places like caves or mineshafts. In Summer, however, they much prefer trees, houses or large chambers, but preferences differ markedly from species to species. Some, along with Frogs, Toads and Lizards, like to crawl into small holes and have hence given rise to the belief that they could survive for centuries in a form of suspended animation, then emerge unscathed. Belfries are not a favourite, despite the common saying, as they are too cold and draughty. The affinity between Bats and Crafters is longstanding and the former have long been believed to be the familiars of the latter, or even the Witches themselves shape-shifted. As a creature of the night, they represent the nocturnal Powers and the ability of the Crafter to 'find their way in the dark'. This means to pursue and discover those secret and hidden things that others cannot, will not, or are too afraid to see. The dextrous flying ability also alludes to the skill of "Night Flight", transvection or spirit-travelling by the practiced Witch, and – although there are no native blood-drinking Bats in Britain – some of the more lurid vampiric tales told about practitioners of the Old Faith. Nevertheless, this fear of our flying friend has not stopped it being used in folk or traditional medicine and I quote here from a medical text published in 1739:

The Flesh of a Bat medicinally taken, is good against a Scirrhus of the Liver, the Gout, Rheumatism, Cancer, and Leprosy, it has greater virtue to cure the above Disorders, when taken after this manner. Take of the Flesh pulverized half a Dram, Powder of Hogs-lice one Scruple, mix for a Dose. Take of the Blood one Dram, Honey half a Dram, mix them, being applied to the Eyes, it cures Ophthalmias, Films, Webs Pearls, etc.

✤ 211 ✤

There is an Oil made of this Bird, which is exceeding good against the Gout, saith Avicenna. Take half an Ounce of the said Gall, Vinegar two Drams, Salt one Scruple, mix them, it is good to wash any part bitten by a mad Dog.

Charming, I'm sure you will agree! However, due to the fall in their population, all Bats in Britain are now protected species and severe penalties follow anyone trying to suck their blood or eat their pulverized flesh.

Seasonal Skies

The start of May can often be relied upon for some outstandingly warm and beautiful weather, which just makes the heart sing to be outside once more, instead of cooped up indoors. However, this rarely lasts and is usually followed by a period of renewed cold and rain, if not worse. The rest of the month can alternate between these two extremes. There are various rhymes that are used to determine the forecast this month, one of the most appropriate being:

If the Oak's before the Ash, then we're in for a splash,
If the Ash's before the Oak, then we're in for a soak.

SScientific forecasters will tell you that this is rubbish, as the Oak invariably puts forth its leaves before the Ash tree does and anyway, cannot predict the weather. However, country folk who have kept records near me have assured me that after 60 years of keeping count, the rhyme is generally true and that the Oak is not always the first to leaf. What we really don't want this month is renewed frosts – which unfortunately do still happen. It is now that the fruit will be setting on the trees and a bad frost will kill off the blossoms or tiny fruits – not to mention the insects that pollinate them. At the first hint of cold weather, cover any fruit trees and bushes still in blossom with a sheet or net curtain overnight; this will raise the temperature enough to stop them 'burning' and still allow the fruit to set.

Talking of the cold, it is still a common saying that you should *"Ne'er cast a clout till (the) May is out."* This causes all sorts of arguments as no one can ever seem to agree on whether the rhyme refers to the month or the Hawthorn blossom, but I have a suggestion which seems to me to work. The rhyme originally referred to the blossom but began before the calendar change in 1752, which meant that the year was actually a bit more advanced, warmer and the blossom was more likely to be out. This is obviously a matter of opinion, but it works for me. Other weather rhymes associated with this month are:

"A wet May brings a good load of hay." This refers to the hay harvest next month and means that there will be good growth of grass and a lot of sunshine in June.

"A cold May and a windy, makes a fat barn and a findy." A "findy" is a good weight of crops and this rhyme forecasts a good harvest, the worse the weather is this month – unfortunately!

"A hot May makes a fat churchyard." For some reason it does seem that a warm May is deleterious to the health of some people and a warm May does make extra work for florists and undertakers.

Finally, the famous rhyme which always seems to suit the tone of May for me: *"March winds and April showers, bring forth May flowers."* Long may this be true for this magical month.

From May onwards we turn to face the South at night and stare into the realms of the Summer stars whose energies now hold the attention of the Crafter. The first and perhaps the mightiest to take our attention, is the constellation of Boötes, variously known as the "Herdsman", the "Ox Driver" or the "Ploughman". This group of stars is to be found following, or pushing, The Plough or Ursa Major – hence its alternative name of "Bear Watcher" – as it circles the Pole star throughout the year. Its main cluster is comprised of five major stars, which can be seen to make up the sign of the Pentagram. Other stars are included in its overall configuration and its main, or alpha, star is known as Arcturus, meaning "Bear Keeper", another reference to its association with Ursa Major/The Plough. In its extended form it is generally imaged as a young man (sometimes a mature man) holding weapons of the chase and/or implements of husbandry, as this figure is both the Warrior and the Farmer. This is a very important constellation in Natural Craft, on many levels. It has been associated with the old British deity Hu Gadarn, who was a culture-bringer and taught the arts of civilisation and cultivation of the Land. As a Hunter/Farmer figure, Boötes resumes the mythos of the Male Powers as it cycles through the heavens and the year. It tells the tale of how the Sun/Son is born, grows, comes to maturity and dies, only to be born again. At this point in the cycle, Boötes represents the Male Powers in their fertile and virile prime, reflected in the image of the Green Man as he peeps from between the sprouting leaves of Oak in the Greenwood. The Pentagram which forms its main configuration can be seen as a gateway, through which the Seeker must metaphorically pass in their quest for further/higher knowledge. It is by accessing and assimilating the Male Mysteries as represented by Boötes that the Crafter is led on to the Female Mysteries behind them, as represented by Cassiopeia and the great interstellar spaces beyond. By following the yearly round, by invocation and meditation, the aspiring Crafter can learn much and travel far with the aid of this anciently-recognised and revered constellation.

Astrologically speaking, the Sun passes into the constellation of Gemini towards the end of May. It lies just North-East of Orion and is about to disappear below the horizon for most of the Summer months. In Classical myth, the constellation represents Castor and Polydeuces (Greek) or Pollux (Roman). These are the twin sons of Queen Leda of Sparta, who later came to be included with the Argonauts on the famous quest for the Golden Fleece. The Anglo-Saxons called them "ge Twisan" and the Anglo-Normans knew them as "Frères", meaning the "Twins" and "Brothers" respectively.

This ties them in with the pan-Indo-European myth of the "Dioscuri" (Twins), found in most Northern European and Mediterranean cultures. The twins may be seen as enemies or close friends/brothers (or even lovers in some accounts) and often serve and support the great Female Powers in some way. The constellation is often imaged as two young men or boys, one holding a club, the other a bow and arrows. These can either be used to defend or attack, each other or those they are serving. In Natural Craft the symbolism can point to the dual aspects of the Male Power, the Light and Dark, Winter and Summer, Hunter and Farmer, etc. and their reflections in us and our energies. It is appropriate that the constellation begins to disappear now, at the start of the Summer, only to reappear at the beginning of the Winter months (roughly), with the rise of that other male constellation, Orion, which graphically symbolises both the energies and the dual nature of the Male divine aspect. As a whole, the constellation was seen also by the Saxons as representing the Giant of Winter, Waendel, who is now ending his reign. The twin (sic) stars Castor and Pollux (the main luminaries in the constellation) which represent his eyes, are now dimming their light and power at this time of year and giving way to the energies of the Summer months.

June

⁂

The Sun rises at approximately 3:51 a.m. and sets at approximately 8:50 p.m. at the beginning of this month.

The image for June, known as The Head of Summer, is as follows:

> *In a mantle of dark Grass green, upon his Head a garland of Bents, King-Cups, and Maiden-hair; in his left hand an Angle, with a box of Cantharides, in his Right the Sign Cancer, and upon his arms a Basket of seasonable Fruits.*

Flora

The Full Moon in June is sometimes named the "Rose Moon" or the "Flower Moon" in alternative calendars and it is certainly true that this is the month when blossoms and blooms of all varieties burst forth in a profusion of colour. Many, many plants flower during this month, far too many to go into here, so I will focus on one of the best-loved of our native species and one which is prominent in magical and traditional lore, namely the Rose.

I have mentioned the use of Rosehips in a previous chapter (see Winter Tide – November), but the flower itself is equally as important. There are 14 species of Rose that are accepted as being native to Britain: four of these – the Dog Rose (*Rosa canina)*, Field Rose (*Rosaarvensis*), Harsh Downy Rose (*Rosa tomentosa*) and Sweet Briar (*Rosa rubiginosa*) are most common and may be seen in most Summer hedgerows. The flowers vary in colour from pure white, to a deep pink, almost red, although there are many modern cultivars and hybrids, many of these actually occurring naturally in the wild. Known variously as "Briar Rose" and "Queen of Flowers", the Rose has long been a symbol of love and the Feminine Powers that rule it. The Classical Venus has the Rose as Her emblem and it is associated also with the secret rites that celebrate the inner teachings of sex magic, the Rose petals being likened to the female labia and used as a glyph for them. Less esoteric is this practice that has been performed by generations of country maidens. To discover if your lover is true to you, you must first secretly pick a single Rose on Midsummer's Eve (or first thing the next morning according to some). Take this home with you, speaking to no one on the way back. The flower must then be laid on a fresh, clean sheet of white tissue paper and carefully stored away until the next Christmas Day. On this day, it should be taken out and examined carefully. If the flower has retained its colour, then the lover's feelings are true and you should wear it and the lover will come to claim you and the Rose. If it has faded then so has the lover's devotion. If this is the case, then another use for the Rose petals (which would need to be picked a-fresh) is to make a "simple" in your Cup of magic. A simple is an herbal brew containing only one plant, but infused with the magic of your desire. White Rose petals should be used for a pure, spiritual love; pink petals for a loving and physical relationship; whereas red petals can be used for purely lustful purposes. Make sure you know what you want beforehand and work accordingly, as mistakes have indeed been known to happen! The Rose is also used to denote those secret things that may not be spoken of outside of closed circles. It was either placed on the table or hung from the ceiling when these things were discussed. This is the origin of the decorative "ceiling rose" that is still used in many homes and of the term "sub rosa" – "under the Rose" – meaning that which may not be spoken of. Medicinally the Rose is the source of the pure essential oil known as "Rose Otto", which has great healing properties. It is used in massage oils, skin creams and lotions and in anti-ageing preparations, as it has a beneficial effect on the skin, in that it decreases lines and wrinkles and plumps up the epidermis. It is beneficial in cases of stress and insomnia, and can be used as an astringent and tonic for the hands and face. It is also a gentle laxative and diuretic. The essential oil is quite expensive, due to the fragility of the petals and the way in which they need to be picked. It takes 2,000 kilos of Rose petals to make one litre of essential oil; they must all be picked by hand to avoid bruising, at dawn whilst the dew is still on them and before the Sun is warm enough to evaporate the volatile oils they contain – so never complain at the price of a pure oil again!

June is also the month when it is considered most efficacious to pick herbs, especially around the Solstice and Midsummer. One of the most magical, healing and well known is St. John's wort (*Hypericum perforatum*). Known simply as "Hypericum" and also as "Faerie Herb", this is a native, perennial plant of open woodlands and meadows. It stands about two feet tall and is crowned with bright, golden-yellow flowers from June to September. The leaves look to have tiny holes in them – giving it the name of "perforatum" – but actually these are small oil glands which appear as translucent dots when held up to the light. It has been known as a highly magical plant for many generations, due to its protective and defensive powers against negative forces. Known as "Fuga Daemonum" ("Flight of Demons") during the Mediaeval period, it was used by herbalists as a smoke to banish foul airs and disease. In the old rhyme *"St John's Wort, Vervain, Trefoil, Dill, Hinder Witches of their will" it is combined with other well known "banishing herbs"* to create a charm or incense against malefic attacks. Banckes' 16th-century *Herball* says that *"If it be putte in a Mannes house there shall come no wycked sprite therein"*. It is considered most beneficial to wear a protective sprig when going to war, and both men and women have strangely also used it to attract the attention of the opposite sex! The herb also has the power to deflect or counteract the ill effects of Faerie magic – hence one of its common names – especially such Midsummer pranks as causing cramps, itching and stitches. Its protective powers are considered to be strengthened by the fact that it 'weeps' a bloodred juice when it is 'ripe'. The herb would be added to the Midsummer Fires – along with other herbs – for the smoke to billow across the land and protect the ripening crops in the fields from disease and evil intent. This red juice actually contains flavinoids, hypericins and essential oils, which make it a very useful herb in healing. I mentioned in a previous chapter (Winter Tide – November) that St. John's wort was very efficacious for those that suffer from depression during the dark months. This is now the time to collect it, dry and store it for the darker times later in the year – although it can be taken at any time of year for those in need. It can be made into an infusion or tincture, as already described, and is exceedingly effective at mitigating the effects of both long-term and short-term depression; much better than Prozac and with fewer side effects. It should not be taken with any other prescriptive medicine however, as there are possible contraindications here and a qualified medical herbalist should be consulted beforehand. It is also much favoured in Herbalism for external use on wounds, burns and sores and for this an oil of the herb needs to be made. These are known as Macerated or Infused Oils and the method of making is as follows. Take a glass jar with a tightly-fitting lid and fill it with the fresh herb, leaves and flowers, top it up with a good vegetable oil such as virgin Olive oil (or, in this case, Sunflower) and give it a good shake, having shut the lid firmly. Place the jar on a windowsill in bright sunshine and leave it there for 10-14 days, shaking once or twice daily. By the end of this time, the oil will have turned a bright, blood-red and is ready for use. Strain the oil off and store in a clean jar, returning the herbs to the place where you picked them or to the compost heap. (This method may be used for most herbs and obviously the resulting oil may be used for magical as well as medicinal purposes. Using this method, the oil lasts a very long while and rarely goes rancid.) The oil is used to rub into wounds etc. as mentioned, and may also be taken internally for menopausal symptoms and menstrual cramps.

Renowned throughout European and British lore is the Elder (*Sambucus nigra*) which is usually in full flower during this month. It is a plant that has an ambivalent reputation, being neither a tree nor a bush, and both honoured and reviled in equal measure. Known in country lore as "Black Elder", "Bourtree", "Boon-tree", "Whistle Tree", "Pipe Tree", "Ellern" and "Faerie Tree", it has long been known to possess both medicinal and magical properties and its use goes back thousands of years. The name "Elder" derives both from the Norse/Teutonic Power named "Hyldemoer" and the Anglo-Saxon "Eldrun", which comes from "Aeld" meaning "Fire". The Hyldemoer was seen as a powerful Earth Mother- type Power and woe betide anyone who crossed or annoyed Her. The association with fire comes from the use of the branches, hollowed of their soft pith, as 'bellows' to blow on fires, but must on **no** account be burnt themselves. The taboo of burning Elder of any kind was strong and disaster would court any that did – even cutting the wood unnecessarily is dangerous without the plant's permission, as I can testify to, myself. Every few years I need to trim the giant plant at the bottom of my garden and, if I don't ask permission nicely and pour a libation of something acceptable, my hands are usually scratched to bits and bleeding profusely by the time I've finished. The Elder is a Powerful – in all senses of the word – plant, hence its ambiguous reputation in traditional lore. It can be a strong ally, but a terrible enemy! Elder leaves and flowers have a very distinctive smell and were/are often used to keep away flies and other insects from animals and dairies. Drovers would use Elder switches to keep away flies and disease from their cattle and Elder wood was favoured for the handles of hearse-drivers' horse whips – another link with the deathly Powers. The Elder is another of the plants closely associated with the Faere Folk, as evidenced by one of its folk names and, particularly at Midsummer, can be used to access their inner realm. Sit quietly beneath an old Elder on Midsummer's Eve, place your back against it and sink into a meditative state. In this quiet reverie, visualise the trunk of the plant as being hollow and filled with steps leading down into the Underworld. Step down in your mind into the depths and you will see what you will see. If you can obtain it, the heartwood and roots of Elder are exceptionally dense and make excellent wands; use these wisely in your dealings with the Underworld Powers and the Faere Folk. The Elder is known also as "Nature's Medicine Chest" and most parts of the plant can and have been used to heal in some form or another. It has been used to charm away warts and vermin, to cure the bites of rabid dogs and to clear the complexions of freckled faces, but it has much greater medicinal virtues than these. It is diuretic, anti-inflammatory, laxative, purgative, emetic and expectorant. It is exceptionally good for colds and 'flu, Winter chills and early stages of fevers with raised temperatures. The berries are generally used in these cases in a tea, tincture, or made into a syrup with sugar or honey, as they are high in both vitamin C and iron. The flowers in particular are good for eye disorders such as inflammation and conjunctivitis, when a cool infusion should be used on pads and placed over the eyes; this can also be used as a wash on the skin in cases of sunburn. The inner bark has been used as an infusion in the early cases of epileptic seizures and also as a gargle in the cases of mouth and throat ulcers. On a lighter and much more enjoyable note – now is the time to make both Elderflower wine and "Elderflower Champagne", as the blossoms will be at their best. Don't use too many in either recipe as this can make the end product smell of cats' pee and not at all nice to drink. Later on, in the Autumn when the berries are ripe, make a wine from the fruits. This is a luscious, thick red wine and is known as **the** Witch's wine. Use as many berries as you like and try adding a few spices in the brew as well; it really warms up a dark evening!

Fauna

As many plants are at the height of their flowering season in June, there are also many active insects about taking advantage of the pollen, and one of the most active of these is the Bee. Most people think either of the Bumble Bee (*Bombus spp.*) or the Honey Bee (*Apis mellifera*) when this creature is mentioned, but there are actually over 250 other species in Britain today, although their numbers are declining rapidly, due to disease and other, unknown, factors. Most species are solitary in nature, which is why most people do not notice them, whereas the Bumble Bee and the Honey Bee are both social animals, living in colonies of varying sizes. The name "Bee" is derived from Old English, but has earlier roots that mean "buzzing" or "quivering", as in fear or terror. The Bumble Bee derives its name from Middle English and means "booming", although it is also known as the "Humble Bee" and the "Dumbledore" with variants on this. The Honey Bee is not a native of Britain, but was an introduced and hybridized species. However, this was so long ago that it is now generally considered a native of these shores; certainly, it will 'go native' if given the chance. It is also known as the "Hive Bee", for obvious reasons. Both types of Bee live in colonies, the Bumble Bee in smaller groups of tens and these are generally found in small holes in the ground. The Honey Bee lives in much larger groups of many hundreds, which generally inhabit man-made hives. They are both 'matriarchal' in nature, having a Queen Bee who mates with the males and produces all the offspring, the colony's only objective being to keep her alive and to feed the larvae she produces. This is done by secreting that wonderful golden-yellow product known as Honey, which I will deal with in greater detail later. They also produce greater or lesser quantities – depending on species – of another exceedingly useful substance, namely Beeswax; again, more on this later. The females of the species do nearly all the work, the males' only role being to mate with the Queen, after which they generally die. It is the worker females that locate the pollen and nectar-bearing flowers and return to the hive to pass on this information, in what has come to be known as the "Waggle Dance". This is a quivering type of figure-eight 'dance' that conveys quite complex forms of information, such as distance of the flowers, direction, and concentration and nature of the pollen found. It is an amazing piece of social development in this creature and one that can only be admired. Once this information is conveyed, sorties are made by larger groups from the hive. The pollen is collected, stored and some turned into Honey for feeding the developing larvae, the rest kept for feeding the colony over Winter. Folklore concerning the Bee is generally focused on informing the hive of any changes in the family that owns it. The Bees must be told when there is a death in the family, who has married or moved away, and when there is a new arrival. If this is not done – and very soon after the occurrence – then the hive will sicken and die, or else it will 'swarm' and leave the family. It is considered exceedingly unlucky to buy or sell Bees, but they may be bartered, borrowed or loaned to others, with payment in kind, not coin. There is a generally little-known tradition in British lore, that the Bee represents the human soul or, at times, may even be the soul itself. This is not represented in any major cultural mythology of these Isles, but is found in lesser-known folk tales, but it is a strong theme nonetheless. The magical connotations of this for the Crafter are worth considering, bearing in mind the attributes of the Bee – a supplier of 'gold' with a sting in the tail; however, if it stings, the Bee also dies.

Although sometimes mating as early as January and producing young about 50 days later, the Fox (*Vulpes vulpes*) usually produces its litter of fluffy cubs around June time, when there is plenty of food to feed the growing brood. If you are lucky, you may see the cubs around now, emerging from the den on a sunny afternoon to gambol and mock-fight under the watchful eye of Mum, as they learn the hunting skills that will enable them to survive in later life. The name "Fox" is Old English, but with a very ancient provenance, and has been linked to the same root as the Sanskrit word "Puccha", meaning "Tail" – the thing that a Fox is known for above all else. Also known as "Reynard", "Tod", "Rinkin", "Laste", "Kliket" and "Faws", the Fox holds a special place in the affections of the British; love it or loathe it, you can't ignore it! It is probably the most successful hunter and omnivore in all these Isles, killing and eating anything it can find and also living off fruit, vegetables and other scavenged carrion. This is the main reason why, although still predominantly a rural animal, some have made a very successful transition to inner city areas and it is now not unusual for people to find a Fox in their back garden. Not that they are easily seen, as they are nocturnal hunters, but the wreckage of garden bins and compost heaps supply a telling tale. The reason for this invasion has been put down to the outbreak of myxomatosis in the rural Rabbit population, hence driving them to look further afield for their main prey. They have lived alongside Man for millennia and have become a part of the folklore of the countryside, particularly in regard to their savage reputation when it comes to killing penned chickens. The reason for this is simple and should be understood before castigating a creature that is simply following its natural instinct. The 'surplus killing' (and Foxes are not the only culprits here) is not entirely wanton, but a means of providing spare food for times of scarcity. In the wild, most of the prey would have escaped and the Fox is just taking advantage of the enclosed space to kill as many as it can for later. It would naturally come back and eat all it had killed, except that Man has already cleared it away. To deter Foxes from your chicken pen, either hang human hair from the netting or pee round the edge – Foxes hate the scent of humans. Foxes are usually depicted as sly and wily, not evil but clever and cunning, even sometimes as loveable. They are highly intelligent and learn very quickly and have often been linked with Witches in traditional lore. It is said that Crafters can take the alternative shape of a Fox – shape-shift in other words – and in this guise raid farms during the night. For this reason, Foxes' heads were sometimes nailed over stable doors to deter them. It was believed that a Fox's bite was always fatal, if not immediately, then within seven years and that a Fox entering the house was a death omen, although this was also applied to numerous other creatures. Strangely enough, the Fox is also linked to the weather; days when there are alternating periods of bright sunshine and sudden showers are said to be a "Fox's Wedding Day". Now June is known as the wedding month and is also notorious for sunshine and showers, but unless this refers to the Fox's ability to trick people, this is a bit of a conundrum. Foxes have never been widely eaten, perhaps because they remind us so much of the domestic pet, but have been used in various folk medicine remedies. Carrying a Fox's tooth is supposed to cure an inflamed leg. Wearing a Fox's tongue (dried!) was a cure for cataracts. Ashes of burnt Fox flesh in wine helped ease liver complaints, and rubbing Fox fat on the pate helped in cases of baldness. For the Crafter, the natural intelligence and skill of this animal is much to be admired and perhaps even emulated in its sheer craftiness. However, the one thing that should never be done is to take the Brush (tail) of a live Fox for whatever reason, magical or no. The Brush is a very special and precious item, conveying certain totemistic and Otherworldly powers on the possessor. This will come to the Crafter in seemingly inexplicable ways when the time is right; it should never be sought for or simply taken.

Although in their larval stages they can spend up to five years living underwater, Dragonflies (Odonata family) live only about 10 weeks once they emerge, around the middle of June, once the air temperature has warmed sufficiently. These beautiful and fascinating creatures have many common names, some of which are "Adderbolt", "Boult", "Devil's Darning Needle", "Edther", "Heather-Bill", "Hoss Stinger", "Peacock", "Snake's Stang" and "Nadder". There are many more, not a few of which either refer to their stinging capabilities (they sting nothing), or their affinity to the Adder (usually they inhabit different landscapes, but I have seen them in the same places). The larvae are voracious feeders and will take anything from tiny freshwater shrimp to small fish, mostly larger than themselves. The adults, once emerged, unlike many other 'aquatic' insects, also hunt and take live prey – mainly other insects – during their brief lives, which consist entirely of mating and laying eggs. The Dragonfly family, which consists of up to 40 species including Damselflies, boasts some of the most beautiful insects in the British Isles, Butterflies notwithstanding. Although they all possess very long, thin and almost sticklike bodies, with huge, protuberant – almost alien – eyes, they also all possess the most iridescent and scintillating wing membranes. In the Far East, where there is much native lore concerning them, the focus is on the red colouring of their wings. In the West, the focus is on the different and heavenly shades of blue to be seen. One of the folk names – "Peacock" – aptly conveys the feeling when espying one of these darting, hovering, flitting creatures at the water's edge and then perhaps landing for a while on a leaf or a reed, with the Sun catching the wings at just the right angle to suddenly project a cascade of rainbows hues to the eye. In traditional lore, the Dragonfly, more so even than the Bee, Butterfly or Moth, has been linked with the spirit or soul. It is seen as a reflection of the liberation and freedom gained by the transference onto the Otherworldly levels. In traditional lore, it is also one of the favourite forms taken by certain types of Crafter when they wish to 'astrally project' during the day. Dragonflies are not night fliers and so this is a perfect vehicle in which to project without detection during the hours of daylight. It also carries the bonus of having a wealth of beneficial connotations as well as the boon of being slightly scary – a good vehicle for day-flying Witches!

Hearth & Home

June is traditionally the month for weddings and the romantic period immediately after the marriage is traditionally called the "Honeymoon". Time used to be measured in "Moons", fair enough, but why the Honey? There are various reasons and traditions for this, some claiming that it was just the 'sweetest' time. However, during this period, copious amounts of Mead – the Honey-based, fermented drink – were drunk, as well as large amounts of Honey itself being consumed. It was believed that Honey increased sexual stamina, endurance and fertility, thus ensuring a successful conception – and not a little pleasure! Honey taken with milk has been proven to increase sperm counts considerably and this is not surprising when you consider the following facts. Honey consists of approximately 38% fructose, 31% glucose (dextrose), 1% sucrose, 9% other sugars, 17% water, and traces of minerals. These minerals include magnesium, potassium, calcium, sodium chloride, sulphur, iron and phosphate. Honey also contains vitamins B1, B2, B3, B5, B6 and C, has a Glycaemic Index of 55, its calorie level is 45% lower than sugar but is 25 times sweeter and it is totally free of cholesterol. All this is produced by the collection of plant pollen – mainly flower-based – by those wonderful Bees. As well as being a great natural health product, Honey has also been considered of great magical use for many centuries. Its rich, golden colour and heavenly aroma have led it to be classed as intensely solar in nature and it has been used in all kinds of spells and charms to increase wealth, health, prosperity, abundance and well-being from time immemorial. Because of its consistency, Honey has also been used as a binding agent in incense making and I would briefly like to look at this aspect here. Because of the abundance of plant material available at this time, both floral and herbal, it is an excellent time to be collecting, drying and storing these items for use later on in the year. Obviously, the plants have their own, individual uses, but many lend themselves ideally to incense making and now is the time to set in a good store. The art of making a good incense is a vast topic and one I have covered in depth elsewhere (see Treading the Mill, Bibliography). Here I will simply give a recipe and instructions for making a particularly seasonal, solar incense, which I have found to work well. Take the following, dried ingredients:

½ measure Frankincense
½ measure Heather flowers
1 measure Honey
½ measure Bay leaves
½ measure Sunflower seeds
½ measure Marigold flowers
½ measure Orange peel
1 pinch Dragon's Blood powder
2 drops Neroli essential oil
2 drops Angelica essential oil

Method:
Place the Frankincense, Sunflower seeds and Orange peel into a clean bowl or mortar and grind them down to a rough

powder with your pestle or other suitable tool. Add the Heather, Bay, Marigold and Dragon's Blood and combine/ grind them together until all the ingredients are of the same consistency. Now first add the essential oils, **then** add the Honey. Mix all together until they are well combined and begin to adhere together (you may need to add a bit more Honey to bind all the ingredients, depending on their consistency, but don't overdo it). You may now leave the incense in a coolish, dark place to dry out, then crumble loosely and store in a clean, dry, screw-top jar. Alternatively, roll the mixture into little individual balls first, before leaving to dry out (this sometimes makes it easier to burn a fixed amount of incense). In this case, wrap the balls individually in tissue paper before storing. It is essential that you allow the mixture to dry out thoroughly before storing, due to the nature of the Honey involved. If all is not totally dry, the Honey acts as a culture medium in which all sorts of wonderful mould life can and will grow and you will have wasted a very good incense – believe me, I know! This incense can be used for a multitude of purposes, either seasonal, blessing or magical, and adds a strong boost to any work in which it is incorporated. Try experimenting with other mixtures and using Honey to combine the ingredients. Maybe a "Honeymoon Incense" including Rose petals, or adding it to your home-made herbal/floral magical oils, either for anointing or including into charm ingredients.

The other main product of the hive which is of great use to the Crafter is Beeswax, which is of course a co-product of the production of Honey. This substance is usually a rich gold or yellow colour in its natural state, although you can buy 'purified' Beeswax which is almost white. This just means that it has been melted and filtered to remove any impurities it might contain, such as Bees' legs or spare wings. It is estimated that about 10,000 tonnes of Beeswax are produced annually around the world and it is used, as it has been for millennia, for making polishes, balms and creams, cosmetics, for sculpting and of course, making candles. It is this latter usage I wish to focus on here. Although candles can and have been made from all kinds of fatty and oily substances throughout history, such as tallow and other animal fats, Beeswax candles have always been prized as the highest quality available and the most expensive. Generally, only wealthy households could afford them, or people who kept Bees themselves. For many centuries both churches and monasteries kept thriving hives, not only for the Honey they produced, but to keep them in candles which, other than rush lights, was the only lighting then available. The village Wise Woman would do no less. Making your own candles is not only very simple, but also a great pleasure. Nothing can beat the scent of a pure Beeswax candle, either during meditation, for ritual or celebration, or just purely for pleasure. There are various methods of making your own candles, and I will give a couple here.

Firstly, there is the traditional 'dipped' method. For this you will need what is known as a "double boiler"; this is a deep, cylindrical pan which fits inside another, larger pan. You cannot heat Beeswax directly as it could catch fire, or evaporate completely, so it needs to be protected from direct heat. You put water into the large pan beneath, and the raw, unmelted wax goes into the deep pan, which then sits inside the larger pan, and the whole thing goes onto the stove to be heated. It's a bit like a deeper version of a bain-marie for melting chocolate etc. These are available either in good cookware shops, or from specialist crafts shops. In days gone by every home would have had one. So, put some water in the bottom pan on the stove and set it boiling, then add the deep pan containing the Beeswax. Do not overfill the top pan with wax as this will expand when heated, and you don't want spillages, especially onto a hot stove. Let the Beeswax melt completely – and this can take some time – then turn the heat down. You only need to keep the wax molten now, so a high heat is not needed. You will now need some lengths of cord to act as wicks for your candles and around which the candle itself will form. You can buy special cords from crafts shops for this, but any **natural** cord will do, cotton or linen being the best. Lengths of string used for tying parcels are ideal, or the cotton string that used to be knitted into dishcloths also works well (I'm showing my age here, but just ask at your local fabric, craft or haberdashery supply shop and they'll know what you mean). The essential thing is that it must be a **natural** fibre as it needs to absorb the wax and burn – synthetics just won't do. Now, decide how long/tall you want your candles to be (as long as it's not longer than your wax pan is deep), double the measurement, add a bit more and cut a piece of cord to that length. Fold it in half and hold it roughly in the middle; you now have the start of two candles. From here on, all you need to do is just dip the cord into the melted wax repeatedly to build up the layers and shape of the candle, keeping the two ends apart so that they don't stick together. You need to let the wax dry between each 'dip', so resting the cord over a stick or pole supported at each end is the best way. If you prepare several lengths of cord, say half a dozen, to start with and work your way through one at a time, the first one will have set by the time you get to the last one and you can begin the process again. This does take some time, so you do need a bit of patience and several top-ups of Beeswax in the pan, but the rewards are well justified, believe me. In this manner, you can build up the thickness of your candles in stages, from the thinnest taper to the thickest 'church' candle – the choice is yours. (N.B. Bear in mind that the thicker the candle you want, the thicker the wick you need for the candle to burn properly.)

The other method takes a lot less time, is more adaptable, but is a bit fiddlier to do. For this method you need a large, flat baking tray and some greaseproof paper in addition to those ingredients used above. Cut out a sheet of greaseproof paper and lay it flat in the bottom of the baking tray. When your Beeswax has melted, pour some carefully and gently onto the paper and wait for it to become semi-set. Next, lay your prepared wick (already dipped and soaked in one lot of wax) along one edge of the wax/paper. Lift the edge of the paper slightly to get the wax to detach itself and begin to roll the wick along the warm wax, pressing down along its length as you do so – the idea is that you want a solid candle, not a hollow tube when you've finished. Leave the whole thing to set and, when cool, trim off the bottom and the wick and you have your candle. You can also buy prepared sheets of wax that you just need to warm through before rolling for this method, but I find melting your own wax to be preferable, as you can incorporate so many more things into it as you go. For example, if preparing candles for a particular rite, celebration or occasion, while the wax is still semi-molten you can add ingredients appropriate to the situation. These can be essential oils, petals, leaves, herbs or powders, either for their scent, colour or magical correspondence. The opportunities are infinite and you can create some truly individual and one-off candles for specific workings.

Seasonal Skies
This month is often known as "Flaming June" and sometimes it even lives up to that reputation, with long hot days of continuous sunshine. However, more often than not the build-up of warmth with the longest of days heralds a stormy month. These are usually short but violent occurrences, with night storms producing dramatic displays of both sheet and forked- lightning and large, heavy raindrops, which can do great damage to burgeoning crops. The ideal for most farmers (and gardeners) is prolonged but gentle rain overnight, which swells the ripening grains of corn and other vegetables but does no damage to the stalks, with good drying weather the next day. This is a delicate time for the farmer as all his hard work and effort is soon to pay off with the forthcoming harvest, and bad weather now could ruin nearly a year's work. Despite the

technological advancements in modern farming, all growers are still dependent on the weather and can do nothing about it. One old saw says *"Calm weather in June, sets the corn in tune."* However, this is contradicted by *"A leak in June sets the corn in tune."* There's just no pleasing some people! It is still a traditional practice in many areas to cover all the mirrors during a thunderstorm and to cover all metal objects. In some places the front and back doors must still be left open, so that if the energy of a lightning strike comes in it has a place to go again without causing any damage. This is still sound advice, as any form of 'caged' energy is likely to explode if it has nowhere to go, particularly in a magical setting. After the storm is over, the canny Crafter will go out looking for the 'thunderbolts' that sometimes come down. These are traditionally the 'earthing' energy of the lightning strike, gift of the heavenly or sky Powers and much valued in magical work of all kinds. These are used for everything from healing to blessing, charming wounds and many other things. In actual fact they are fossilised forms of, mostly, iron pyrites which appear in a long bolt-like shape, reminiscent of a rounded spearhead. They actually have nothing to do with storms at all but, curiously, are often found in greater numbers after a really spectacular show, just where the lightning seems to have hit the ground!

This is the month of "Haysel" ("sael" means "time" or "season") known to the Anglo-Saxons as "Mowmonth". It is when the mowers would be heard whetting their scythes preparatory to cutting the standing grasses into long swathes as they made inroads into the greenery. Next would come the "tedding" of the hay, turning it over to dry more evenly and setting loose one of the most beautiful of natural perfumes, that of fresh cut and drying hay. This used to be followed by the carting – the tossing up of the bundles onto the hay cart with the long pitchforks – and carrying the crop off to be stacked for the Winter. These days it is formed into enormous rolls and covered with black plastic – now where's the magic and charm in that?

Looking Southwards once more into the Summer skies at night time – and avoiding the lightning! – we see the constellation of Hercules. This is a large, scattered figure, which has its culmination at midnight during June. It is not a particularly obvious cluster, with no stars brighter than third magnitude, but may be found by reference to the brighter constellation of Vega, which lies immediately to its East. Its main star, Ras Algethi (Arabic for "Head of the kneeler"), averaging a magnitude of 3.5, is a red giant, one of the largest stars currently known and is 600 times the diameter of our Sun. Hercules is generally imaged as a mature man, kneeling, with one foot on the head of a dragon (constellation Draco in the heavens, which it does 'stand' on), bearing a club in one hand and an Apple branch in the other. This is indicative of the well-known Classical Labours of Hercules and denotes the Golden Apples of the Hesperides and the slaying of the Nemean Lion and the Lernaean Hydra. However, this particular constellation does appear to have a much closer link with British tradition than many other so-called Classical constellations. The chalk hill figure carved into the ground at Cerne Abbas in Dorset is known locally as "Helith" or "Helis" – a name associated with solar Powers – and is held locally to be the earthly representative of the constellation Hercules. The "Long Man of Wilmington", another chalk hill figure, is also thought by some to be a similar representative. The age and function of these figures is still hotly debated, but Tradition is quite certain of their use and function – they are the representatives of the height of the Summer/Solar Powers and have been venerated and used as such in public and private practice for as long as Tradition can remember. Local fairs have been held on these sites, both at May Day and more particularly at Midsummer, for many centuries and courting couples have often taken the opportunity to have sex on appropriate parts of the figures' anatomies at certain times of year, to partake of the energies felt to be present there, particularly those of fertility. So despite whatever modern research throws up as to the age of these figures, magically and energetically speaking, they have a direct link to the energies of this particular constellation. They are used at certain times of year and particularly at the moment, for specific purposes. These need not be for purely physical fertility either, as Natural Craft is interested in more than just the procreation of the physical body. That these openly-public – and clandestine – rituals have value and worth is amply demonstrated by the fact they have been practised, and still continue to be practised, up to this very day. The individual Crafter may make use of the energies of this culminating constellation of Hercules by acknowledging them during their own Solstitial or Midsummer rites to great benefit.

At this month's Solstice, the Sun metaphorically passes into the sign of Cancer the Crab, paradoxically for this particularly solar time of year, ruled by the Moon! It is the least conspicuous of the zodiacal constellations, having none of its stars brighter than the fourth magnitude. Its main luminary Acubens, meaning "Claw" is only rated at 4.3. It lies between the constellations of Gemini to the West and Leo to the East, covering only a small patch of sky as far as the human eye is concerned. However, it has a most interesting feature in that the Beehive Cluster (M44) appears to be contained within its body. Bearing in mind the fecundity of the earthly Bee at this time, the appropriateness of this constellation's pre-eminence at this time of year is remarkable. This cluster is also known as Praesepe ("the Manger") and is a group of some 50 stars of the sixth magnitude and fainter, 520 light years distant from Earth. They are visible to the naked eye as a misty patch in the centre of Cancer, three times the diameter of the Moon. This is highly significant at this time of year, because of the release of the fresh, solar energies on the inner planes, in that the ancients saw this feature as a key station marking the gateway for the descent of souls into physical incarnation. Given that the incarnating soul brings with it fresh ideas and knowledge and is nurtured by the energies of the Otherworld, the symbolism of the Bee and the Manger could not be more apposite. Moreover, some traditions hold that the pattern of the main stars in the Beehive is reflected in the shape of the courtyard in front of many "long barrows", the womb/tomb features of megalithic Britain. Cancer is also linked to the constellation of Hercules in Classical myth, in that it was sent by Hera to pinch his toes and distract him in his battle with the Lernaean Hydra. Hercules crushed the Crab underfoot and, as a reward Hera elevated it to its present position in the skies. There is much to be considered and learned from a deeper contemplation of the traditions of this constellation, which would be of great use to the individual Crafter in the pursuit of their own journey.

Times & Tides

St. Barnabas was traditionally a farm labourer, who owned land in Cyprus where he became the patron saint, and his day was celebrated on June 11th by Barnaby Fayres. Before the calendar change in 1752 this was the longest day and, like St. Lucy's day, the date was kept after the change, thus making it estranged from its original significance. This was traditionally the start of the haymaking time and on this day it was customary to deck churches and houses with Roses and Sweet Woodruff. These *"being made up into garlands or bundles and hung up in the houses in the heat of the Summer doth very well attemper the air cool and make fresh the place to the delight and comfort of such as are therein."* (John Gerard, 1633). This day was also known as "Barnaby Bright", after the little jungle:

Barnaby Bright, Barnaby Bright,
Longest day and shortest night.

St. Vitus' day is on the 15th of the month and, apart from the fact that a rheumatic condition is named after him, very little is factually known about him. He was apparently born in 290 CE and martyred in 303 CE, but all other details are open to discussion. St. Vitus' Dance is the name that came to be given to the condition now called rheumatic chorea, which is a nervous disorder characterised by twitchings and jerkings of the body. His cult was very popular in the late Middle Ages, when his devotees would dance before his shrines in homage – possibly also lending to the Dance nomenclature. He is the patron of comedians, dancers, actors and epileptics and is also said to protect against animal attacks and lightning strikes. In this latter role it is often said:

If St. Vitus' Day be rainy weather,
It will rain for thirty days together.

So St. Swithin has competition!

The main focus of this month is undoubtedly the Summer Solstice, which takes place around the 20th/21st/22nd. This sees the culmination of the Sun's long journey to its highest point and furthest Northern rising and setting points in this hemisphere. Like the Winter Solstice, this period has a long and chequered history in these Isles but, unlike that other event, does not seem to have been viewed in a particularly religious light, rather in a celebratory and protective manner. The traditions surrounding the Summer Solstice necessarily revolve around fire and light and this can be seen in the surviving practices around this time. I say 'around this time' as, historically, most celebrations and events took place over a period of time, usually around 23/24 June (St. John's Eve/ Day, known also as Midsummer's Eve and Day), or either time separately, or again on 28/29 June, the Eve and Day of the Feast of Saints Peter and Paul. The actual Solstice itself seemed to be of lesser importance – date-wise – than the other marked days. This may have something to do with the shifting calendar, but also that until recently the emphasis was not so much on the moment of the Solstice itself – that period when the Sun 'stands still' – but more on the time when it starts moving again, after its apparent pause. This had obviously been noted for many thousands of years previously, as the rising and setting points of the Sun throughout the year had been well marked and observed, so it was not the point of Solstice that was important, but the recommencement of movement after it. This bears out the sound practical magical tradition of only using the moving tides to work on, rather than the points of stillness, as there is then no impetus to drive the magic. However, back to the actual traditions.

Most folk practices involve fire in some way. This is either as great bonfires or as parades using torches or wheels made from straw, lighted and rolled flaming down hills to mimic the motion of the Sun. The bonfires (i.e. "boon" or "good" fires, although some did involve the use of bones) were often lit on the windward side of the fields, where the smoke would be blown across the ripening crops to bless and protect them in the vital next few weeks before harvest. It was during this time that bad weather, disease or blight could be disastrous to the people's living for the whole of the next year. Protective and beneficial herbs, such as St. John's wort, Vervain, Mugwort, Gorse and Heather were thrown onto the fires in great quantity to add their good magic to the billowing smoke. And, just as in certain places at Roodmas, the cattle and sheep were paraded through the smoke and dying embers to bless and protect them also. Likewise, the flaming torches, again often composed of Gorse and magical herbs, were paraded or danced round the fields sunwise, through the streets and houses, and the embers were kept as magical talismans. They were used either to put on the family hearth, or kept and scattered on the Land with the seed of the following year's planting. This was a time of great anticipation of the bounty to come and people would put out tables in the streets, set with bread, meat and drink, to share with their neighbours, friends and foes alike.

The other traditions at this time, particularly those of St. John's/Midsummer's Eve involved the honouring and placating of the Faere Folk, just as at Roodmas. Midsummer's Eve is one of the three "Spirit Nights", along with May Eve and All Hallows, when the veil between the worlds is said to be at its thinnest and interaction with the Otherworld(s) can take place. This, again, was a time of great danger and trepidation, as the Faere Folk were not always benign when it came to dealing with humans and some were downright malignant. There were many different 'tribes' of the Good Folk or Good Neighbours and one had to know how to deal with and keep them all happy. Many are the cases of children being kidnapped and replaced with Changeling babies by irate Fay who had not received what they considered to be their just due, as the legendary play by Shakespeare, *A Midsummer Night's Dream*, shows. There are many old traditions bound up in this play and the Bard was a man who knew his Craft, in more ways than one. It is a long held and strong belief amongst both Traditional and Natural Crafters that there is a strong link between Witches and the Fay. Witches are seen as a race apart, having preserved a trace of Elven blood through the ages, either genetically or spiritually, known as the "Red Thread". Elfhame – the home of the Faere Folk – is said to be the place where Witches or Crafters go when they die, there to rest with their kin and, indeed, some say that the Faere Folk are only the spirits of the Dead waiting to be reborn. Some Crafters have reached such a level of advancement that they do not need to come back again and remain in the Land of Elfhame, to act as spirit guides and teachers to those that do incarnate again. This is an aspect of Witch lore generally ignored and shunned by most modern pagans, but they ignore it to their detriment and lack of further advancement in the Mysteries.

St. John's Eve was also a night on which many divinations were practised, there being greater recourse to the knowledge of the Otherworlds, when helpful spirits might be walking abroad. Sprigs of the Saint's own wort were placed under pillows to bring prophetic dreams.

Infusions of Vervain were drunk before meditation under sacred trees to divine the future, either for oneself or one's lover. Herbs were burnt in the fires and the smoke was watched carefully to see what it would foretell. All of these methods and more were, and still are, used to determine what the Fates (Fays?) had in store. It is also the night to collect Fern seed, which is reputed to confer invisibility if correctly harvested, and also the "coal" under the root of the Mugwort plant, which has various magical properties. Divination at holy wells, springs and shrines was also conducted on this night, the waters being believed to possess magical, healing and protective properties at this time. Offerings were made to the spirits in the waters and bowls would be taken home to splash on the doorsteps and windowsills to keep away any malignant entities that might be abroad that night. Some of the water would also be kept, infused with the magical herbs and used later in the year at times of need, such as blessings and healings, cleansings and protections.

Esoterically speaking, this is the time when the new tide of energy is released on the inner planes at the Solstice: that of ripening and maturity. This will be earthed or manifested in the physical realm around the end of July or beginning of August, hence ushering in the time of harvest and the collection of the ripened fruits and grains. It is the time of greatest Light and Energy, which is acknowledged and celebrated with joy and thankfulness, but it is also noted that the shadow is not far away. Whereas at the Winter Solstice there was hope and eagerness for the lengthening days and light, now the days begin to grow short and soon there must be death and decay. Ever is it thus; in Death there is Life, in Life there is Death. There is no sharp change in the flow of energies however, but a gradual altering in the feel of the tides, a gradual shifting in the energy patterns after the Solstice, which makes it clear that the seasons are gradually changing. It is this change that the Crafter looks out for and attempts to work and be in tune with, rather than impose a constructed format on a natural rhythm. Although not a specifically religious time in the year, the Crafter now honours the Rose Queen, Sovereignty, the Female Power in the Land. It is She that is otherwise known as Mother Earth, but is so much more than that. She is not a gentle Power, but can inflame the head of the poet and seer and set the mind alight with prophecy and insight. She it is who determines who will be Her consort and, marrying Him, creates him Summer Lord. She is the Queen of Elfhame and Lady of the Fay, ruling Her Otherworld folk with a gentle yet strong hand. She is wildly sexual in nature, as is the heat of passion at this time of year. She is to be found in the intoxication of the heavy Mead wine and the heady smell of the Heather ale that is brewed at this time. Love and beware Her and you may just survive Her embrace. As for the Lord of Summer, the Male Power in the Land, at this time of year He shows His pranksterish nature and delights in games and deceits of all kinds. He knows His time is short and will soon be ended by the sweep of a sharpened sickle. He is to be seen both in the natures of Shakespeare's Puck and also in His master Oberon. Just as the former is said to be the son of the latter, they are merely aspects of the same being. The Bard took Oberon from the German Elf King "Auberon" or "Alberich", who ruled the dwarven-smith's fires in the Underworld. This links Him then with those other smith Powers like Wayland and Tubal Cain, prime images of the Witch Lord in British Craft imagery and practice.

As at Midwinter, most Crafters will have their own practices to perform, but I offer the following as an alternative or addition to those practices, for any that care to use them.

On the Eve of the Solstice or Midsummer, whichever suits your practice better, journey to a place of natural water and collect a bowl of it. This may be a local holy well or shrine or a local source of spring or river water, whatever suits you best. On your return, try to collect sprigs of St. John's wort, Vervain and Mugwort from the wild, otherwise obtain them as best as you can, but try to get them fresh and wild. Once back home, divide the herbs in half and place one half in your bowl of water, setting the others aside. Put the bowl of water outside in the Sun until you are ready for it. Kindle a censer of appropriate incense for the time of year – perhaps using the recipe I suggested earlier – and cast on your remaining herbs, keeping back one sprig of St. John's wort. Now take this incense around your home, sunwise, asking the Powers for cleansing and purification of any ills that may have become attached to it over the past year, that will affect the coming season. (If you have a detached property, take the incense around the whole outside; if not, take it through each room in the house, but try to keep to a sunwise direction wherever possible.) Return to your starting point, put down the incense and take up a pure Beeswax candle. Using a magnifying glass, or similar, light the wick of the candle (it is important that the candle is lit this way, so do not use any other artificial means, but persevere until you are successful – effort in magic is always rewarded). Place the candle in a holder and take this all around your home, once again sunwise wherever possible. Use words of your own and call on the Powers to bring the light and warmth of the Sun to your dwelling. Return to your starting place beside your bowl of herb water. With all your concentration and focus, raise the candle on high, then bring it downwards, as if bringing down the power and strength of the Sun with it. Douse the candle in the water and **see** the water become charged with the energy and life of the living Sun. Put down the candle-holder and take up the bowl of water, dipping the fingers of your active hand into the water and anointing your forehead with the charged liquid. Now go around your home once more, sunwise, sprinkling the magically-charged herbal waters wherever you go. You may use words of your own once more to pronounce or call a blessing, or you may just see ripples of clear energy being cast about as you go; the choice is yours. When you have finished, pour the remains of the water into a jar or bottle and stopper it well; keep for future magical use when needed. Before retiring for the night, do not forget to leave out a small bowl of milk or cream for the Faere Folk, with a few whispered words of blessing and comradeship. Place your remaining sprig of St. John's wort under your pillow and sleep tight.

July

✤✿❋✿❋

The Sun rises at approximately 3:49 a.m. and sets at roughly 8:18 p.m. at the beginning of this month.

July, known also as the Chief Head of Summer and, like June, as the Hay Month, is imaged thus:

> *In a Jacket of light Yellow, eating Cherries; with his Face and Bosom Sunburnt; on his Head a wreath of Centaury and wild Tyme; a Scythe on his shoulder, and a bottle at his girdle: carrying the sign Leo.*

Times & Tides
Until we get towards the end of the month and the possible beginnings of the harvest traditions, July is

not generally known for its festivals. Most of the focus of this month would normally have been on the drying and stacking of the hay and of weeding the cornfields, prior to harvesting. However, there are a few dates that are worthy of note for the Crafter, both in the past and today, that may be marked in a solitary or group manner.

July 3rd is traditionally the beginning of the Dog Days, which last for 40 days until the August 11th (although Bede puts the start at July 14th). This marks the rising and setting with the Sun during this period of the Dog Star, Sirius, the main luminary in the constellation of Canis Major (although the actual, heliacal rising of Sirius varies widely from year to year). We now enter the height of Summer and the period of greatest heat, when it is said that the seas boil, wine ferments in the cellars, standing waters are set in motion and dogs go mad. (Sirius is derived from the Greek "Serios" which means "scorching".) This is obviously not necessarily the case, but we do now enter a time when the temperatures seem to rise to an almost unbearable level – with records being set these days it seems every other year – and the atmosphere holds a sticky, muggy feeling that can't be shaken. This has nothing to do with the esoteric nature of the time however, and that is what the Crafter would tend to focus on. The import of the rising and setting of Sirius with our Sun at this time of year – apart from any other mythological connotations – is that it brings an influx of 'fire-related' energies and qualities to bear. The star Sirius is equated in some traditional systems with the rune Kenaz, and this period initiates some very special attributes that the Natural Crafter may wish to work with. "Kenaz" has the meaning of "Torch", the flaming light that illuminates the darkness, both literal and metaphorical. In this case, it is the light of **inner** illumination which is meant, in the darkness of ignorance, illusion and materialism. The root of the word Kenaz also gives us the Gaelic "ken", which refers to "kenning" or "knowledge" and also supplies the root of the term "cunning" in Old English. This relates to the modern term "Cunning Man", one who has knowledge of certain (esoteric) subjects. This in turn all relates to that aspect of the Male Powers known as the Master of Light, the Cunning Smith at His forge in the Underworld. He is also, paradoxically, the transcendent "Light Bringer" of Traditional lore, who bequeathed the spark of divine life and sentience to the emerging human race. So, it can be seen from this brief exposition that this is a period of time when the Crafter may wish to take advantage of this influx of fresh 'fire', to enhance and inform their own workings of a more internal or mystical nature.

I suggest here a form of working that interested Crafters may wish to use at the rising of the Dog Star, and also at any other time during this period. Please note: it is not without risk in itself, as an overindulgence in the energies invoked could lead to an imbalance in the psyche of the one overusing it, so a certain level of caution is required. Don't forget, there is a reason why this time is especially associated with madness, in humans as well as dogs!

Perform this rite as close to Sunrise on the 3rd as you can, but after rather than before, if not at the exact time.

After you have hallowed your space as is your usual practice, stand for a moment in contemplation of what it is you wish to achieve with the energies you are about to attempt to contact. Take three, large deep breaths. Light a central (Beeswax) candle on your altar (in the North), using the following words or similar:

Old Master of Cunning, you who bears the Torch of Knowledge between your horns and the Light of Wisdom within your gaze, be present at this my work and look with favour upon my Arte. Grant illumination within me as I honour the rising of the Dog Star.

Take the candle and go to stand facing the East. Cross your arms over your breast, bow deeply then rise and say:

A Star rises in the East, Sirius, Torch of Knowledge. Primal Fire that creates and sustains the Universe, Inner Light that dispels the Darkness, dwell within me.

Pause for a moment here, then assume the "stadha" (rune stance) of Kenaz: feet together, facing the East, active hand raised holding the candle, passive hand lowered, palm out flat, thus your arms form a 'V-shape' on its side. Intone *"Kenaz"*, slowly three times, then lower your hands.

Now place the lighted candle between the horns of your Stang, set it in the centre of your space and Tread the Mill to the following chant or similar:

The Torch is raised between the Horns, Hail the Flame in the East!

Continue until you feel a light trance begin to occur. Return to the East of your space and sit down. Breathe in and out three times, through the right nostril only, holding the left one closed; then continue breathing normally and raise your own internal Fire.* When this is achieved to your satisfaction, reach out mentally with your charged and enhanced senses and make contact with the energies of the newly-risen Sirius, touching your Fire to that of the Star – carefully! Remain in this state for as long as you feel is appropriate, but remember that the energies you are dealing with here can lead to imbalance and madness – you are purely seeking knowledge and inspiration! (In actual practice it is rare that anything shocking occurs; it is more likely that you will make some interesting connections within your work, or achieve some deeper insights.)

When you have had sufficient contact, or the contact breaks naturally, gently lower your own Fire and bring it 'back to earth'. Take a few normal breaths to fully balance and stabilise yourself then rise, bow to the East and say:

> *The Torch is raised within me and the Fire is lit. Old Master be present in my Work and my Arte.*

Return to your altar and offer a toast, then close down in your normal fashion. (*Techniques for trance work and raising the inner fire are given in my previous work *Treading the Mill*, see Bibliography.)

July 22nd is the feast day of St. Mary Magdalene and the day on which Roses are traditionally supposed to start fading – modern hybrids excepted of course! As mentioned previously, the Rose has always been symbolic of the feminine divine Powers and, although the Magdalene is not believed to be of divine origin, her true role in history has long been debated and theorised over. Apart from all the modern speculation stemming from the book *The Holy Blood and the Holy Grail* and all its followers, particularly those like *The Da Vinci Code* and its ilk, Mary Magdalene has long been thought to have been the wife of a historical Jesus and the bearer of his children, from at least the early Middle Ages onwards. Although sadly and badly misrepresented by the established Church as both an adulterer and a prostitute (based on a deliberate misreading of the gospels), she is believed to have been a woman of property and wealth, a landowner in her own right and possibly of royal blood. This is too difficult to prove these days – secret documents uncovered notwithstanding – and would not be of huge importance to a Crafter anyway. No, the Magdalene's prime role to those of Natural Craft is as an exemplar and servant of the divine feminine qualities, such as those representative of the Lady of the Land, of Motherhood, as Priestess and as Queen of the Inner Realms. What importance or impact this has on the individual Crafter is for them to say, but Mary Magdalene stands as one of three Biblical

Marys that echo many of the divine triplicities in our own cultures, and is therefore worthy of note and honour. I would suggest that this day, occurring at high Summer as it does, would be a fine time for a pilgrimage to one of those places or shrines at which she is honoured. Take the opportunity for a little meditation and contemplation on the place of the Magdalene in Natural Craft. Light a candle and sit in quiet solitude and the results may well be quite surprising and revealing.

On the 25th of the month, the feast day of St. James the Apostle is celebrated and it is on this day that it is traditional to start eating the new season's oysters (although the season proper does not start until September). The shell of this marine crustacean is very similar to the badge traditionally worn by pilgrims making the journey to St. James' main shrine at Compostela in Spain, namely the Scallop shell. This was anciently the badge of those people devoted to the Female Powers, particularly those that had prominence over the seas and waves. It is therefore coincidental that many pilgrims took ship for their journey from the lost city of Dunwich, the famous metropolis that sank beneath the waves off the coast of Suffolk in stages, starting during the
Middle Ages and continuing to the present day. As patron of Horses and colts, St. James watches over those on pilgrimage and protects them and he is also said to have defeated the Arch Mage Hermes Trismegistus and stolen all his esoteric knowledge. The pilgrim on his journey to Santiago de Compostela, whose route is said to represent the Milky Way, thus symbolically takes on the role of the defeated mage and strives to realise the divine knowledge within himself. Indeed, it was for this reason that many pilgrims began this journey, not to actually worship at the shrine of James at all. On a lighter note, the Ragwort plant was called "St. James' Wort", because it was believed to cure "staggers" in horses and I will look at this plant in greater detail later on.

❉ 249 ❉

Finally, at the end of the month, on the 31st in fact, we come to the traditional date for the celebration of the festival of first fruits, that of Lammas Eve. As I have mentioned previously, this may or may not actually be the time when the first harvest is cut and as a Natural Crafter takes their lead from what is actually going on at the time, I will delay talking about this feast until the next chapter, when it may be more timely (or not!).

Fauna

Of the six species of Owl seen in British skies, the Barn Owl (*Tyto alba*) is probably the most immediately recognisable, if not most often seen. Answering to many different folk names, amongst which are "Berthuan", "Billy Wix", "Gillihowlet", "Hoolet/Howlet", "Padge/Pudge", "Scritch or Screech Owl" and "Ullert", it is at one and the same time a most beautiful and a most dreaded creature. The name "Owl" dates from the Middle Ages and this particular one has been called "Barn" since the 17th century. It receives this name mainly because barns are its main residence and indoor hunting ground, although it will nest in many different habitats and hunts widely abroad at night also. There is little difference between male and female, both having a wide, heart-shaped face, golden/buff coloured upper parts laced with silver grey and white underparts, and are often difficult to tell apart. Their main prey is the Bank Vole, closely followed by Mice and Shrews, although they will take any smallish rodents they can find. In times of shortage the young will even turn cannibal, consuming their smaller, weaker siblings if the parents cannot provide enough food. This said, one would imagine that they would be the farmer's friend, particularly at this time of year when there is great damage caused to the burgeoning crops by mice in the fields. However, not a bit of it and they have been persecuted almost to the point of extinction in recent years, although they are now making something of a comeback. They are a creature that has always been associated with the night and all that goes with it. In some cases this has led to the "Wise Old Owl" personification, particularly in children's stories and folk tales but, unfortunately, more often it has led them to be viewed with a superstitious awe and dread as harbingers of death and doom. This is possibly understandable as, seen flying overhead at night, drifting by on ghostly white wings whilst seemingly a beautiful sight, once they utter the hissing screech for which they are famous, they can put a chill into the hardiest of hearts. They have been associated with the Female Powers from a very early period, particularly those of Night, Fate and Destiny. Indeed, the Summer Queen/Rose Queen's alter-image is sometimes depicted as a great white Owl. Because of this maybe, they have been both loved and reviled, particularly the latter and their dead bodies, or parts of them, have been used as apotropaic charms for many centuries. These were hung up over barn doors or houses to keep away bad luck or night spirits and even the mention of an Owl in certain circumstances could bring about death or disaster. They have not, as a general rule, been eaten regularly, but the Barn Owl has played its part in folk medicine and remedies. It is said that if an alcoholic is given Owls' eggs to eat, then he will henceforth detest the taste of drink. Owls' eggs, once charred and powdered, were used as a remedy for poor eyesight and Owl broth used to be given as a treatment for whooping cough. The strangest remedy may be the following: take a Barn Owl and pull off all the feathers, salt it well and leave it for a week, then put it into the oven and bake until it is like a mummy, after that, beat it into a powder, mix with boars' grease and apply to any limb afflicted with gout, and a cure is certain. Or, you could also use it for epilepsy or madness! One wonders whose?

Another animal that is making a great comeback in these islands, where it has been hunted for centuries, is the European Otter (*Lutra lutra*). Known also as the "Water Dog", "Dratsie", "Lutria", "Ote" and "Tyke", the Otter is an animal that is at home both on land and in the water, both freshwater and salt, and can be seen in many of our riverways about now if you are very lucky. It was thought once to be almost on the verge of extinction, but is now increasing in numbers, mainly in the South-West of Britain, the Highlands of Scotland and in East Anglia. It is a fairly large animal, a "dog" (male) Otter reaching about four feet from nose to tail and a "bitch" or "queen" (female) reaching about three-and-a-half feet. Both have a double-layered coat, with long hair on the outside and a thicker, softer layer on the inner. This traps a layer of air and warmth whilst in the water and gives a swimming Otter a gorgeous silvery sheen when seen from below. Although the Otter is at home both in rivers and the sea, it must periodically return to the freshwater to leach the salt out of its fur to retain its consistency. This pelt used to be highly prized by hunters, being of the equivalent value to an Ox or Deer skin and eight times the value of a Sheep or Goat, although it was never usually made into clothing. This pelt was also valued in Natural Craft for its supposed magical qualities, being said to aid the art of shape-shifting, to preserve the magic of healing herbs, to be an antidote against fever and smallpox, to safeguard against drowning and also to be able to heal any wounds it was placed over. It was also of great use in childbirth – somehow! Like the Toad, the Otter is also rumoured to possess a stone in its head, which is known as the "Pearl of Wisdom". This comes from catching the Salmon of Knowledge in the waters of the Underworld in traditional lore. The word "Otter" comes from Old English, deriving originally from a Greek term meaning "Water Snake". This is a very accurate description if you have ever seen a line of Otters following one another along a river; it does indeed look like a giant snake undulating through the water. As mentioned already,

Otters have been widely hunted but it appears for no particular reason other than sport, and up until very recently. The activity was only outlawed in the 1980s, but water pollution and illegal hunting still claimed many lives up until the end of the 20th century. Despite popular opinion, the proliferation of released North American Mink into the British countryside did not have a large impact on Otter numbers. During observed encounters, the Mink appeared to give way and retreat their territory before the Otter. Like most other animals, the Otter has been used for various purposes, both medicinal and non-medicinal. Its flesh was the subject of great debate as to whether it was meat or fish during the Middle Ages and hence as to whether it was lawful to eat it on Fridays or not. The pulverised liver was used to stop haemorraging and bowel fluxes, and the dried testicles, once powdered and drunk in water, were said to cure epilepsy – but then wasn't everything! From personal experience, the greatest benefit of contact with Otters is that of utter joy and abandon. Seeing them play along a river bank and in the water, thinking themselves unobserved, brings on a feeling of complete freedom, but to experience the spirit of an Otter in the Otherworlds is a transport of delights. To run, jump, slide, tumble and leap without a care in the world is a 'pearl beyond price' and a memory to be treasured all ways.

Very common at this time of year, indeed, during most Summer months, is the Long-Tailed Field Mouse (*Apodemus sylvaticus*), also known by the more common name of "Wood Mouse". Unfortunately, this last name is a bit of a misnomer, as they are more likely to be found in grasslands, fields, gardens and hedgerows than woods. However, they were so-named some centuries ago by the great naturalist Linnaeus and it has stuck. This tiny rodent has a long-established archaeological record and is a true native of Britain, unlike other species of Mice, such as the House Mouse (*Mus musculus*), which are much more recent imports, only arriving with the Romans or even later. The Field Mouse is about three-and-a-half to four inches long, has brownish-yellow fur, small ears, a pointed snout and a tail as long as its head and body combined. Unlike its cousin, the Vole, which is mostly vegetarian, the Field Mouse is omnivorous. It will take whatever it can find, although insects, fruits and grains are its preferred food – grains especially now as they are ripening in the fields. In turn, it is itself the prey of many larger animals, especially Owls, Foxes and Cats. They breed mainly from May to November, in litters of six to eight and the young are born in grass-lined nests below the ground. The word "Mouse" comes from Old English, but its roots stretch much further back, via Latin and Greek, to the origins of the common Sanskrit word for "Thief", the original being to do with stealing. Wood Mice are extremely common and extremely numerous, occurring throughout the British Isles, unlike the Yellow-Necked Mouse (*Apodemus flavicollis*), a very closely-related species. This is found mainly in the South-East of England and in the Severn Valley, ironically enough mainly in woodland. Predictably enough, the Field Mouse, like Mice in general, has long been used medicinally for a wide range of ailments. These include an antidote for bedwetting, for whooping cough, sore throats and fevers. They could be roasted, boiled, fried or dried and reduced to a powder, then given in some sweet-tasting drink, mixed with honey or jam and put in a sandwich, or simply tied up, alive, in a bag around the neck. When the animal died, it took the disease away with it. Mice have long been considered as Witches' familiars, or themselves shape-shifted, and as such considered to be an ill omen. They were supposed to have been kept in boxes and fed on a drop of blood and the Witch could not die until she had passed them on to a relative or her successor. (This last is indicative of the "Passing of Power" which is such a strong point in Hereditary and Traditional forms of Craft.) If a Mouse were to run across a sickbed or to squeak behind the headboard, it was sure to mean the death of the patient. If they were to enter the house in any significant number, the only way to get rid of them was to speak to them politely, explaining that their presence was not wanted … and suggest someone else's house that they should go to instead! In Craft lore they are representatives of the Underworld Powers, being able to cross from Upper to Lower realms at will via secret passages. They are heralds of blessings from those same Powers, as all wealth and luck are considered to be in the keeping of those cthonic entities. They are bringers of health and healing and should not be harmed for any reason, or the luck, wealth and blessing of the home will be damaged.

Seasonal Skies

As mentioned above, July is mainly known for the Dog Days, which are usually considered to begin on the 3rd of the month. The Romans considered that the Dog Star, Sirius, which rose and set with the Sun approximately during this period, reinforced the heat of the Sun and so caused the greatest Summer heat at this period. Of course, all the stars put together do not give us a fraction of the heat that we receive from our own Star, and the Sun sets half an hour later at the end of the month than the beginning anyway. It is true however, that we can get the most violent Summer storms at this time – just when the crops don't need them – which can cause quite severe damage. Storms in recent years have caused severe flooding across Britain and have totally destroyed the grain harvest in some areas – more on the importance of that in the next chapter. Many people can be affected by thunderstorms. Some (like many Natural Craft Practitioners) find them exceedingly invigorating, whilst others cower away and take cover. The approach of a storm can cause headaches in many people and restless behaviour in animals and birds, both domestic and wild alike. This is one reason for storms being regarded in folklore as something more than just a natural event. They have often been considered to be manifestations of the anger or displeasure of the higher Powers and this is not surprising considering their effects. A typical discharge of lightning can contain the equivalent of 1,000 volts of electricity and a heat build-up to more than 10,000°C. . The superheated air expands rapidly and this is heard as thunder. Because of the difference in speed between light and sound, thunder is always heard after the lightning flash, the time lag depending on how far away you are. If standing right by the lightning strike, the thunder will sound as a deafening bang right overhead; however this is not advised in the open air! Forked lightning travelling from cloud to ground can be over a mile long, whilst lightning travelling from cloud to cloud can be several miles in length. Church bells were often rung during storms, as they were believed to have the power to avert the negative forces causing the storm. This is an 8th-century blessing used to consecrate the bells to that end:

> *Whenever this bell sounds, let the power of enemies retire. So also the shadow of phantoms, the assault of whirlwinds, the stroke of lightnings, the injury of tempests and every spirit of the storm winds.*

The Crafter so inspired may use this formula today on their own handbell, if used, for similar purposes.

St. Swithin's Day, on the 15th of the month, is undoubtedly the most well-known and notorious weather day of the year. The popular belief is that if it rains on this day, it will continue raining for the next 40 days.

> *Oh St. Swithin if thou'll be fair,*
> *For forty days shall rain nae mair,*
> *But if St. Swithin's thou be wet,*
> *For forty days it raineth yet.*

If indeed it does rain, the saint is said to be blessing the Apples for the future harvest, for, as the old saying goes: *"Till St. Swithin's Day be passed, the apples be not fit to taste."* St. Swithin himself was a humble monk, who was Bishop of Winchester from 852 to 863 CE. He suggested that when he died his body should be buried in the churchyard where the rain from the church eaves could fall on him, as suited his sense of humility. However, in 971 CE, an attempt was made to move his body to the inside of Winchester Cathedral, which was considered a much more fitting place for a man of his holiness. It is said that the spirit of this saintly man was so disgusted, that he made it rain for the next 40 days and nights, until the monks gave up the effort of moving his remains and left him in peace. A new shrine was, however, added above his tomb in 1962, to no discernible detriment in the weather!

Looking to the South-Eastern skies after dark at this time of year, the constellation of Aquila the Eagle can be seen low on the horizon. Aquila is a fairly small constellation, culminating at midnight in July, which appears to be flying Eastwards across the Milky Way. Its brightest star, Altair, forms one apex of the Northern hemisphere "Summer Triangle" of stars. The others are Vega in Lyra and Deneb in Cygnus, the brightest being Vega. This triangle can be seen throughout the Summer months and marks the revolution of the celestial season in a most dramatic way overhead at night. It is well worth seeking out and viewing as it wheels across the heavens and marks time in a most natural manner. Aquila is associated in Classical myth with the abduction by the Eagle (Zeus in avian form) of the beautiful youth Ganymede, and his later ravishing by the lustful Olympian. However, there is a more apposite legend for the Natural Crafter at this time, which is the story of Prometheus and the divine fire. Prometheus was one of the last remaining Titans – the race of giants that represented the primaeval energies of creation – and a special patron of early humankind. He taught the Arts and Sciences to Man, which was forbidden by the more recently-emerged deities, and also brought 'Fire' down from heaven to them, concealed in a hollow tube (Torch?). This last 'crime' was punished by having him chained naked to a pillar in the Caucasus Mountains and sending the Eagle, representative of Zeus and the younger Powers, to tear out and devour his liver every day. As a Titan and immortal, Prometheus's liver grew back every night, only to begin the terrible punishment again the next day. Eventually he was forgiven and allowed to be released by Hercules on one of his quests. The severe nature of this punishment is borne out by the alternative names of "Falcon", "Vulture" and "Griffon" that this constellation has borne over the centuries. This story is most appropriate at this time of year, as the essential meaning of this tale indicates the same principle as that of the Fire from Sirius that we have looked at earlier in this chapter. Prometheus can be seen as an aspect or type of the primaeval Lord of Light, who gifts the emerging human species with sentience and the divine spark of knowledge. That he is cruelly punished for this act is typical of the latterly-emerging Powers, who wished to keep the human race subject to their own whims and commands. The original, chthonic and primaeval Powers have always been the friends of Man, if only we would recognise this and see through later propaganda to the truth.

Around the 22nd of the month we pass into the influence of the constellation of Leo, one of the most easily recognisable in the night sky. Its major star, Regulus, is also called "Cor Leonis" and is a 1.4 magnitude blue-white star, so is easy to spot, just South of the 'pointer' stars in The Plough. "Regulus" means "Little King" and "Cor Leonis" means "Lion's Heart", this star cluster having been viewed from ancient days by nearly all Western cultures as the figure of a Lion. Leo is very closely connected to this time of year – apart from any astrological association – as the Ancients associated it with the star Sirius and the raging heat that they thought it produced. Ancient physicians thought that when the Sun was in this sign medicine was a poison, and even a bath equally harmful: "*In these Dog Days it is forbidden by Astronomy to all Manner of People to be let Blood or take Physic. Yea, it is good to abstain all this time from Women.*" The weather-wise also said that thunder foretold sedition and the deaths of great men – yet another reason to avoid Summer storms! The Lion has long been adopted as a symbol for the Sun, which is another reason for it to be associated with the heat of this time of year, and also as a symbol of royalty and the monarchy, hence its adoption onto coats of arms and extensive use in heraldry. Indeed, during the 12th century in England it was the only animal shown on Anglo-Norman shields. Leo is also said to be the Lion in the tragic tale of the lovers Pyramus and Thisbe, retold and made famous (infamous?) by Shakespeare in the play within a play during *A Midsummer Night's Dream*. The story tells how their parents forbade them to marry and so the two one day made a plan to meet outside the city, beside a certain mulberry tree with white berries. When Thisbe came to the meeting place Pyramus was not there, but she was startled by a Lion, bloody from a kill. As she ran away, her veil slipped and fluttered past the Lion which snatched it with its paw. When Pyramus arrived he saw Thisbe's torn veil, bloody from the Lion and assumed that his love had been killed. In anguish, he killed himself with his sword. Thisbe ran back and flung herself on her dead lover's body before taking the sword and thrusting it into her own flesh. Their blood coloured the white mulberries red and they have remained this way ever since.

Flora

Although much used in Midsummer rites, Vervain (*Verbena officinalis*) usually comes into flower during July. It is a hardy, herbaceous perennial plant, with a square-sectioned spindly stem above lush grey-green leaves, growing to about two feet tall. The small flowers are a lilac or mauve in colour and open in succession up the stem. Known also as "Herb of Grace", "Enchanter's Herb", "Herba Veneris", "Juno's Tears" and "Holy Herb", it has been used for both magical and medicinal purposes for millennia. A favourite of the Druids, they used it in an infusion to wash their altars prior to making sacrifices. The Romans used it to scatter on their altars to sanctify them and dedicated the plant to Venus. It was one of the prime herbs of Anglo-Saxon times, being much favoured by clergy and common folk alike for all kinds of ills and ailments. In particular it was used in their Holy Salve, and the Elizabethans were addicted to its use in love potions and philtres, for which it is ideally suited. All parts of the plant are used and traditionally it must be picked at the rising of the Dog Star, Sirius, when the light of neither Sun nor Moon is in the sky. It must be plucked with the left hand only and a libation of honey must be left in its place to appease the Earth Mother. One would usually pluck enough to last all year and anything remaining would be cast onto the Midsummer Fires the following year and fresh herb picked after. It is a plant very well disposed towards people and will do its best to aid them, if treated with respect and consideration. Magically it is used mainly as a protective charm and for cleansing a place or person. It can be made into a strong infusion by steeping in wine or spirits, which is then used as a wash or sprinkled around a place or person. Warriors would keep a piece about them when going into battle, either sewn into their clothes or worn in a bag, and sorcerers would bind a piece round their brows during ritual to protect from demons. It was hung up in the house to protect against evil spirits, either tied up in bundles, bags or poppets and these are a good defence especially against predatory or parasitic entities. It is a protection against black magic and wards off bad dreams if hung around the neck, and will aid in casting a glamour to hide from enemies, especially when prepared as an ointment. In fact, it is a very good all-round magical plant to have about the home and no Natural Crafter should be without it. Medicinally speaking, it is an antispasmodic for relief of tension and stress, and a stimulating relaxing nervine with affinity for the liver and kidneys. It is traditionally used with good effect in cases of epilepsy and asthma and helps combat infectious diseases, strengthening the immune system. It helps in cases of post viral fatigue syndrome (ME) and jaundice, and also helps promote the flow of milk in nursing mothers. It is a very good wound herb and a wash can be applied to all types of cuts, scrapes and bruises. It is a very easy plant to grow and spreads rapidly, so a small pot or tub growing outside the back door would be an excellent way of having a sure supply when needed fresh; infusions may be made of dried material at any time of year.

Mugwort (*Artemisia vulgaris*) is another plant that is much used in protective and warding rites and also has a long and venerable history of usage. It has many folk names, some of which are "Muggers", "Muggons", "Felon's Herb", "Sailor's Tobacco", "Witch Herb", "Moderwort" and "Maiden's Wort". Its common name – "Mugwort" – comes from the Anglo-Saxon term "Mucgwyrt" or "Muggia wort" meaning "Midge Herb" and this gives us the clue to one of its main uses. It has been used to rid the house and closets of pests and mites for centuries and, along with its close cousins Wormwood (*Artemisia absinthium*) and Southernwood (*Artemisia abrotanum*), it constituted one of the traditional "strewing herbs" that were laid on the floor to discourage fleas and bugs up until very recently. According to folklore, there is a most potent "coal" concealed in its roots, which should be picked on St. John's Eve and will act as a most effective amulet against all types of venomous serpents and poison. This coal is in fact the dried and acidified remains of old roots, which may be used as an amulet if you so wish. It has also been taken internally to rid the body of worms and other infestations, but has most generally been used medicinally for 'womens' problems'. As a menstrual regulator, it has a strengthening effect on the uterus and so helps with irregular periods, menopause and difficult childbirth (both to promote ease of labour and to expel the placenta afterwards). This is the main reason it derived its genus name of "Artemisia", as it was dedicated by the Ancients to that Power and the ease of all female problems. An 18th-century entry in a Household Book describes the following: "*For a poor Country woman in Labour to hasten their birth. Take 3 handfuls of Mugwort, 12 cloves whole and boyle them in a pint of white wine half an hour, then Strein it and let the party drink it blood warm at a draught, you may gather Mugwort and dry it in a chamber and soe keep it all the year which is as useful as the green is.*". Because of these effects it should not be taken during pregnancy. On a lighter note, it has been used to flavour and preserve ale before the advent of Hops, and also as a smoking alternative for tobacco. The latter also has a magical use in that it helps to see the spirits; this should only be done in moderation as an excess can be painful! There was a widespread belief that it could give strength and protection, especially to travellers, and many would place some in their shoe to this end, some even going so far as to state that it would help a man to walk 40 miles before noon, without stopping or becoming tired. Magically speaking, it has two main uses: one for divination and the other for protection and banishings. For use in divination it should be made into an infusion (often along with Wormwood), and your crystal, mirror, bowl or whatever should be washed in it prior to use. Its juice was often smeared on the back of scrying mirrors to enhance their properties, or the dried or fresh herb placed into the back of the frame. It was placed under the pillow at night in order to receive prophetic dreams and the tea was drunk to aid in clairvoyance (it is very bitter though, so do be warned). Added together with Wormwood again, it was used as an incense which was burnt during scrying sessions to great effect, if a somewhat smoky and 'heady' one.

To use the herb for banishment and cleansings, it is usually employed as an incense, by itself. Mugwort is the **true** British "smudging" herb, **not** Sage as is often stated. The Sage that is used by Native Americans in their rites and copied by European 'wannabe shamans', is not the same as our European Sage (*Salvia officinalis*). American Sage is a form of Artemisia (*Artemisia tridentata*), properly known as Sagebrush; therefore using British Sage would not have the same effect (although it can be used as a mild cleanser). Mugwort is normally used dried and burnt on charcoal as an incense for banishings, but you can make a kind of "smudge stick" after the Native American manner if you so wish. (In fact, this style or method has been utilised long before the current craze for all things 'shamanic'.) You must get some stalks of the fresh herb and hang them up to dry for a while until the leaves are limp, but the stalks are still pliable. Next, plait the stalks and leaves together, combining as many as you wish until you have the desired thickness, tying them all in tightly with fine twine as you go. Hang the completed plait back up again out of the Sun to dry and there you have a British stick of native smudge. Use in the usual way. Mugwort can be used to clear spaces of negative influences, ward off negative or evil spirits, or ward off illness and disease. It should be burnt before all major works of exorcism and afterwards to seal the space. As an alternative to an incense, Mugwort may be dried and ground into a powder and either spread around an area or person, or made into sachets or pouches. It tends to have a consistency more wool-like than powder, so is a good binding agent when used with other herbs. It may also, like Vervain, be used as a wash or spray, particularly made from a strong decoction, and is traditionally effective for clearing spaces where restless or hostile spirits of the deceased linger, especially at funerals!

As mentioned above, the Ragwort plant (*Senecio jacobaea*) is known as "St. James' Wort" and is generally in flower during July. It is also known as "Staggerwort", "Stammerwort", "Stinking Nanny", "Stinking Willie", "Yellow Tops" and "Mare's Fart", which gives us a hint that it is not altogether well-liked wherever it grows! This plant is actually the bane of most livestock farmers lives, in that it is poisonous to both cattle and horses. Sheep can tolerate the mature plant in small amounts and eat it with relish, but they too can succumb to its effects. Cattle and horses will not eat the growing plant, but they will eat it when it has died, and dried out and it often finds its way into hay fodder and suchlike if extreme care is not exercised. Green or dry, it causes insidious and irreversible cirrhosis of the liver, but this may not be apparent in the animal for quite some while, by which time the damage is done. The poison in horses can build up over several years and can start with what appears to be skin problems and walking difficulties with their hooves. Hence some of the common names such as "Staggerwort" and "Mare's Fart" – all effects of inadvertently consuming the plant. It is said that Ragwort reached Scotland, where it is particularly hated, in the fodder of the Duke of Cumberland's horses, hence the nickname "Stinking Willie". This may or may not be true, but the Highlanders have made full use of Ragwort since, as a type of rope may be made from the fibres of the stem – like Flax or Nettles – and these ropes were used to tie down the thatching on their roofs. Its tough stems were also used in basket making and weaving, and dyes of bronze, green and orange may also be extracted from the plant. It is almost the only food of the striking black and yellow caterpillar, larval stage of the Cinnabar Moth and, as it has an extremely bitter smell when crushed, it was sometimes used to layer corn stacks with, to deter mice and rats. Strangely enough, despite its poisonous nature, it also has quite a long and venerable usage in herbal medicine, for both humans and animals alike. It was used in poultice form to treat "quinsy", an old term for a sore throat; it was applied to boils to bring them to a head, and for unknown swellings of the breast in the 18th century. Ragwort was employed in treating burns and scalds, and coughs and cuts, as well as rheumatoid arthritis; ulcers, inflammations and fistulas were all likewise treated with Ragwort. As it contains pyrrolizidine alkaloids and various volatile oils, it is these days limited to external treatments; it is used in ointment form for gout, lumbago and sciatica. A lotion can also be made of one part flowers to 10 parts alcohol (vodka, gin etc.), and applied externally only. According to folklore, Ragwort is much favoured by the Faere Folk, in that they used it to shelter safely from the rain. In common with many Witches, they also used the stems to ride upon and in this manner would skim the surface of the water as they flew from island to island around the coasts of these Isles! Witches would ride the weed as a horse and speed over mountains and crags in their Midnight revels and fiendish doings, all at the beck and call of their dark Master.

Hearth & Home

July is the time when many flowers and herbs are at their peak and vegetables and soft fruits start to become ready for picking and eating. It is also the time when traditional pickles, preserves and herb or fruit vinegars are started, to get in a long maturation process before the Yuletide season, when most of the edible types are enjoyed, as there is no fresh produce around. The herb and floral/ fruit vinegars can be used on salads, in sauces and other culinary preparations, but can also be used in more esoteric fashions, such as ingredients in things like Thieves Vinegar and cleansing washes or protective sachets. I would first like to give an example of a delicious method of keeping the flavour of Summer through into Winter and then move on to other, more versatile suggestions.

This method of preserving Summer fruits is simple, but needs top-quality fruit and works best with organic produce (preferably that you have grown yourself). You can also use organic sugars with this, just to keep the purity going. As the seasons progress, you can add more soft fruits as they ripen – and sugar – just make sure to add a bit more alcohol each time, just to keep the fruit covered. Remove and replace the plate each time.

Method:

Wash and remove the stalks from two pounds of Strawberries and place whole in a large bowl. Sprinkle with one pound of golden caster or granulated sugar and leave to stand overnight. Next day, tip into a large, sterilised jar – one of the old-fashioned sweet jars works best. Pour on 1¾ pints of Rum or Brandy and stir into the mixture well, making sure not to break up the fruit in the process. Put a plate (or similar) on top of the fruit to keep it submerged. Screw the top on tight and leave in a cool, dark place for at least a month, but preferably until Yuletide. As time goes on you may add more soft fruits as they become available, things such as Cherries (including stones), Raspberries, Plums, Peaches, Greengages and Redcurrants or Blackcurrants, stirring them in carefully each time. If you like, you may wish to add a little spice for an extra flavour, such as some ground Cinnamon or a few Cloves, but not too much as the flavour will get stronger over time. When ready this can be served simply with cream or ice cream, or it makes a luxurious base for a fantastic trifle at your Yuletide festivities. Alternatively, try pouring some over the traditional Christmas pud, lighting the liquor and standing well back!

Fruit and herbal vinegars have always been found in the Natural Crafters' larder. They give a most unexpected lift to salads and sauces, are useful for making up drinks and, as already mentioned, can form the basis of magical sprays, washes and lotions. Here is a basic method for making up a herbal vinegar, which you may adapt and use as and how you need to. Collect the herbs as their nature requires, roughly shred them into a screw-top jar and add as much white wine vinegar as the jar will hold. (You can make this up with single herbs or a combination, depending on the end requirement.) Leave the herbs to infuse for two to three weeks, in a warm, dark place, shaking the jar every time you pass by. Taste the vinegar after this time (if non-toxic of course!), and, if to your satisfaction, strain the liquid off from the jar into a clean bottle and add a sprig or two of one or more of the fresh herbs. Seal and keep away from direct sunlight until you are ready to use it. This will keep for two to three years, but if not used after one year, it's best to tip it on the compost heap and make a fresh one each year.

The method for a fruit vinegar is slightly different and here is one using Raspberries, but any soft fruit of this type may be used now.

Method:
Take two pounds of Raspberries and two pints of red wine vinegar. Place the fruit in a bowl, crush slightly and pour the vinegar over the fruit. Cover and leave for a week, stirring daily. At the end of this time, strain the fruit through a jelly bag or piece of clean muslin, discard the fruit in a useful manner and measure the liquid left. For every pint of liquid take one pound of sugar and place both in a preserving pan or saucepan. Stir to dissolve the sugar, boil for 10 minutes and bottle in sterile bottles when cold. Seal tight and store in a cool place away from direct sunlight. These types of vinegars are excellent in the Winter Tide for colds, sore throats and sniffles, when diluted with hot water and, later on in the year, the same method may be used for Elderberries and Blackberries.

Lavender generally reaches its peak during July and there is nothing more reminiscent of Summer than the smell of this fragrant flower, tucked into the back of a drawer or in the wardrobe, softly scenting your clothes during the cold, dark months; it also keeps the moths away as well! Rather than use the flowers loose, or in the well-known Lavender bags that most of our grandmothers used to sew (well, mine used to make them all the time!), here is an alternative that is equally traditional – dating back at least to Elizabethan times – that can also have a more magical use as well. To make a Lavender Wand, take nine strong stems of Lavender, freshly cut from the garden (dried stems are too brittle), tie them tightly together with a long, narrow ribbon about four times the length of the stems, just under the flower heads. Now, double back the stems, one at a time and weave one end of the ribbon between them. Nine, being an odd number (and with many other connotations as well), the warp of the stems should appear in alternate bands with the ribbon in cross threads, giving a pleasing woven effect. Continue weaving down to the bottom of the stems after you have completely enclosed the flowers' heads inside the cage, then take both ends of the ribbon and tie them off together, round the end of the stems. You should now have a sweet-smelling, fragrant wand, that may be placed in amongst your clothes, wherever you please, or even worn as a Summer buttonhole. Lavender, also known as "Spike", as well as having many useful, medicinal properties, is also much loved by the Faere Folk. This wand can be used in actuality when dealing with them to great benefit, for Crafter and Fay alike.

And so the Summer Tide draws to a close and we start to look towards the ripening and harvesting of plans, ideas and crops that we have planned for and planted earlier in the year. Having ridden the rush and tumble of the bubbling energies of the Summer, we now need to take a somewhat more mature approach to things and slow down slightly. The reaping and harvesting that is soon to take place can be a marathon, rather than a short sprint and we need to conserve our energies more during the Autumn Tide.

THE AUTUMN TIDE

꙳꙰ꙟ ✤ ꙟꙡ꙳

We now reach the final season in this particular annual flow of tidal energies and begin to reap the fruits of all the previous ones, before we start the round once more. Autumn is the time for ripening and harvesting, when all the seeds that were sown in the earlier seasons now come to fruition, on many levels. We now collect and store away the produce to see us through the dark times that we know will be just around the corner. Autumn is also the time for cutting down and pruning back, giving up those things that are no longer needed and, dare I say it, for sacrifice of some of those things that we hold dear, in payment for those good things that we have just received. The Natural Crafter knows that nothing is gained by nothing, and that a portion of all that is harvested belongs to and must be returned to those Powers that helped originate it. This can sometimes be painful and quite harsh, but it sets up the right conditions for future harvests, when the sacrifice will be repaid.

Like all the seasons, Autumn does not suddenly start on a certain date, but slides in when it will and occurs at different times in different parts of the country. Traditionally it has always begun with the grain harvest. "Haerfest" is the Anglo-Saxon word for Autumn and gives us our word "harvest". This timing may not be applicable at all in some areas, in which case different criteria need to be used. The season culminates with the end of the Apple harvest, which ushers in the time of All Hallows and the beginning of Winter.

During this Autumn Tide, it is not only the Wheat, Barley, Oats and Rye that will be gathered in – weather permitting – but also the later-fruiting trees like the Damson, Plum, Apricot, Walnut and Hazel. Blackberries will be about from the beginning to the end of the tide, with all their taboos and provisos on picking, and the Sloes will begin to ripen on the wickedly-pointed Blackthorn trees. Flowers like the Poppy and Goldenrod will bloom briefly and die back, setting seed for the next cycle, and the leaves on the trees will give their wonderful Autumn colour-show, then begin to gently slide from the branches. Under the denuded boughs, Mushrooms and Toadstools start to poke their heads through the ground and sprawling between the two, the shiny, purple/black Belladonna berries reach full ripeness.

It is time for a stocktake in the home during this season; what is worth keeping and what needs throwing out. This is not the spring cleaning of earlier tides, but more on the lines of maintenance. What do I need to keep during the dark months, what will serve me and provide for me, and what needs to be cherished and protected so that it can flourish again after the turning of the tides? Traditionally some of the year's harvest – be that grains, fruits, nuts or berries – are preserved and kept, either to feed on through the Winter, or to sow again in Spring. Indeed, Autumn sowing is also a long-standing practice and this can also be applied to the home in the form of projects and activities that need starting now, if they are to be completed by the Spring. Other things too need to be cherished, such as the energies of the previous harvest(s), so that they can be put to good use once again when Spring comes around once more.

Wildlife will be taking full advantage of the glut of food at this time, either putting on stores of excess fat for those that hibernate through the Winter, or storing away caches of provisions for those that do not. The season can be long so there is no hurry, but it must be done or else starvation and death can result. For those animals, mostly birds, that are Summer visitors only, or who come to these shores just to breed, it is now time for them to begin their, mostly, long and arduous journeys home. Swallows and Swifts begin to leave in August, closely followed by the Cuckoo, and later on the tribes of Geese that go honking through the skies at night, like a pack of spectral hounds on the chase. Nests and burrows will be dug afresh or cleaned out after the long warm tide and fresh straw, hay, twigs or other lining materials will be collected and laid by, ready for the bleaker times ahead. The Game hunting season begins during this tide and some of our wild cousins, less nimble than others, will make a welcome addition to the Crafters harvest pot. You can always tell when Autumn has arrived by the activities of our natural brethren, and the wise Witch pays close attention if they wish to follow the seasonal tides closely.

The weather may continue to be warm and balmy for many weeks yet – indeed, our Summers these days are turning into very mild Autumns – and temperatures may still reach to the heights. However, the days now become noticeably shorter and the evenings begin to creep in closer. Then we change the clocks back at the end of October for that return to 'real' time and we can really tell the difference. The benefit of the longer nights is that there is more time for stargazing once again and we can see the circle of the heavens turning overhead in greater detail. The constellation known as The Great Square of Pegasus is prominent throughout the Autumn months and we are treated to one or two fine meteor showers as well. Andromeda sails high and clear and at the end of the tide, the great hunter, Orion, begins to rear his head once more, and we know that the seasons have changed once again.

August

✤✿ ✣ ✿✤

The Sun rises at roughly 4:25 a.m. and sets around 7:46 p.m. at the beginning of this month.

August, known for many centuries as the Harvest Month, has this traditional image:

> *A Young Man of fierce and Cholerick aspect, in a Flame-coloured Garment; upon his Head a garland of Wheat and Rye, upon his Arm a Basket of all manner of Ripe Fruits, at his Belt a Sickle. His sign Virgo.*

Times & Tides

The festival of Lammas traditionally celebrates the **start** of the grain harvest. This is when the **first** sheaf of corn is cut and customarily begins on August 1st, although in reality, location and weather may change this to a greater or lesser degree. Lammas comes from the Old English term "Hlafmaesse", meaning "Loaf Mass" and refers to the ceremony of the blessing of the first bread made from that year's harvest. This was done both in thanksgiving and in hopes of a fruitful and bountiful harvest to come. The main crop to be harvested around now was and is Wheat, but other cereal grains such as Oats, Barley and Rye are also ripening and will soon need to be cut, if this has not begun already. This period is the climax of the farmer's year and unless one has lived or worked on a farm, it is difficult to understand the excitement and trepidation that is felt at harvest time. The grain, which was drilled in Spring or last Autumn, is now red-gold straw, bowed down with heavy ears of corn which need to be cut and stored before it can be ruined by bad weather or disease. There is excitement because all the hard work has now come to fruition, and trepidation because it could all be ruined by just one bad storm. In times past, the Company of Reapers who had entered into agreement with the farmer at Whitsun to do the work as a complete whole, took over their responsibilities now. "Earnest Money" had been given and taken through their "Lord", who was their leader. He came first in everything, setting the rules of the harvest, the hours to be worked and the amount of ale allowed to be drunk during the long, hot, thirsty days. His second in command was invariably known as the "Lady", no matter that it was quite frequently a man. First came the golden Oats, then the brown ripe Wheat, followed by the flaxen Barley and the rich and ruddy sweep of the Clover.

Lammas both celebrates the first loaf and attempts to ensure the safe bringing-in of the rest of the harvest. Various traditions and customs have evolved over the centuries to honour and celebrate this time in the different regions of the British Isles. These include fairs and gatherings of all kinds, most of which are far too well-known to describe here, as we are concerned mainly with the overall flow of energies. We are here talking about natural, seasonal occurrences and tides and so the beginning of the harvest period is not tied to a specific date for the Natural or Traditional Crafter (or farmer for that matter). For these folk, what is important is the initial manifestation and earthing of the energies that were released at the Summer Solstice, namely those of ripening and maturity, which mark the beginning of the harvest tide (and Autumn). This manifestation will continue over a period of time and is not fixed to a specific calendar date. The occurrence of this will naturally vary from place to place, and also depend on what type of crop – if any – is being harvested. Therefore, it cannot be said for the Natural Crafter that the feast of Lammas occurs on the 1st of the month, only that it may do so. Once the harvest has begun however, it would be a natural thing for the Crafter to celebrate in the local fields (where possible) with rites which would include dancing, chanting and trance work to the Powers in the Land and the Ancestors. All this would be finished with a healthy dose of sex in the open air and an enjoyable feast of first fruits. The trance work involved in these rites would involve taking messages to and bringing them back from the Powers which govern the Life in the Land, and possibly some form of sacrifice in gratitude also. This is an important aspect of the Witch's practice and one that is often neglected these days by people who follow more modern traditions. It is not always – or ever – necessary to give a life for a life, but often a little blood-offering of one's own is appropriate for the personal harvest being reaped. This is particularly so if it is a bountiful one, and the Natural Crafter would not baulk at this, recognising the reciprocal bond between themselves and the Powers they work with. The sex performed in the fields is not purely for enjoyment's sake – although that's nice too – but to encourage the ripening of the rest of the harvest and to ensure the earthing of the energies of the season. (Recent scientific studies have shown that sexual activity in the presence of growing plants both increases growth and brings on fruition, so the traditional practices at this time of year have a sound, practical basis.)

As already mentioned, Natural Craft attempts to work in tune with the rhythms, Spirits and Powers of the Land, on all levels, and if you happen to live in an area that does not have a grain harvest, how can you have a Loaf Mass? Moreover, if the worst has come to the worst and the grain crop has been ruined by drought, disease or flood, what is there to celebrate? The answer is that you either do not celebrate this festival at all – it is not compulsory after all – or acknowledge the earthing of the energies released earlier in the year in a way that is appropriate to you, personally and in your area. Harvest your own tide and the produce that is around you on your part of the Land in your own way – make it relevant. Furthermore, there is more than one theme involved in this time of year. There is obviously the celebration of the cutting of the first grain harvest, but there is also the need to ensure that the rest of the harvest (of whatever kind) is completed successfully. There is also the theme of sacrifice: that of giving back that which has been gained, in payment and in preparation for future harvests. This is valid both on a group and individual basis and is a major consideration in those areas that do not have a grain harvest. Consider those things that you set in motion at the Spring or Vernal Equinox, just as the grain was planted then. They should be beginning to manifest themselves around now – if they have not already done so – and you may wish to consider this when deciding how or whether to celebrate this feast. You must decide whether you wish to celebrate a purely 'earthly' harvest, or acknowledge the manifestation of other energies as well as, or instead of, them.

Having said all this, there are obviously many different ways in which Lammas may be acknowledged or celebrated, with widely-differing versions around the country, but nearly all of them will involve the use of bread or a loaf in some way, if only as a symbol. Most people will have their own methods for celebrating this time, ritual or otherwise, in a group or as an individual, but I would like to make a few suggestions for you to consider or include as you do so.

Whether you live in a grain-producing area or not, try to make your own small loaf of bread (or roll) if at all possible, from the best and most natural ingredients that you can obtain (or have grown yourself). As you mix the ingredients, knead and roll the dough, pour into the loaf the knowledge that this is the culmination and manifestation of all those things that you have set for yourself to achieve in the seasons just passed. It is not just representative of an actual, grain harvest. This may be magical, material, romantic, financial or whatever. Know that this loaf represents and is the embodiment, the manifestation, of all that you have achieved – your own harvest. You may wish to form the dough into a specific design or shape representing these things before you bake it, or just leave it as it is. Bake it as carefully as you can, trying not to burn or overcook it. When it is done and cooled, you may perform the following small rite, by yourself or in company with others, as part of a larger rite or meal, or simply by itself.

Lay the loaf on a platter on your table or altar and set beside it a Cup of full-bodied red wine. Call to yourself whatever Powers or Spirits you work with to witness the rite and to take part in it, without being too flowery! Place your dominant hand over the bread and say these words, or similar:

> *Here is the First Loaf, symbol of this year's harvest. It is the result of all that has gone before, from the planting of the seed, through the growth of the work, to the ripening of the effort and the reaping of the intent. It is good and I/we give thanks for it.*

Cut the bread in half with your Knife and lay half aside in a separate bowl, saying:

That which is taken must also be given. As a true Son/Daughter of the Old Faith I return a portion from whence it came.

Place your dominant hand over the Cup and say words to this effect:

Here is Wine, fruit of the vine and Blood of the Land. May the Powers see that it is honoured for what it is and accepted in gratitude and sacrifice.

Pour a libation of wine over the bread in the bowl, mix the two together and anoint the foreheads of all present with a dab of the mixture. (Afterwards, this must be taken out to a natural place and poured directly onto the ground, with whatever words or prayers you feel suitable. It is a sacrifice and a giving back in gratitude to the Powers for some of the benefits They have seen fit to give you.)

Now, break the remaining bread and distribute it amongst all present, or take a piece for yourself if alone. With full awareness of what you are saying and doing, say the following or similar:

I take and eat this Bread in acknowledgement of this year's harvest.

Eat slowly.

Pass the Cup around and/or take a drink from it yourself, saying the following or similar:

I take and drink this Wine, in gratitude for this year's harvest.

Savour the drink.

Take some time to consider your 'harvest', and the significance of what you have just done. Proceed to complete the rest of your rite, party or meal with enjoyment and a full knowledge of the season and its meanings. (You have, in effect, just performed a simple Loaf Mass, in recognition of the First Fruits, encompassing the true meaning of the time of year.)

On the 11th of the month, we come to the end of the Dog Days and, hopefully, the intense heat that comes with them. The period of 'madness' comes to an end, whether metaphorical, magical or actual, and we can continue our work in a much more balanced and reasoned fashion. One could almost say that the energies released at the rising of Sirius have reached their maturity too, so if you have worked with these then a time of harvest would also be appropriate here.

The festival of Hecate is traditionally celebrated on August 13th. Although She is one of the Greek Powers and obviously not native to these Isles, She has long been venerated by the Witches and Crafters of Britain and still is. Her worship was brought here in Roman times, or maybe before that by the Greek traders to these shores. (Behind Her stands an even more ancient deity, Tanith – who was brought here possibly by the Phoenician traders of millennia ago – and they share many similar characteristics and symbols.) Shakespeare gives Hecate as the patron of his Witches in the "Scottish Play", where She is clearly a Power to be reckoned with, and most of the focus of Her festival at this time is, historically, dedicated to propitiation. It is considered that if She is not satisfied, then She will send storms to ruin the ongoing harvests at this time. She is traditionally venerated at crossroads – one of the customary meeting places for Crafters – where food and other offerings to Her should be left in silence. One should then turn around and walk away, without looking back, as no one could confront Her face to face. Her main symbol is the Torch, which illuminates the darkness of ignorance and She is known as a female leader of the Wild Hunt, which is in keeping with Her pre-Olympian origins as one of the most ancient of Powers. With this in mind, a small lighted candle may be left with Her offerings, if it is felt safe to do so.

St. Bartholomew has his feast day on the 24th of the month, which is an important day in weather lore (see later). Little is factually known about this Apostle, although he is said to have taken the gospel to India, where he is highly revered. Traditionally he was martyred by being flayed alive and then crucified, whilst in Armenia, which, rather gruesomely, led to him becoming the patron of tanners after his death! (He is also patron saint of cheese merchants and plasterers for some reason.) The festival in August has been a traditional occasion for markets and fairs, and such a fair serves as the scene for *Bartholomew Fair*, a play by Ben Jonson.

These fairs would mark the end of one period of work for many people, and them being available for new work. These were often known as "hiring fairs" or "mop fairs" and marked one of the main cross-quarter days in British social and legal reckoning. Contracts for work or other things often only lasted for one year, so the celebratory period towards the end of harvest was an ideal time to take stock, change jobs if you wanted to, or get rid of lazy workers and hire some new ones if you were an employer.

In days gone by the grain harvest would usually come to an end roughly around the end of the month, although in many cases it continued well into September. These days it probably only takes a couple of days to harvest the grain with the huge machines available, even in the vast fields where the crops are now grown. However, the end of the harvest is still a very important period, in that it is now time for a brief rest and respite from the heavier work and, in days gone by, the farmer would have provided the Harvest Home supper for all the workers. As Thomas Tusser (the 16th-century poet and farmer) has it:

In Harvest-time, harvest folk, servants and all
Should make, all together, good cheer in the Hall,
Once ended thy Harvest, let none be beguiled
Please such as did help thee, man, woman and child.

In my native Suffolk and parts of Norfolk, this is referred to as the "Horkey Supper", but it has a long and venerable history throughout many parts of Britain and under many names. The last sheaves would have been loaded onto the wagons, with the "Lord" of the harvest sitting on top. The last sheaf would have been cut (see later for customs surrounding this) and held up high in honour on the way back to the farm. The women and children would finally have been allowed into the fields for "gleaning" (picking up the dropped ears of grain after the harvest, an important extra source of food in poverty-stricken rural areas, as many of them were), and the rabbits hiding in the centres of the fields would have been caught for the pot. If the weather was fine then trestles and benches would be set outside for the feast; if not, a barn would have been cleared, decorated and the tables set up in there. The farmer would have provided the best of all foods for the workers, which would have included hams, muttons, geese, cheeses, breads (of course), vegetables, fruits and gallons of home-brewed ales and ciders. Much toasting would have gone on, particularly to the farmer, the Lord and the last sheaf, installed in a place of honour, probably twisted, plaited or 'dressed' in some manner. Sadly, this custom has nearly died out in today's modern economy, but you can still find one or two farmers who adhere to the old ways, in more than one fashion!

Flora
Normally to be seen in the fields of golden Wheat at this time of year, are the bright scarlet petals of the native Poppy (*Papaver rhoeas*). It is often called the "Common Poppy" and its other names include "Corn Poppy" and "Field Poppy", but it is also known by the more descriptive and evocative names for this time of year of "Thundercup", "Thunderflower" and "Lightnings". This is because it was thought that to pick them at this time of the year would provoke storms and ruin the crops. Conversely, whilst they remained unpicked, they acted as a talisman to keep the

crops safe from Autumnal downpours. This Poppy is a native annual (or rarely, biennial) that has a thin, spindly root and stalk, that grows to about two to three feet tall. It grows on any disturbed and fertile soil in full Sun, and is obviously associated in most people's minds with the corn and harvest. It has symbolised both fertility and death for thousands of years, wherever it has been found. It is associated with both the Female Powers of the crops, growth, ripeness and harvest and also with the Spirit of the dying Male Powers that are sacrificed at this time of year, so that the people may eat and plant fresh crops for the next year. The milky-white juice that comes from the stem and head when they are cut symbolises the milk of a lactating mother, and the blood-red petals are associated with the death of the year's crops as they graphically fall to the ground. Although possessing slightly narcotic properties, the Common Poppy is nowhere near as strong as the Asian White Poppy (*Papaver somniferum*), from which is derived both the sticky latex that produces opium and, curiously, the Poppy seeds that are used for cooking; these are non-toxic and non-narcotic. In magical practice, it is mostly the seeds or seed heads that are used. Carrying the dried seeds is said to promote fertility and attract good fortune and prosperity, and to become pregnant the seeds should be added to all food that is eaten. The dried seed heads may be emptied of their contents and used as the receptacles for spells; the request should be written on a small piece of paper and inserted into the seed head and placed under the pillow at night. The Powers should be invoked to bring about the desired end and, if you dream of the spell in the night, then your work will be successful. Medicinally, the plant is not much used these days, but it does have its values. An infusion may be made from the leaves and petals which has a soothing effect on sore throats and chests and can also be used to treat catarrh, hay fever, asthma and other respiratory ailments. A few crushed Poppy heads added to a linseed poultice will reduce pain and swelling. Although not possessing the same sedative qualities as the White Poppy, an infusion of the petals in milk was given to infants to aid sleeping, and dummies were also dipped in the seeds and given to babies to suck when teething. The seeds are good to chew for headaches, particularly hangovers (the Poppy also being known as the "Headache Flower"), and neuralgia and toothache have also been successfully treated with Poppies. Both Gerard and Culpepper recommended the Common Poppy for treating the pain of pleurisy, and syrup of wild Poppies remained in the *British Pharmaceutical Codex* until as late as 1949. Of course, one of the most well-known uses for the Poppy these days is as a symbol of remembrance on Armistice Day on November 11th each year, in honour of the dead of the two World Wars; red is the general colour worn for the fallen soldiers, although white poppies are now worn by those who wish to honour and remember the dead, but do not wish to condone the violence of war.

In contrast to the blood-red of the Poppy, the bright, golden-yellow of the Goldenrod (*Solidago virgaurea*) in flower shines out this month. Also known as "Woundwort", "Aaron's Rod" and simply as "Solidago", this native plant is a member of the Daisy (Compositae) family. It is a perennial, growing best in hedgerows, open woodland and rocky places and is also popular as a cottage garden plant. As its name suggests it has a wand-like form, with an upright, flexible stem and neatly-arranged, lance-shaped, toothed, dark green leaves. It can grow up to five feet tall and is crowned by sprouts of short branches, each bearing three or four small, daisy-like bright yellow flowers. Bees adore these flowers and it is estimated that if an acre of land was planted with Goldenrod, it would supply 100 hives with their Winter stores. The stems of this plant have traditionally been used as divining rods – hence one of its folk names – and have long had the reputation of discovering hidden springs of water, as well as deposits of silver and gold. The wand should be taken during the flowering season and dedicated to the Powers of the Underworld, bathed in spring water, then dried out thoroughly before use. However, in some parts of the country it is considered unlucky to bring it into the house, or even to have it growing in the garden! Goldenrod's generic name "Solidago" means "to make whole" and for generations it has been used primarily as a wound herb, mostly in ointment form. It has marked astringent and antiseptic qualities and, applied externally, the pulped plant will arrest bleeding and prevent infection; it is even believed to halt gangrene and tetanus when used in this manner. Used in infusion and taken internally, it helps to reduce high fevers and promotes sweating and is also a fine tonic for digestion, nausea, vomiting and weak stomachs. It is also used specifically for hay fever, jaundice and morning sickness. It has marked dissolvent properties, which has led it to be prescribed effectively for disorders of the kidney and bladder, specifically for stones and gravel therein. It is a herb which goes in and out of fashion quite regularly and Gerard comments, in 1597: "*I have known the dry herbe which came from beyonde the sea sold in Bucklersbury in London for half a crowne an once. But since it was found in Hamstead wood, even as it were at our townes end, no man will give half a crowne for an hundred weight of it.*" And yet the plant, as he continues to say "*no doubt have the same virtue now that then it had, although it growes so neere our owne homes in never so great quantity.*" Nothing really ever changes now, does it!

Creeping along the ground, below the much taller plants above, can be found the Cinquefoil plant (*Potentilla reptans*). Although this genus of plant has over 300 different species, the one that is usually referred to in native lore is this one, the "reptans", known also as "Crampweed", "Five-finger Grass", "Five-leaf Grass", "Synkefoyle", "Five Fingers" and "Gooseweed". This plant can be found on grassland, waste places, along roadsides and in gardens. The reddish runners, sometimes confused with Wild Strawberry (*Fragaria vesca*) to which it has a passing resemblance, will soon invade your herb garden and attempt to choke the other plants if not watched carefully. Its long-stalked leaves are composed of five hairy leaflets (hence the name) and the single flowers are golden-yellow in colour, flowering between June and September (the wild Strawberry has white flowers and three-lobed leaves). The leaves will curl up during rain or when the Sun goes in, so protecting the tiny flowers within. A great favourite of Mediaeval Witches and sorcerers, Cinquefoil was used for a variety of magical purposes, particularly for protection and curse breaking, although it was also used as a bit of a Jack-of-all-trades. However, its main usage was (and still is) in compounding the famous "Flying Ointment". Many, many different recipes are extant for this salve, most of which are highly toxic and composed of noxious ingredients derived from fevered Inquisitorial imaginations; they will only send you flying off into a coma if used in their given state. However, there are various, safer, options that rely more on practice and application, with a little help from the – non-toxic – herbs, and such a one is the following. This is a modern version of an old recipe, the original involving such things as lard, pig fat and soot, which are quite unnecessary, not to mention messy, and this works just as well.

Take half an ounce of dried, chopped Valerian root and place it in an enamel pan. Add one cup of vegetable oil and **warm** through gently for two hours, stirring occasionally. After this time, strain the liquid through a fine sieve, discard the Valerian somewhere appropriate and return the oil to the pan. Add a handful of fresh Chamomile flower heads, a handful of fresh Skullcap herb, a few fresh Lemon Balm leaves and a handful of fresh Cinquefoil leaves. Return the pan to the heat and once again **warm** the mixture through, stirring occasionally, for a further 20 minutes. After this time, again sieve and discard the herbs and return the oil to the pan, replacing on a gentle heat. To this oil now add half an ounce of pure grated Beeswax and let it melt in, stirring gently. When it has all amalgamated, pour the mixture into a clean, sterilised jar(s), screw the lid(s) on tightly and allow to cool until set. (You may like to add a couple of drops of Benzoin essential oil as a preservative before screwing on the lid(s), as it helps to keep it for a long time.) Store in a cool, dark place. Before using any ointment you have made, always perform a patch test to see if you have any reaction to it. Dab a little of the salve onto the soft skin on the inside of your elbow and leave for 24 hours. If there is any redness, swelling or rash, do not use the ointment as you are possibly allergic to one or more of the ingredients. If there is no effect, you may safely use this in your work, rubbing a little on the insides of your wrists, temples, neck and thighs each time you wish to 'fly'.

In addition to this, Cinquefoil has also long been used in herbal medicine for its astringent, antispasmodic and tonic properties. It is a favourite herb of the Romany people and is used for its powerful sedative effect (possibly why it is used in the above ointment – to induce sleep and trance). It is particularly effective in cases of hysteria, epilepsy and, it is claimed, schizophrenia. It is an excellent painkiller, an infusion being used for topical applications in cases of cuts and wounds, and internally as a gargle for sore throats and swollen tonsils. A cordial may be made, which is much more pleasant, instead of the standard infusion, by steeping a handful of the fresh herb (or three ounces of dried) in a litre of German Hock wine; take a wineglassful each morning and night. In addition to all the above, as evidenced by one of its folk names, it has also been used to treat muscular cramps and aches of all types, evidently to great effect.

Hearth & Home
As mentioned earlier, there are very many customs surrounding the end of the harvest, as well as the beginning, not the least of which is in dealing with the last sheaf of corn to be cut. Contrary to most popular opinion, there was no general practice when dealing with this item, but customs varied greatly from one end of the country to

the other and were not part of some cohesive whole. In some areas, the last sheaf of corn to be cut was viewed with fear and trepidation, as the abode of some evil spirit. In others, it was venerated and cut with much ceremony, then preserved until the following year. In yet others, there was no particular importance attached to it at all and it was cut down along with the rest of the harvest. Some people viewed it as embodying the spirit of the harvest, but this was by no means a universal concept and to say that it was viewed as the Earth Mother would also be stretching this too far. The names by which it was referred to were also very different, depending presumably on how it was viewed: the "Neck", the "Carlin", the "Dame", the "Bitch", the "Mare", the "Maiden", the "Hare", the "Dog", the "Wolf", the "Bride", the "Cailleach", the "Bogey" and the "Ben" were all names applied to the last sheaf. Therefore, there is no way that they could all have adhered to some common concept of what it represented. This is true also of what has now come to be called the "Corn Dolly", the decorative, plaited- straw figures that appear in abundance at craft fairs at this time of year. The practice of making these figures had practically died out long before the Second World War, but was revived in the 1950s and 60s and has turned into the 'tradition' that we have today. Originally the term "Dolly" was unknown and these figures were called such things as the "Corn Baby", "Corn Maiden", "Kern Babby", "Babby" or nothing at all. Like the last sheaf, they did not necessarily represent the spirit of the corn or the fertility of the land, let alone the Earth Mother, Ceres or Demeter as some writers would have had it. They were decorative celebrations of the end of the harvest, varying greatly in size from about hand-sized to several feet high. Again, these figures were treated differently in different areas. Some were given places of honour at the Harvest Supper, kept until the next year and then replaced. Some were hung up in the barns and then ploughed back into the fields in the Autumn or Spring sowing, being seen as some kind of protective charm. Yet others were used to taunt neighbouring farms with the fact that "we've got our harvest in before you", then cast back into the fields. The shapes and forms that existed, although widely varying, were also nothing like as complex as we see today either and were often very rough, rural figures made at the drop of a hat. However, different regions did have their own styles and were known for them, but two forms were almost universal: one was the Cornucopia and the other was the Drop Basket.

Whatever the origin and meaning of the original dolly, many Crafters make their own, for their own celebrations and their *own reasons at this time of year an*d I would like to describe here one method that you may like to try for your own celebrations. I shall describe the Drop Basket, as this is fairly simple and doesn't use too much straw to begin with.

The straw that you use must either be fresh, or have been laid flat in water for 24 hours beforehand to temper it and make sure it does not snap when you bend it. Take five, long pieces of the straw, with good even heads and cut them with sharp scissors just above the first leaf node (only the top part of a straw is ever used for Corn Dolly making). Tie them firmly together with raffia just below the heads, then turn the straws upside down, so the heads are pointing downwards. Hold the heads gently but firmly in your passive hand and spread the straws out flat with your dominant hand so that they are evenly spaced like the spokes of a wheel. Number the straws to yourself from 1 to 5 in an anti-clockwise direction, or mark the numbers on if you find that easier and clearer. Starting with straw 1, bend it across 2 and 3 to place it between 3 and 4. Move the straws in your hand a quarter-turn clockwise. Straw 3 is then bent across 1 and 4. Lay straw 4 across 3 and 5. Lay straw 5 across 4 and 2. Keep moving the straws in a clockwise direction as you work. Bend straw 2 across 5 so that it lies parallel to 1. Bend straw 1 over 2 to lie parallel with 3. Straw 3 then goes under and over 1 to lie parallel with 4. Continue this way, bending each straw over the next two and moving the second up and over in the same way. Keep turning your dolly as you work.

Whenever you come towards the end of a 'weaver' straw, cut it off at a corner of the weave and push the thin end of a new straw into the centre of the old one (it goes in more easily if you cut it slantwise first). While you continue in this way, laying the moving straw parallel to the straw two beyond it, the dolly will widen. When it is about half as long as you want it to be, begin to overlap the moving straw; this will gradually decrease the width. To finish off you will need to be working with three straws at least eight inches long, so add new weavers if it is necessary. Bend the straws upwards and tie them firmly with raffia. Plait the three longest straws together and bend them round to make a loop. Tie the loop with raffia to the two other straws, close to the end of the weaving. You may tie a red ribbon around the raffia below the corn heads, and hang the Basket from its loop. (This may sound complicated in description, but is actually quite easy when you are doing it – just give it a try. There is a drawing of the finished Basket in the illustration to *The Autumn Tide* at the beginning of this section, for reference.)

This form of dolly is both decorative and very useful in that, if required, the Crafter may insert items into the body of the dolly, representing anything they desire, depending on how the Crafter views the item. For example, if the individual does view the figure as a representative of either the Spirit of the Harvest or the Earth Mother, then either a small piece of paper with a written request, blessing or prayer to either may be inserted into the dolly, or other items such as flowers, pieces of bread, whatever; I'm sure you get the idea. This may then be kept, or not, until next year, or play other roles in your rites if you so wish.

Finally in this section, something to fill the inner body during the Harvest Supper at the end of the month, namely a good bowl of Frumenty. This is also sometimes called

Furmenty, it can be served hot or cold, and was a traditional part of the end of harvest feast, made with the grains of whatever was the local crop, or whatever grain was available. There are many variations to this recipe around the country, but here is one from my region, using Wheat (treat other grains the same). You will need:

Ingredients:
1 teacupful clean new Wheat (washed thoroughly)
4oz mixed dried druit
2oz flour for thickening
2 pints milk
2oz sugar
nutmeg to flavour
cream for serving

Method:
Cover the Wheat with one pint of the milk in a bowl and put into a slow oven or slow cooker and leave overnight (or all day if serving in the evening). Transfer to a saucepan and add the rest of the milk, sugar and a little grated nutmeg. Thicken with flour mixed with milk, add the fruit and bring to the boil, then simmer. When the fruit has softened remove from the heat. As said, it can be served hot or cold, always with cream and maybe with a tot of rum or brandy!

This dish has been described as "gruel with its best clothes on"; having never tasted gruel I can't comment, but Frumenty certainly gets my vote.

Fauna
Although they are native residents and are to be seen all year round, if you are sharp-eyed and lucky, the lower angle of the Autumn Sun now catches the beautiful plumage of the Kingfisher (*Alcedo atthis*) in a stunning lightning flash as it dives from its perch into a slow-flowing river or stream. This strikingly coloured bird has an orange/red underbelly

and an apparently electric blue plumage on top, although this is purely the result of light refraction and it appears duller out of bright sunlight. It was originally known just as "Fisher" (a name that still survives in dialect, particularly in Yorkshire), but this became "King's Fisher" in 1318 and the now common name "Kingfisher" in the 18th century. However, for such a strikingly coloured, much loved and enjoyed bird, it appears to have no other folk names attached to it. They fly rapidly, low over water and hunt fish from riverside perches, occasionally hovering above the water's surface. They are vulnerable to hard Winters and habitat degradation through pollution or unsympathetic management of watercourses. They are widespread, especially in Central and Southern England, becoming less common further North, but following some declines last century they are currently increasing their range in Scotland. Kingfishers are found by still or slow-flowing water such as lakes, canals and rivers in lowland areas. In Winter, some individuals move to estuaries and the coast; occasionally they may visit garden ponds if of a suitable size. Both male and female birds excavate the nest burrow into the stone-free sandy soil of a low stream bank, usually about two feet from the top. The birds choose a vertical bank clear of vegetation, since this provides a reasonable degree of protection from predators. The nest tunnel is usually three to four feet long, and the two-and-a-half-inch diameter is only a little wider than the bird itself. The nest chamber at the end has a slight depression to prevent eggs rolling out, but no material is brought into the nest. Two or three broods are raised in quick succession, normally in the same nest. Kingfishers rarely eat their catch as soon as they have caught it, but spend some time striking it on their perch or a nearby rock, to ensure it is stunned, before swallowing it head first; they are particularly careful with spined fish, such as Sticklebacks, and make sure they kill these first, rather than stun them, so that the spines cannot be raised as they are being swallowed. For such a beautiful and fascinating bird there is little lore attached to them, other than a couple of curious pieces of erroneous natural history. It is said that they do not moult and that their skins never decay, possessing the power to preserve any material that they come into contact with. Giraldus Cambrensis, writing in the 12th century, has this to say about them: "*It is remarkable in these little birds that, if they are preserved in a dry place when dead, they never decay; and if they are put among clothes and other articles, they preserve them from the moth and give them a pleasant odour.*" The other curious piece of natural history told about them is that, if a dead and dried Kingfisher is hung up indoors, it will swing round until its beak points towards the quarter from which the wind is blowing; this was common lore up until quite recently. It was even said that it would point one way during fine weather and the opposite direction when it was raining. How curious! As with most animals in these Isles, although it has seldom been eaten for its taste alone, it has often been used medicinally. John Keogh, writing in 1739, has this to say about the Kingfisher: "*The potestates of the Flesh cure consumptions, being taken to the quantity of three ounces for a dose. The flesh pulverised taken in any proper vehicle, to the quantity of two drams at a time is good against the epilepsy. Also the Heart, being dried, and hung about the neck of an infant, is said to drive away the said disorder.*" One wonders, with all these cures for epilepsy how it ever managed to persist into this day and age!

The "Glorious Twelfth" of this month is the traditional date on which the Grouse (*Lagopus lagopus*) hunting season begins. Our native Grouse is the Red Grouse, which now exists in its own subspecies of *Lagopus lagopus scoticus*. Where once it was the only species of endemic British bird, it is now a subspecies of the circumpolar Willow Grouse. Colloquially also known as the "Brown Ptarmigan", "Gor Cock/Hen", "Heath Cock", "Moorfowl", "Moor Game", "Moor Pout", "Moss Hen" and "Red Game", it is one of the few species that retains the same colour plumage all year round, where others normally turn white during the Winter months. They are fairly small birds, about the same size as a Bantam chicken, and the name "Red Grouse" is appropriate as the plumage of the British bird is typically a dark red-brown overall, although there are some local variations. The bird's generic and specific name of "Lagopus" is derived from the Greek "Lagos", meaning "Hare" and "Pous", meaning "Foot", because of its distinctive feathered legs and claws, similar to those of other members of the family, such as the Ptarmigan and the Capercaillie. The predominance of the word "Moor" in many of the common names for this bird gives the clue to its usual habitat and indeed, like others in its family, it has a specially-adapted digestive tract that helps it cope with its almost entirely heather-based diet. This tough, fibrous plant is not easily broken down and hence needs this adaptation, even though it is mostly the fresh, green shoots and buds that are eaten (the developing young however will take insects if they can get them). The male Red Grouse is unique in its nesting behaviour. In all other species of Grouse, only the female takes responsibility for the young; however, the male Red often takes over the care of the family by staunchly defending his territory and his young. Males have even been known to attack humans who come too close to their nests whilst they are brooding hatchlings. It may or may not be coincidental in this case that the male's call is usually given as "go-back, go-back"!

August 12th was chosen as the start of the shooting season in this case to coincide with the end of the breeding season but, in times gone by, it had a lot to do with other concerns too. Parliament in London always made sure that it was in recess by then for the Members to make their way North for the sport. It has only been in the last 150-200 years though that the Grouse has been any sort of game bird with a following. This occurred after the introduction of the railways, enabling better access to the moorlands and heaths of the North of England and Scotland, and the introduction of the breech-loading shotgun which gave quicker action for the 'bagging' of more game. Before this period, it was really only local people who bothered, especially as the larger hunting estates had not yet been created by the forced relocation of much of the populace and the change in management of the heathland. This is one of the main reasons that very little is heard of the Grouse in literature until this recent period; certainly, it bypassed the main luminaries such as Shakespeare and his ilk. As already stated, Grouse is a game bird, and any decent cook will tell you that game birds need to be hung for five or six days before eating. This seems to offend some people these days, with modern sensibilities, but they should try eating it freshly killed. "Hanging" is important for game birds, to enable the tough fibres of the flesh to break down; this makes the meat more tender and improves the flavour. There are no hard and fast rules on how long to hang the birds, as much depends on the weather and the taste of the consumer. An August bird may need hanging for only three or four days, whereas a bird shot in January will hang for two or three weeks and still be in perfect condition. Traditionally the meat should be hung by the tail feathers until it rots off them and falls of its own accord; by this point the meat may be green and crawling with maggots, but that's how it's done!

An animal that is to be seen in fields and hedgerows in increasing numbers at this time of year is the Rat. There are two species of Rat in Britain, the Black (*Rattus rattus*) and the Brown (*Rattus norvegicus*), the latter being by far the more common, although also, by far the more recent incomer. Neither species are 'native', the Black Rat arriving sometime during the first millennium, ultimately from Central Asia; the Brown Rat arriving much later, the first recorded instance being just before 1730, from the same ultimate origin. The Black Rat has been almost supplanted by the Brown, the Black being smaller, slower to breed and less adaptive to modern poisons. The Brown is a prolific breeder, will fight vociferously for its own, or any other, territory and has developed much greater immunity to the usual poisons such as Warfarin. The Black Rat has never really taken to the open countryside and is mostly to be found in old houses and on board ships, hence its common names of "Roof Rat" and "Ship Rat". The Brown Rat has colonised almost every available space, is totally omnivorous and is known as the "Common Rat", "Hanoverian Rat" and "Norway Rat" (these latter names are due to the erroneous assumptions of their origins in early years). As well as being well known for infesting barns, haystacks and farms in general, taking full advantage of the spilled grains and seeds at this time of year, there is one other thing that Rats are mainly known – and loathed – for. This is the spread of the Bubonic Plague during the Mediaeval period, when almost half the population of Britain was wiped out; and later for the spread of the Black Death, which was only halted by the Great Fire of London in that major metropolis. Without going into these tragedies in detail, suffice it to say that recent investigations relieve the pressure on the Rat a bit. Although it is well known that they indeed helped to spread these noxious diseases via the infected fleas and lice that they carried (and still do in some areas of the world), the rapid spread of the disease throughout Western Europe now leads many scientists to believe that it was not Rats alone that were responsible for its distribution. Other factors such as human fleas (which do not infest Rats), tainted water and airborne infections may also have had a great effect, especially as it is now thought that different types of disease other than Bubonic Plague may have been at fault. However that may be, Rats have always had a sinister reputation and hence have always been linked in the popular imagination with Witches. This may, in fact, be the whispers of quite a strong connection with Natural Crafters, as many in the past, and today, have Rats as familiars and companions. Historically many Witches were convicted and condemned for this 'peculiarity', simply because they enjoyed the close connection that can exist between human and animal in this instance. Rats are highly intelligent, creatures of habit, ready to learn and, in the case of Black Rats, very tidy and fastidious in their manners. In times gone by, many a Crafter would have a pet Rat to aid him or her in choosing a tarot card for divination, or selecting one grain from a random selection of seed, with which to foretell the future. Also, Witches were credited with the power of shape-shifting into tailless Rats in their nocturnal journeyings and were likely to visit friends, and enemies, in this form to do them good or ill. It was also said and believed that, like Mice, Rats were the souls of people who had passed over and had foreknowledge of things to come. Hence they were the first to know if a ship were sinking, or would leave a house if a person there were about to die (although it also has to be said that the reverse was also considered to be true, in that Rats entering a house in any number foretold the death of one or more of its inhabitants). To Crafters and Witches themselves, Rats, again like Mice, have always been seen as closely connected with the cthonic Powers and in some senses their representatives. They are not to be shunned or feared, but to be acknowledged for their abilities and uses, watched for signs and thanked for their guidance when it is asked and received. To revile such close companions and representatives of the Powers is not only foolhardy, it is just asking for trouble for the conscientious Witch, no matter what common wisdom may say – the Crafter lives beyond this and walks to their own tune.

Seasonal Skies
August is a month of exceedingly changeable weather, when it can basically do anything you can think of: one minute it will be swelteringly hot, the next pouring with rain. In general though, it is the month when we see the disappearance of the thunder and lightning, as the old rhyme says:

If it sinks from the North,
It will double its wrath;
If it sinks from the South,
It will open its mouth;
If it sinks from the West,
It is never at rest;
If it sinks from the East,
It will leave us in peace.

The 11th of the month, as already mentioned, is generally viewed as the end of the Dog Days, but it initiates the peak period of the Perseid Meteor Showers, which are most active from the 11th – 13th, generally reaching their height on the 12th. This shower, as the name implies, appears to originate in the area of the constellation of Perseus, being associated with the Swift-Tuttle comet. In the Mediaeval period they came to be called the "Tears of St. Lawrence", who was one of the seven ancient Deacons of Rome and whose feast day is the 10th of this month. This shower can usually be relied upon to provide a good display and even around the time of the Full Moon a fair number of shooting stars will be visible. If you look up into a clear sky in the early hours of the 12th you will be very unlucky not to see several meteors, and this is a good time to use the stellar energy towards creating a beneficial environment for yourself during the Autumn and in the Winter Tide to come.

The 24th of August is St. Bartholomew's Day, as mentioned previously and is another of those weather 'prognostication' days. It is said that St. Bartholomew brings the cold dew.

All the tears that St. Swithin can cry,
St. Bartlemy's mantle wipes 'em dry.

And:

If St. Bartholomew's Day be fair and clear,
Then a prosperous Autumn comes that year.

If the weather is settled on this day then a fine Autumn is promised.

Looking high up and just to the West of South in the night sky, the fairly faint constellation of Ophiucus can be made out, with a bit of patience. Its main star, Ras Alhague, is derived from the Arabic for "Head of the Serpent Charmer" and this is the main association for this constellation ("Ophiucus" itself means "Serpent Holder"). The Serpent that he charms, or carries, falls to either side of him; to the West is its head (Serpens Caput) and to the East its tail (Serpens Cauda). These were originally an integral part of one and the same constellation, but now seen as separate figures, albeit entwined or combined. Classical myth concerning this figure revolves around the story of the divine healer Aesculapius who was supposedly the son of Apollo, and his descendant Hippocrates, the "father of modern medicine", whose symbol is of course the Serpent-entwined staff. This attribution holds true in native lore also, as the Serpent is seen both as a representative of the stellar energies and also of the cthonic Powers, in whose hands lay the secrets of the healing – and wounding – herbs. Indeed, it has long been held by Witches that Serpents have a consummate knowledge of herbal medicine, being familiar with the properties of all the plants in their immediate area. A healer would only need to watch the movements and habits of the snakes to divine the uses to which the herbs should be put (this also involves quite a bit of arcane knowledge on how to deal with snakes, but that's a whole different story. For practical notes on snake-handling see my previous work *The Devil's Plantation*, see Bibliography). The fact that the figure in the constellation – usually imaged as a mature man – is seen to be carrying (or charming) the snake, indicates that he is the bearer of the knowledge that the Serpent carries or symbolises. This figure has been identified with that of St. Benedict, founder of the order of Benedictine monks in Western Christendom, who, with his followers in the

6th century, inspired and continued the learning of the Greeks and Romans in so-called Dark Age Europe. This connection with wisdom and learning is also an attribute of the Serpent, so would fit a scholar and healer to perfection. Both Aaron and Moses have also been identified with this constellation, because of their Serpent associations – the first because of his staff, the second on account of the Brazen Serpent in the Wilderness – and so we can see that the symbolism is pretty well established and fixed. For the Crafter or Witch who wishes to deepen and strengthen their knowledge in the above areas, they would do well to work with the energies stemming from Ophiucus at this time and include this constellation in their overall working patterns and seasonal rites.

Known to the Anglo-Saxons as the "Maedden", the constellation of Virgo is astrologically important from about the 23rd of the month, until roughly the 22nd of September. From time immemorial this constellation has been depicted as a young woman, holding a sheaf of Lilies in one arm and a sheaf of corn (Wheat) in the other; she is frequently also winged, but not invariably so. She has been associated with just about every Virgin deity known (in the original sense of a woman who is complete in herself and independent, not beholden to any man, and not in the modern sense of "virgo intacta"). This includes the Virgin Mary in Christian mythology, but particularly those who have to do with the grain crop and the harvest. Classically she is Persephone (Proserpine) the daughter of Demeter/Ceres and very closely entwined with the grain Mysteries anciently held at Eleusis, just outside of Athens. In native lore she is most closely connected with the harvest period and the "Maiden" of the Wheat-field, otherwise known as the "Kern Babby", or the last sheaf of Wheat to be harvested. It is her influence that is magically held in the twisted plaits of straw that are nowadays called Corn Dollies, and not the so-called Queen of the Harvest, Grain Spirit or fertility Spirit. The fact that the last corn standing is frequently called the Maiden is indicative of this. This is also born out in the astrological timing of this 'sign', in that the original harvest season would frequently have lasted until at least late August, if not into September, rather than the two or three days it takes on modern farms (although at the time of writing, 21st August, there are many fields of Wheat nearby that have yet to be cut, due to the rainfall this month).

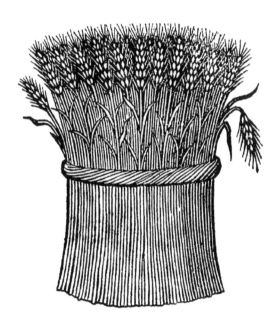

September

✣✤✣ ✤ ✣✤✣

The Sun rises at approximately 5:14 a.m. and sets at approximately 6:45 p.m. at the beginning of this month.

September, known to the Saxons as Barley Month and otherwise commonly as the White Straw Month, has the following image:

> *A merry and Cheerful Countenance, in a Purple Robe, upon his Head a Wreath of red and white Grapes, in his Left hand a handful of Oats, withal carrying a Horn of Plenty, full of all manner of Ripe Fruits, in his Right Hand the Sign Libra.*

Flora

As we move further into the Autumn Tide, we start to see the beginnings of the "second harvest", that of the later-fruiting trees and the hedgerows. One of the most prominent, well-known and loved of the latter fruits is the native Blackberry, or Bramble (*Rubus fruticosus*), which is actually a member of the Rose family. Known colloquially as "Blegs", "Black Heg", "Bumble-Kite", "Mushes" and "Gout-Berry", this is a plant that is both loved and feared by all who know it. Loved because of the succulent berries, but feared because of the wicked spikes and thorns on its stems. It is a common, sprawling shrub, native to Britain and can be found in many subspecies and microspecies all over these Isles. Producing small white or pink flowers from May onwards, the first fruits begin to appear in early September and continue into October and later, giving a very long fruiting period indeed. The first fruits appear at the tips of the shoots, changing from green to red then a deep purple-black colour and are the biggest, juiciest and most tasty; these are the best for making wines and liqueurs. The later fruits ripen backwards up the stem and are better for jams and jellies, but the ones at the very back of the stem will not ripen at all before Winter and some still have blossoms on them as the first snows fall. The shoots will bear fruit for two or three years, but will then wither away to make room for newer, fresher stems. This is a plant that spreads both by seed from the fallen fruit, but more so by suckering and rooting its stems along the ground and, once established, is exceedingly difficult to eradicate, which is why it makes such good hedges and barriers.

It has long been a plant with supernatural overtones, classed as one of the sacred plants by our Iron Age forebears, and always associated with the Faere Folk as belonging specifically to them. There is a taboo on picking the fruit after a certain period, usually given as the 29th of the month, Michaelmas, but the date varies from region to region; some say October 10th (Old Michaelmas) and others Hallowmas. The reason for this is generally stated as being that when Lucifer was expelled from heaven, the Blackberry was the plant that he landed on and he was sorely troubled by its thorns; in return for this treatment he either spat or pissed on the fruit, hence spoiling them after this date. This prohibition is actually sound common sense as, after a certain time, the fruits tend to go mouldy rather than ripening properly and could cause some serious internal troubles if eaten. In keeping with their Otherworldly reputation and spiky nature, Brambles have often been planted on and around graves, to stop the unquiet dead from walking. Conversely, the 'whippy' stems are used in Natural Craft to clear away unwanted energies in an outdoor place or along a path. The stems are stripped of their thorns for a distance along the thicker ends, bound together and this end is held, whilst whipping the springy ends back and forth, sweeping or clearing away the 'undesirables'. The leaves can be picked ritually, with prayers and offerings to the Faere Folk and made into a tea or infusion to make contact with them. This is especially effective if sitting near or under a Bramble bush at the time – mind the thorns though, on all levels! Blackberry wine is a superb drink and rivals Elderberry as a Witch wine in the Cup at this season, but here is a recipe for something a little stronger and quicker to make: Bramble Brandy.

Method:
Fill a large, screw-top jar with ripe Blackberries (having gently washed and shaken them dryish first), then top up the jar with a good quality Brandy of at least 70% proof and screw on the lid. Give it all a good shake and leave it all to amalgamate for about 14 days, shaking regularly, just as if you were making a strong tincture. At the end of this period filter off the liquid through a jelly bag or a few layers of muslin into a container and discard the residue left over conscientiously. Leave the liquid to settle for about 24 hours, then pour off the clear liquid again,

leaving any sediment behind. For every one pint of liquid take eight ounces of sugar and dissolve it in a quarter of a pint of water over a gentle heat, to form a thick syrup. When cool, add this to the Blackberry mixture, stir together well and bottle, leaving to mature for a couple of months. This should be ready about Yuletide for a delightful little tipple beside the fire on long Winter nights!

Blackberries are very high in vitamin C, malic acid, tannins and pectin and the leaves are highly astringent, tonic and diuretic. The berries have long been used in herbal medicine as a treatment for colds and coughs, cystitis and dysentery, haemorrhoids and as a gargle for sore throats and mouth ulcers when taken as a tea. An infusion of the leaves can be used as an enema or wash to cleanse open wounds, and also on cuts and scratches to disinfect and seal them. Gerard recommends a lotion of Blackberry leaves be used to heal sores on the *"privie parts"*!

Appearing in the fields and woods and under the hedgerows at this time of year are all kinds, manner and variety of Fungi. Usually known to us mortals as either Mushrooms or Toadstools, there is actually no scientific difference between the two – they are both Fungi; some just happen to be more edible than others! Actually, the parts that we see above ground are the fruiting bodies of the Fungus proper, a complex net of delicate threads called the Mycelium, which grows around the roots, leaves, trunk, body or whatever of the host plant or animal, in the case of rotting flesh. Fungi are a class on their own, exhibiting traits of both plant and animal and do not contain chlorophyll. Hence they are unable to manufacture their own carbohydrates and must live off those manufactured by other plants or animals, living or dead, which gives them immediately a somewhat sinister reputation. They are active all year round and the fruits can be found at any time, the conditions being right. However, they are most conspicuous in the Autumn when the majority of varieties put forth their fruits, enabling them to release their spores into the atmosphere and so reproduce. Although Fungi have no use for sunlight directly, they are to be found in areas where there is a good supply of it, as that is where the majority of their hosts will live. Hence they are mostly to be found on well-rotted vegetable matter that has had direct sunlight, such as the edge of woodland, forest glades that are well lit and in open fields and gardens. They also like warmth and damp, so a fine Summer followed by a mild, wet Autumn will see Mushrooms and Toadstools in abundance. These two terms are generally used to denote poisonous (Toadstools) and non-poisonous (Mushrooms) forms of Fungi but, as stated, this has no basis in science. However, for convenience sake I shall continue with tradition and use these terms here, with their stated meanings.

There are some 3,000 species of large-bodied Fungi growing in Britain, only about 20 or so of them being seriously poisonous. Some other species may cause severe stomach pains, diarrhoea or vomiting, or be too tough or fibrous to be edible, but are not actually deadly to humans. Most of the rest are edible in some form or other if you are careful and cook them properly; indeed, many are delicious and are a sadly-neglected form of food in this country. Correct identification is the key to picking any Mushrooms in the wild and I shall not attempt to go into all the rules and regulations here, as you cannot learn to identify an edible Fungus from a book, only from someone with great knowledge in the wild itself. A well-illustrated field guide to Fungi can give you a basic idea of what you should be looking for, but there is no substitute for practical knowledge, as many Mushrooms are identical to Toadstools and vice versa. Many is the budding gastronaut who has ended their career after only one misguided foray into the woods. Having said that, many areas organise "Fungi Forays" these days, with experienced guides to help the novice learn what to look for and what to avoid and I would thoroughly recommend that you go on one of these. There are a great variety of succulent Mushrooms waiting to be discovered at this time of year, among them the Bracket Fungi, Blewits, Ceps, Chanterelles, Agaricus varieties and others, which make excellent eating. These can be eaten fresh, having first observed any peculiarities of their species, or preserved in various ways for later enjoyment. The two main forms of preservation are pickling and drying. If pickling, simmer the Mushroom lightly in water for 10 minutes, drain and put in jars, covering with ordinary pickling vinegar and screw on the tops. These will keep well for up to a year. If drying, cut prepared Mushrooms into half-inch slices (or keep whole if small varieties) and string onto fine cord. Hang up in a warm place with a dry current of air until ready. They are dry when they are crisp to the touch and can be crumbled easily in the fingers. To use, either soak in water overnight, or boil in water for about 20 minutes.

The use of psychotropic/hallucinogenic Fungi in the Craft is a vexed question these days. Yes, they were used in the past and their use has a long and venerable history, both for magical and medicinal use, and some still use them to this day. But the knowledge of their correct use and application is largely a lost body of lore in this country and those few who do know keep that knowledge a closely-guarded secret for very obvious and practical reasons. This information is held by some Traditional Witchcraft orders as a separate body of lore within the tradition; these are known by some as the "Dark Orders" and training is only offered to those worthy of the knowledge. Many of the Amanita genus of Fungi, such as the Death Cap (*Amanita phalloides*), the Destroying Angel (*Amanita virosa*) and the Panther Cap (*Amanita pantherina*) are highly toxic and can cause agonising and prolonged deaths; others of different genera are just as deadly. It is not 'cool' to experiment with toxic substances if you do not have the requisite knowledge or support and my advice is to leave well alone if you don't. It is a wise Witch who is able to achieve trance states of their own effort without vegetable help – and also a live one!

Right through this month the fruit of the Apple tree will be ripening and becoming ready for the picking and the season normally extends until the end of October; this is the traditional "third harvest" and culminates at All Hallows. The native Crab Apple tree (*Malus sylvestris*) is an ancient and venerable plant, grown here from at least the Bronze Age, as ripened Apples have been found in coffins unearthed from this period. The fruit is quite round, small – about the size of a good Damson – and very sharp and tart to the taste. It doesn't make a good eater, but is excellent for jams, jellies and chutneys as it is very high in pectin content. It is a relative of the Rose (indeed, they are from the same family of plants) and, like its cousin, can sometimes bear sharp thorns, so beware when picking the wild fruit. The cultivated Apple (*Malus domestica*) is a much more recent arrival, coming over with the Romans and later being 'improved' upon by Mediaeval monks in their walled orchards. The fruits of the native Crab Apple are known variously as "Scroggs", "Gribbles", "Bittersgalls", "Sour Grapes" and "Fruits of the Underworld" and the cultivated types derived from them now come in many hundreds of varieties. Unfortunately, many hundreds more have been lost, due to the fact that many orchards were scrubbed up during the Second World War to grow subsistence crops, and never replanted. However, there is a concerted effort by many growers these days to reclaim the older varieties, particularly for cider making, for which they are excellent. Apples do not grow true from seed, which is why you will see them grafted onto older rootstock and if stray seeds sprout and grow into trees, they are known as "wildings" and can produce an amazing variety of fruits, being a mixture of various parent stocks and 'throwbacks' from centuries ago. If gathering anything from an Apple tree for magical purposes and the tree is in an orchard of any size, the oldest and most venerable tree in the orchard – known as the "Old Man" – must be approached and asked for permission first, otherwise just ask the tree you are collecting from. The wood of the tree is a lovely creamy-white in colour and is excellent for carving into many forms: Cups, Wands, Staffs, Statues or Bowls. The bark should be left on it whilst drying the wood out as it has a tendency to warp otherwise and any 'leftovers' should be kept for incense making, as the wood has a most pungent and sweet aroma. Apple logs on a fire in the home are an ancient and beautiful way to scent and perfume the house. The beautiful pinkish-white blossom may be picked early in the year for use fresh in love potions, blessings on weddings or for all purposes of fertility, but it is the fruiting season we are concerned with here and that wonderful product of the tree, the Apple itself.

This item has been used in the magical arts from time immemorial, usually being associated with the Female Powers and connected with the themes of love, desire and fertility, although it can also be used for bewitchments, cursing and enchanting. Cut an Apple in half crossways and you will see the mystical pentagram stamped within it, a true sign that it is of magical origin. At this time of year the Apple has many uses, apart from the obvious ones of making wines and ciders, jams and chutneys. As an item in itself, it is both a foodstuff and a source of drink, from the juice, so may serve the Crafter as both Cakes and Wine within the one item on the altar. It may be placed at the directions in the sacred space during Autumn, as offerings to the Spirits and Powers of harvest time and can be used in many forms of magic in itself. If using it in this manner, carve your desire into the fruit with your Knife, either in words or in the form of a symbol, invoking the appropriate Powers as you do so. If the spell is to do with yourself, eat the Apple there and then, taking the magic into yourself, and leaving the core and pips at the foot of the tree you plucked it from in thanksgiving. If the spell is to do with the material world, place the carved and charmed Apple either in a graveyard, or other place of power and sanctity, there to rot and release its energy for your work. If you wish to affect another person, carve your fruit appropriately, go to some wild place and roll the fruit along the ground in the direction of the person you wish to charm, calling on the Powers as you do so. Leave the Apple where it stops and walk away without looking back.

Apples have long been used for various medicinal purposes, mainly because of the fruit acids they contain. They are an excellent digestive, calming and soothing many stomach complaints to do with overeating and are a great help in cases of constipation, particularly in those people that have to sit down a lot whilst they work; raw, ripe, juicy apples eaten at bedtime is best, or stewed if you prefer it. The acids in the Apple not only help the digestion, but also help break down other foods whilst eating, hence the sauce used with meats such as pork and goose and, in times gone by, also with cheese. Apples are an excellent mouth cleanser, being just tough enough to move back the gums, so that the acids can clean the borders and are also beneficial in keeping plaque at bay. They are good to eat, raw and grated first thing in the morning as an antidote to morning sickness and almost totally negate the growth of calculi (gall, kidney or bladder stones), best taken in small but frequent drinks of unsweetened cider. Rotten Apples are still used as a poultice for sore eyes in some areas, whilst the juice from Crab Apples, which is rich in tannins, is useful in cases of chronic diarrhoea.

I shall give the final word to the 16th-century poet Barnaby Googe, who put it like this:

> *The Apple declareth his ripeness by the blackness of his kernels. They are gathered after the 14th of September, or thereabout, according to their kinde, and not before the Moone be seventeene daies old, in faire weather, and in the afternoone: Those that fall from the tree must be laid by themselves. It is better to pull them, than to shake them, lest they be bruised in their falling. They are kept in faire lofts, vaults or cold places, with windows opening towards the North, which in faire weather must be kept open.*

Seasonal Skies
Natural Crafters and Traditional Witches look for the Harvest Moon more than any other. Her brightness is exceptional, seemingly close enough to touch and often puts all but the most brilliant of stars out of view. Farmers would find it a useful lamp for harvesting the remainder of the crops after dark and in addition, it was used as a barometer, before modern weather forecasts (which are invariably wrong anyway!).

> *If the Moon show a silver shield*
> *Be not afraid to reap your field,*
> *But if she rises haloed round*
> *Soon we'll tread on deluged ground.*

Others call this time the Hunter's Moon, but that belongs more properly to the darker days of October, when traditionally the meat supplies for Winter would be laid in. However it may be, this is undoubtedly the *"season of mists and mellow fruitfulness"*, when the dew falls heavily in the morning and there starts to be a definite and noticeable nip in the air when you wake. The 1st is known as St. Giles' Day, on which Partridge shooting commences, and if this is a fine day, the weather will continue to be so all the month. September is noted for its generally settled weather and is a month of gentle change, although *"If acorns abound in September, snow will be deep in December."* But we needn't worry about that quite yet!
September 14th is Holy Cross or Holy Rood Day and is normally considered excellent weather to go a-nutting (collecting nuts that is, not accosting innocent bystanders!). Also, as the old rhyme goes:

> *If dry be the buck's horn*
> *On Holy Rood morn,*
> *'Tis worth a chest of gold.*
> *But if wet it be seen*

Ere Holy Rood e'en,
Bad harvest is foretold.

Normally the majority of the harvest would have been collected by now, so it would have been a bad year anyway if it still needed bringing in. By the 21st, which is St. Matthew's Day, the saying changes however to *"St Matthew brings on the cold dew, St. Matthee, shut up the bee!"*. So we can assume that the thermometer is beginning to drop and preparations must be made to protect those of a more delicate nature. The Autumn Equinox also occurs each year around the 21st and is often a turbulent time, weather-wise, so sudden drops in temperature, sharp winds and storms that blow in out of nowhere and are soon over are not to be unexpected. St. Michael's Day on the 29th is twinned in lore with that of October 16th in the saying *"If it does not rain on St. Michael and Gallus, the following spring will be dry and propitious."* Surely a good sign and one to be looked out for.

If you are lucky enough to see through the encroaching Autumn mists and have clear skies at night, now is the time to look for the constellation of Pegasus. Look to the South-East after dark and you will see the Great Square of the main body culminating at Midnight during this month, with the alpha star of Andromeda (which we will look at next month) in its North-Eastern corner. The alpha star of Pegasus, Markab, is a blue-white star whose name means "Saddle", implying anything that bears a rider and is to be found in the South-West corner of the Great Square. The Eastern edge of the Square roughly indicates the North-South meridian line that passes through the Equinox Points and if you duplicate the Square immediately below itself, you will find the position of the Vernal Equinox Point. In Classical mythology, Pegasus is the offspring of Poseidon and the Gorgon Medusa, and who rose from her spilt blood, fully formed, when the latter was slain. The winged horse was said to have helped the hero Perseus in his attempts to free the captive Princess Andromeda and was also later the mount of the hero Bellerophon. When Bellerophon attempted to reach heaven on the back of Pegasus, Zeus became angered and cast him off his steed's back, placing the flying horse in the heavens instead. The constellation has also been seen in later times as the Ass upon which Jesus rode into Jerusalem, and also as a representative of the Archangel Gabriel.

In British lore, this constellation has been associated with the white, chalk horse figures cut into the hillsides of the Land, and with the many springs that are said to have flowed from the pawing of the horses' hooves. A number of traditions also state that the horse was 'dancing' at the time, which may indicate the movement of some form of energy through the Land during this period. This connects the lore with that of the Serpent, or serpent energy, in the Land and the energies associated with it at ancient, sacred sites, particularly wells and springs. Many of these sites were used in the past as meeting places for Crafters and Witches at significant times in the year, and some still are. Esoterically, this outpouring of water, especially at this significant time of the year when the constellation of Pegasus reaches its culmination, can be equated with the release of the new flood of energies at the Autumn Equinox. These energies can be said to flow from stellar or astral origins, to manifest later on our Earth, or the earth plane, bringing about natural changes in the seasons, landscape and tides of the year. The wise Crafter knows when these things happen and works with the tidal flows, the better to have their desires and efforts realised both in this realm and the higher levels they may aspire to. The (winged) horse has always been a symbol of higher aspirations, transporting the aspirant along the path to their goal and now is the time to set the seeds of a future harvest, leaping onto our flying steeds and flying off into the turmoil of the approaching Equinoctial energies.

Around the 22nd of the month, the Sun enters the astrological sign of Libra, imaged as a pair of scales in the form of a hanging balance. The three stars that make up this constellation have not always been seen as a separate symbol, but were once associated with the constellation of Scorpio (see next month) and known as the "Scorpion's Claws". In fact, the name for the alpha star in Libra, Zuben Elgenubi, is Arabic for "Southern Claw" and a reminder of this time. However, Libra has been seen as a separate constellation for at least 2,000 years, as the Sun, passing into this sign at that time heralded the Autumnal Equinox (unlike today, due to the shift in star patterns). The symbol of the balancing scales obviously denotes this special time of year; coincidentally so does the alpha star, which is actually a double or binary system, visible through a decent pair of binoculars. A minor legend in Greek times names this constellation as "Pluto's Chariot", in which he carried off Proserpine into his Underworld kingdom; this ushered in the time of mourning by her mother Demeter, hence bringing on the onset of Winter and is thus also an indicator of the Equinoctial passage. What all this means for the Natural Crafter and Witch, is that it is a prime period in which to use the energies of this constellation in rites of rebalancing and harmonizing of energies within oneself. I will speak further of this later in this chapter, but it is well to note that the symbol of the balance may be used to great benefit at this turning point in the tides of the year.

Hearth & Home

All through the year, the Natural Witch has been working with the Spirits and Powers that are concerned with the home and domestic life, asking for blessings and protection on all their undertakings and attempting to ensure prosperity under their roof. It is now time to say 'Thank you' and give something back in payment for all that has been received. This is the time in the year when the Crafter naturally sits back and takes stock of all that has gone before and weighs up what they have achieved and what has yet to be done. It is the time of the second harvest, as already mentioned, when the natural world is giving of its bounty in great dollops – if we are lucky – setting seed with the ripened fruit, to create the conditions for future harvests to come. It could be said that the first harvest, in August, was man-made, cultivated, whereas the second harvest in September is the product of the Land's generosity. There is an open invitation for those that follow a natural path to join in and celebrate at this time, before the darker days of Winter take over once more. At this time, for those that follow this path, there is a great flurry of activity as wild produce is collected from the woods and fields and our own vegetables and fruits are collected from the garden. This is the time of pickling and preserving, as we cannot possibly use up everything that is harvested before it all 'goes off' and, in times gone by, this was the only way of keeping all the produce to use later. I well remember Blackberrying forays into the countryside with my parents and brothers when I was younger, usually on disused airfields in East Anglia, and it is something that I still do to this day, nearly 50 years later. It's all very well to just throw everything in the freezer when you've picked it in these days of 'mod cons', but making your own preserves is a great joy; there is still something magical about standing over a great pan of steaming and bubbling fruits, maybe whispering a few 'preservatives' of your own into the mix, and later having great rows of multi-coloured jars full of tasty treats in the larder. Now is the time to make use of all that is available and give some back in gratitude for all that you have received throughout the preceding year. This is the origin of the real Harvest Home, separate from the Horkey that was celebrated after the corn was safely harvested, and the forerunner of the modern harvest festivals, still celebrated in many schools and churches today. I will give here a couple of my favourite recipes that you may like to try and will then give some suggestions for a Crafters' "Harvest Thanksgiving" dinner.

It is quite easy to make good preserves, chutneys, pickles etc. if you use fresh, sound and slightly unripe produce. Watery vegetables benefit from soaking in brine after being prepared and before pickling, as this crisps and firms them and removes the excess moisture, which can make a preserve very soggy. Do not allow any metallic substance to come into contact with pickles or vinegar, as this will turn them 'off'. Ensure all pickles are completely covered with vinegar and if any part shows signs of being bad, pour out the liquid, replace the offending article with new and cover with fresh vinegar, adding fresh spices at the same time.

Apple Chutney
Ingredients:
¾lb brown sugar
1lb cooking Apples
¾lb raisins
¾lb onions
1 tsp ginger (ground)
1 tsp cayenne pepper
1½ tbsp salt
1pint pickling vinegar

Method:
Peel and core the Apples and put them, along with the onions and raisins, through a mincer. Put the vinegar and sugar into a pan and bring to the boil, at which point immediately add all the other ingredients. Stir until all is well mixed and bring back to the boil. Turn down the heat and simmer for 20-30 minutes, stirring occasionally, making sure the mixture doesn't 'catch' on the bottom of the pan. When ready, put into warm, sterilised jars. Allow to cool before screwing the lids on tightly.

Hedgerow Cheese
This is obviously not a cheese, but sets very like a soft one, hence the name. Basically, this is an amalgamation of any wild or cultivated fruit that you can lay your hands on, such as Elderberries, Sloes, Blackberries, Plums, Haws, whatever, plus the addition of Crab Apples to set the mixture; use one pound of Crab Apples for every pound of hedgerow fruit.

Method:
Wash and roughly chop the Apples and place in a large pan; gently wash and remove the Elderberries from the stalks; wash and pick over Sloes, Blackberries and any other fruits and discard any that are 'off'. Place all in the pan and add one pint of water for every three pounds of fruit. Simmer until all the fruit is soft, then sieve the fruit and discard the pips, skins etc. Measure the pulp and for every pint, add one pound of sugar; place all back in the pan, boil to setting point and skim. Pour into warm sterilised jars and cover in the usual manner. This has a thicker, more old-fashioned consistency than jam, but is richer in flavour and can be used when baking cakes too.

Bramble Dessert
Ideal for a harvest supper and as an offering to the hearth spirits – if you can bear to spare any that is!

Ingredients:
   2lb cooking Apples
   12oz Blackberries
   4oz granulated sugar
   8oz fresh breadcrumbs
   4oz soft light brown sugar
   4oz butter

Method:
Peel and core the Apples, slice and put in a pan with the Blackberries and a little of the sugar. A very little water may be added now. Stew gently until all is soft. While the fruit is cooling, mix the breadcrumbs with the brown sugar; melt the butter in a fresh pan and add in the breadcrumb mix, stirring well. When this mixture has also cooled, layer the fruit and then the breadcrumb mix alternately in individual glass dessert bowls. Finish with a layer of crumbs and chill for two hours before serving. Decorate with cream if you wish!

St. Michael's Bannock

In addition to the above recipes, this is another traditional dish that is eaten at this time that you may like to add, either to your ritual repast or to your Harvest meal. Originally an Irish soda bread-type dish, it has long been eaten in England at Michaelmas and lends itself well to the themes of this time.

Ingredients:

⅔ cup Barley meal
⅔ cup Oat meal
⅔ cup Rye meal
½ cup plain flour
½ tsp salt
2 tsp bicarbonate of soda
2½–3 cups milk
3 tbsp honey OR brown sugar
¼ cup raisins OR sultanas
2 eggs
1 cup cream
4 tbsp melted butter

Method:

Mix the Barley meal, Oatmeal, Rye meal, flour, bicarbonate of soda and salt together well in a large bowl. Stir in the milk, honey or sugar, and the fruit. Turn the mixture out onto a well-floured board and knead just long enough to make a soft dough. Add more flour or milk, if required to get the consistency right. Roll the dough into a circle about eight to nine inches in diameter and half to three-quarters of an inch thick. Wrap lightly in waxed paper and leave to rise for about 20 minutes in a warm place. Mix together the eggs, cream, and melted butter. Heat a griddle or a large frying pan and grease it lightly. Unwrap the dough. Paint one surface of the bannock with the egg mixture, and place the bannock with the painted side on the griddle. Cook over a moderate heat until brown. Paint the upper surface of the bannock with the egg mixture. Flip over and cook the other side. Keep turning it over and painting the bannock until each side has been painted and cooked three times, when it is then ready to serve. St. Michael's Bannock is good either served plain or spread with butter and honey.

Any and all of the above may be served at your Harvest Thanksgiving supper (stuffed mushrooms to start?), with the main course being the traditional (Michaelmas) goose, although if this is too difficult to find at this time of year – as it often is these days, unfortunately – duck is a nice alternative and is just as traditional and acceptable. Plan to have your supper at least a few days **before** the actual Autumn Equinox when the new energies will be released. The Equinox is a very magical time and needs different observances; this is a thanksgiving meal and is prepared for a different purpose. You should aim to have a group of like-minded people with you for this meal, if you can; those that understand what you are doing, or whom you work with magically, and who can really join in with the spirit of the meal. Make a big thing of it and enjoy it; this is not a sombre affair but a joyous celebration of Nature's bounty and it would be niggardly to observe this time half-heartedly. Play music throughout the meal time, something like traditional folksongs or Mediaeval feasting music. Just before you start the meal, when all have sat down, make a statement to the effect that this meal is held in honour of the domestic Powers and Spirits who have helped, protected and worked with you over the past year. Dedicate the meal in their honour and ask that they be present and join in with you. Have a separate bowl laid ready on the table and place the first/best portion of every dish into the bowl, before anyone else eats. Then set to and enjoy your repast. At the end of the meal, take up the bowl and go around the house with it, visiting all the places where you have requested help or protection during the past year (or maybe just to the four directions if this is possible). At each place, say a little prayer of gratitude and leave a portion of the food from the bowl on a saucer or similar. When you have been all around the house return to your hearth (or equivalent) and place the bowl down there (as long as it is safe to do so and you can keep all pets away, for a while at least). Give a slightly longer and more formal prayer of gratitude and leave the bowl there overnight, or as long as you safely can. Then enjoy the rest of the time with your friends before retiring to bed. In the morning, collect up all the individual offerings that you left around the house, take the bowl of food out into your garden (or nearby your home if you do not have one) and discreetly turn out the remains onto the ground, with simple whispered words of thanks. Turn and walk away without looking back.

Fauna

I have already mentioned the Goose in connection with this month and would now like to look at this bird a little closer. Various kinds of Geese are to be seen in Britain, a lot of which are migrant visitors here and rarely breed, including the Canada, Brent and Barnacle Goose, the Bean, Pink-footed and White-fronted Goose. However, the true, native, British resident Goose and the ancestor of all our domesticated species, is the Greylag Goose (*Anser anser*). Known also as the "Fen Goose", "Grey Goose", "Marsh Goose", "Stubble Goose" and "Wild Goose", it has been a resident breeder here for many thousands of years. The word "Goose" is possibly of Indo-European origin and was in use as early as 3000 BCE, the modern version having changed little since Old English. The female bird stays as "goose", whereas the male is known as a "gander" (originating from the Old English "gandra" of a similarly ancient provenance), and the young are termed "goslings", itself a Middle English term. They mate for life and are extremely devoted couples, performing a complicated ritual dance, known as a "triumph ceremony" each time they meet. They have been kept by man for at least 4,000 years and, during that period, have provided meat, eggs, feathers and fat as well as being used as quite vicious 'guard dogs' and early warning alarms. They have given rise to many, many common expressions in the English language, such as "goose pimple", "goose flesh", "gooseberry", "goose step", "cooked his goose", "can't say boo to a goose", "goose that laid the golden egg" and numerous others. In fact, the Goose has insinuated itself into our culture to such an extent that it is hardly even thought of any more.

In common with the Swan, many "Celtic" areas of Britain had a strict taboo on the eating of Goose flesh, although it was kept for religious sacrifices. This is in sharp contrast with the more "English" areas where the eating of this bird was the norm, right up until the time of the Victorians, when the introduced American Turkey overtook it in popularity. Queen Elizabeth I was a firm devotee of goose and tradition states that it was she that began the custom of eating goose on Michaelmas Day (29th), in honour of the defeat of the Spanish Armada. In actual fact, goose had been eaten on this day long before this time, purely because of seasonal practice. After the Autumn harvest of the corn, Geese were let out into the fields to fatten up on all the dropped grain left behind, hence one of the colloquial names, "Stubble Goose". There was such a glut of fat Geese by Michaelmas that it would have been inconceivable not to celebrate the feast without one on the table. This was also the time of year when annual rents and tenancies would have been renewed and poor farmers would often have given their Landlords Geese in lieu of money, and these would need to be used in some manner. In many places it was thought unlucky not to eat goose at Michaelmas, because hard times for the family would otherwise follow.

In British and European lore in general, the Goose has always been symbolic of soul flight, often being connected with the Wild Hunt later in the year, and in traditional lore it is particularly associated with the Female Powers of Winter and Night. Many of our old folk stories, children's rhymes and nursery tales, which often stem from the Grimm Brothers' collections of Teutonic Lore, hark back to these beliefs. For example, a widespread countryside comment when it snows states that *"the Old Woman is plucking her Geese"*. Another well-known rhyme is "Goosey Goosey Gander", still much repeated, but less well known is that it possibly hides a reference to the Goose as a sexual symbol representative of the female generative powers. A dead Goose was traditionally carried in bridegrooms' processions as they were being escorted to the bridal chamber on the wedding night. Another old rhyme states:

> *Grey Goose and Gander,*
> *Waft your wings together,*
> *And carry the Good King's daughter*
> *Over the one-strand river.*

Academia seems not to know who the king, or his daughter, was, or what is meant by the "one-strand river", although agreeing that the rhyme is very old. For those of Traditional Craft though, there are some interesting symbols here that are very well known.

As is usual with native animals, most have built up a large, traditional medical use around them and the Goose is no exception. Goose fat or grease has long been a standby for Winter colds and coughs and there are still people around who can remember having it smeared all over their chests, then being sewn into their underwear for the Winter (it also makes the best roast potatoes too). In the 17th century the following advice was given: *"The fat of a Goose tempered and mixed with a Spyder and Oyl of Roses together, being used as an Ointment on the breasts, preserveth them safely, as that no milk will coagulate or curdle in them after any birth."* Not that I'd recommend that these days, nor indeed the following from the 18th century: *"The dung is a specific against the jaundice, it helps to cure the scurvy, dropsy, gout and green sickness, it also opens all manner of obstructions in the womb, liver and spleen ... the dung which is green, and gathered in the spring is the best."* But who would want to try that now?!

As far as magical uses go, apart from the usual use of animal parts in associated esoteric practice, the only specific recommendation is as follows: burn the feathers of a Goose in the flame of a Beeswax candle and waft the smoke around a haunted or bedevilled place and the smell will drive all malignant energies away. I'm not surprised – have you ever smelled burning Goose quills!

One of the most beautiful activities at this time is to take an early morning walk, just as the Sun is rising and see the light shining on and through the myriad of Spiders' webs that appear in abundance across the fields and trees, as if by magic. Of course, they've been there all year round, but they seem much more noticeable now, covered in dew with the light lancing through them. (In actual fact there are more around at this time of year, as the female is trying to attract the male for mating.) The Spider belongs to the class Arachnida and the order Araneae, there being some 600 species native to the British Isles, most, apart from the more familiar, being individually identifiable only by the expert. The Spider is differentiated from the Insect by having only two main body parts at most, no wings, no antennae and invariably, four pairs of legs. They lay eggs which hatch into miniature versions of the adults, called "spiderlings", which do not undergo any metamorphosis to the adult stage. Mature specimens vary in size from the Money Spiders only a sixteenth of an inch across the legs, to the two largest species, the Great Raft Spider (*Dolomedes plantarius*) and the Cardinal Spider (*Tegenaria parietina*), which can measure more than five inches across. The modern word "Spider" is from the Old English "Spithra", meaning "a spinner", but previously this animal had been known by the Middle English term of "Cop", meaning "a top" (as in spinning); the term "cobweb" descends from this. The older name is reflected in the myriad colloquial names for the Spider, such as "Aftercrop", "Attercop",

"Eddercop" and "Ottercop" and their vaiations; others include "Arain", "Hatter", "Meratoo", "Shepherd-spinner" and "Willie-buck". Considering the fear and utter terror they can inspire in some people, the Spider is one of the most benign of creatures in Britain. They are carnivorous but do not spread disease, feeding on flies and other insects that most people find distasteful. Whilst a few foreign species can be extremely poisonous, apart from the Water Spider (*Argyroneta aquatica*) few British Spiders are able to give even a painful nip.

In traditional lore, Spiders are invariably associated with the Powers of Fate and Destiny, those who spin and create the patterns of Life and Death; it is not surprising therefore to find them linked closely in the popular mind with fortune or poverty. It is considered extremely unlucky to kill a Spider, or even to break its web if it is still on it, and dire consequences are said to follow if this happens. One of the best-known sayings is *"If you want to live and thrive, let the Spider run alive."* If you see a Spider spinning a web, someone will give you a gift of new clothes. To find one of the tiny Spiders on your body or clothing is reckoned very fortunate, hence these are named "Money Spiders". One either has to throw the animal over the left shoulder, or as I was brought up to do, twirl it on its thread three times around your head and return it to where you found it. However, the same care over the Spiders' wellbeing is not taken when dealing with the realms of folk medicine, as always. They are thought to be especially beneficial in warding off the effects of the ague or malaria, and also whooping cough in children, the cure being applied in various ways. Generally, the Spider or Spiders (usually three) had to be suspended around the neck in a cloth bag; as long as the Spiders lived the illness or cough would persist, but as soon as the creature(s) died the patient would recover. Rolling them in honey or butter before swallowing them was sometimes recommended and this was also said to relieve the effects of rheumatism too. Sometimes they were contained in a bag and hung from the mantelpiece, the cure again being effected when the creatures died. However, by far the most common use for the Spider was its web. This was considered a sovereign remedy for cuts and wounds, if applied directly to the opening. This treatment has been used for centuries and was mentioned in the works of the Roman historian Pliny the Elder; some Crafters and country folk still use this form of 'sticking plaster' and swear by the results. Cobwebs were also used after dehorning cattle, the sticky threads being placed over the cuts to stem the flow of blood; this was also done when fighting Cocks were de-combed prior to a contest.

On a lighter and more compassionate note, finding an abundance of cobwebs in the morning is thought to foretell fine weather for the day and seeing Orb Web Spiders sitting at the entrance to their creations is said to be particularly favourable. Stormy weather is forecast by the filaments on which the web is suspended. If a storm is coming, you will see the Spider shorten the hanging thread; after the storm has passed, it will let the thread out again. Bear this in mind particularly around the Equinox this month!

September is still the traditional month for eating Oysters, being the first month with an 'R' in it (native Oysters spawn in Summer and are therefore not caught and sold between May and August inclusive). It is said that Julius Caesar was a great lover of Oysters, like many Romans, and that the main reason that he invaded these Isles was to get his hands on our Oyster beds, which were known to be some of the very best – and still are. Colchester, in Essex, has an Oyster ceremony in September (held since the 14th century, the modern version dating from 1845) which marks the opening of the Oyster fishing season. There is a ceremony of drinking a Royal toast with thimbles of gin and eating pinches of locally-made gingerbread. (Woburn in Bedfordshire and Galway in Eire also hold festivals during this month.) There are four European Oyster species, but the British native, the Common (Flat) Oyster (*Ostrea edulis*), is by far the most numerous and important. The Oyster has for millennia had a reputation for being an aphrodisiac and this may be based on the animals' own sexual proclivities. Some species remain sexually constant, some are born bisexual and then orientate one way or the other, but the native Oyster is usually born male and then oscillates backwards and forwards during its lifespan. However, they do always spawn at the Full of the Moon.

Traditionally Oysters are eaten raw, with either lemon juice or raspberry vinegar, but always alive and this puts many people off, including me (I can't even stand them grilled!). It may be because of this that they have a very dodgy reputation for the stomach, but it is equally possible that the large amounts of either Guinness or Champagne that are traditionally quaffed with them may be to blame. Either way – treat with caution! At one time the Oyster was almost a staple in most people's diets and considered most ordinary; huge midden heaps of abandoned shells have been found in a wide range of locations and time periods throughout the British Isles. They were eaten in every conceivable way, cooked and raw, and with every conceivable accompaniment, most notably with ham, beef or bacon. These days they are considered to be a delicacy and eaten mostly by the fairly well off or only on special occasions.

The most famous side-product of the Oyster is obviously the pearl and there are various types of these. The pearl is the result of the introduction into a living Oyster of a small particle of sand, or similar, which irritates the living animal. To relieve this irritation, it is covered with a secretion produced from the entire surface of the Oyster itself, containing aragonite and calcite, bound together with an organic compound known as "conchiolin". (This secretion also covers the inside of the Oyster shell and is what has come to be called "Mother-of-Pearl" in this form.) Over a period of time, this nacreous substance will increase in layers and thickness, hence producing what is termed a "natural pearl"; if the sand is introduced artificially, it produces what is known as a "cultured pearl". The larger and more perfectly spherical is the natural pearl, the greater its value, and this is also dependent upon its final colouring. The finest pearls are pure white, or with a slightly pink or cream hue, but other colours exist and the most prized of all are the black pearls, because of their rarity. Like most things in this world, the Oyster, its shell, Mother-of-Pearl and the pearl itself have all been used at one time or another in forms of medicine. The Oyster, as said, has been used mainly for its aphrodisiac properties, but has also been taken because of its supposed life-prolonging capabilities. The harder constituents have usually been reduced to powdered form and used likewise, particularly the pearl, especially by the noted seer and physician Michel de Notredame (Nostradamus). He advised taking them to counteract the effects of poison and to reduce malignant tumours.

Natural Craft values the pearl otherwise. Because of its associations with the Sea and the Moon, it is seen as a representative of the Powers behind and controlling their energies and tides, and is used with respect and discretion. As the larger examples of the pearl are quite rare and expensive, examples of these are often passed down lines of family or Tradition, worn as meaningful jewels on special occasions, or used as particularly effective scrying objects. If one should come your way by chance, consider yourself blessed and use it in an appropriate manner.

Times & Tides
St. Giles' Day is September 1st as mentioned above and the saying goes that Giles finishes the Walnuts – meaning they are now ready to be picked. St. Giles was a Greek of noble birth, born in Athens in the 8th century and brought up as a Christian. The story goes how he once saved some sailors in danger of being crushed upon some rocks, by his prayers, and was venerated thereafter. He was a very important saint in Mediaeval times and significant trading fairs were held

upon his feast day in Winchester and Oxford. As well as being associated with ships and the sea, St. Giles is also remembered for becoming a companion of the animals of the forest – a theme close to the hearts and minds of many Natural Crafters and Witches. On the front of Norwich Cathedral there is still a carving of the saint with a Deer leaping up to greet him.

The Autumnal Equinox occurs each year around the 20th/21st/22nd of the month and, like the Vernal Equinox in March, is a time of great change on the inner, or astral, levels. It is the change over from the time of the predominance of the Light to the Dark, when the hours of Night will now be longer than those of Day and the Sun rises due East and sets due West once again. Like the Vernal Equinox in March, this time in September has also accrued a lot of pseudo-ancient, modern pagan names and is mainly celebrated as a harvest festival and time of thanksgiving to the Powers for their bounty – even if They have not been particularly bountiful that year. Most of the traditional pastimes that were associated with this event have become transferred to Michaelmas, which I will look at later in this chapter. However, to the natural Crafter and Traditional Witch, this Equinox is once again a time for individual, magical work on quite deep levels, not for revelry and feasting, their celebrations having mostly already taken place. As with the Vernal Equinox, the Autumnal Equinox releases fresh, new energies with a great deal of magical turbulence on the inner planes, but this time we are at the other end of the year and it is the energies of dissolution, decay and death that are now being unleashed. They will manifest on the earthly levels around the time of All Hallows, when the great remembrance of the Ancestors is observed, although their influence will be increasingly felt before then.

At the moment however, it is time for the Crafter to work with the new energies magically and set the seeds for any long-term projects that they wish to see manifest by or around the time of the Equinox next Spring. I have already discussed the 'hows' and 'wherefores' of this in the chapter on March, and the same procedures and techniques may also be employed at this time. However, there are other factors that need considering at the Equinoxes too and these are the much-discussed, but little-understood, terms of Equilibrium and Balance. Although the dictionary definition of them can be the same, in magical practice they can end up being very different. In short, and in magical terms, Equilibrium can be seen as the (re)calibrating of one's internal energies, so that they are all as synchronised and in as harmonious a condition as they may be. Balance is a momentary occurrence where continually moving, changing, opposing or contradictory forces are in harmony, before moving on again in their own way. Basically, Equilibrium is a process and condition, whereas Balance is a point – I hope that makes a very complex subject clear.

At this time in the year, after all the experiences, workings, manifestations and actions of the previous months, the Crafter can feel themselves and their internal energies to be in quite a state of turmoil – like the traditional weather patterns around the Equinox. Now is a good time to achieve Equilibrium, at the Balance of the opposing energies, the better to make themselves ready for the work and trials of the dark times of Winter ahead. (This practice may obviously also be observed at the Vernal Equinox at the opposite end of the year.) There are many ways and methods of achieving this, but I offer here one adapted from Traditional sources which the reader may like to attempt. A word of caution here; if performed properly, with focus, attention and application, it can stir up some surprising and unsettling emotions and energies in the Practitioner – don't worry if this happens, it is quite normal and means you're getting it right. Just proceed and go through and you will emerge quite safely on the other side.

This is best performed out of doors if at all possible, but is suitable for indoor adaptation. At Sunset on the day of the Equinox, prepare your working place as normal, placing in addition a scrying tool (crystal, bowl, mirror etc.) and a fresh Apple at the centre of your space before you begin, then create your working space as is your usual practice. Stand in the West, facing outwards and make a statement to the effect that at this time of balance, of light and dark, you are going on a journey to harmonise your own personal energies, the better to pursue your work ahead. Through the turbulence of the birth of the new energies of decay and death you will make your way to your own point of Balance and return with a fresh perspective. Turn then to your **left** and begin to walk the edge of your area widdershins, gradually and slowly spiralling inwards to the centre of your space, taking seven circuits of the area to achieve this; this is the Serpent Path that spirals inwards. Whilst you go, focus on the fact that you are going on an internal journey, to the centre point of yourself and that once there you will readjust the focus of your energies and, perhaps, obtain a glimpse of your future work or purpose. Take this slowly and do not rush. Once at the centre, sit down comfortably, facing West, and take up your scrying tool. You should now, metaphorically speaking, have placed yourself at what is variously called the Grail Castle, the Hill of Vision or, sometimes, Avalon the Apple Isle. In Traditional lore this is the dwelling of the Lady, She who spins and weaves the patterns of existence and is also called Fate by some. It is the home of all potential and possibility and where all is held in Balance – the eye of the storm. Place yourself mentally here and gaze into your "speculum", acknowledging any internal turbulence and focusing on that momentary point of Balance that is now possible. You may see images, receive sensations or emotions, or you may feel a shifting of energies within you; whatever happens, go with it until you have reached your own sense of stasis and the feeling(s) you receive have subsided. At this point, pick up the Apple and dedicate it to the Powers you work with, honouring them and yourself in communion at this point. Eat half the Apple and leave the remainder as a libation/offering. When you feel ready, stand up and retrace your steps, spiralling outwards seven times, **clockwise** around your area, until you have reached the point where you began. Upon your return, give thanks in your usual manner and close down your working as is your normal custom.

September 29th is the Feast of St. Michael and All Angels, more traditionally known as Michaelmas (pronounced Mikklemus). This is one of the Quarter Days of the year and in times past was one of the most significant dates in the country calendar. It was traditionally the day when farm tenancies changed, when rents fell due, and also one of the days when jobs were changed. Huge gatherings were held across the country, known as "hiring fairs", where all manner of financial transactions took place, debts were settled, new labourers were taken on – or dismissed – and much merrymaking took place. In those areas that did not have a Lammas Fair, this was the equivalent (sometimes even in addition too). The traditional Goose would be much in evidence, either for sale as livestock or in the form of cooked flesh. The day is a Christian feast derived from the remains of the earlier Autumn Equinox celebrations. Saint Michael, Prince of All Angels, is an Archangel who was the leader of the army of Yahweh during the war in heaven, casting Satan out of Paradise (landing on the Blackberries), as featured in the Old and New Testament. He is one of only two angels named in the Bible, the other being Gabriel. As early as 1014, the laws of England's King Ethelred prescribed a three-day fast for all Christians before the feast. In the Middle Ages, Michaelmas was celebrated as a holy day of obligation, but along with several other feasts it has gradually been abolished since the 18th century. Michaelmas also used to be the day in England for choosing magistrates and bailiffs, whereupon the people used to go into the streets and throw cabbage stalks at each other, in a ritual called the Lawless Hour.

Following this the bailiffs paraded through the town. Local rulers were esteemed in a way similar to angels, and as Michael was the leader of angels, it was deemed appropriate to choose leaders on this day.

The 29th is also celebrated by some Crafters as the feast day of Gwyn ap Nudd, honoured as the ruler of the Dead and King of the Faerie realms, the White Lord under the Mound. He is the leader of a pack of spectral hounds, known as the Cwn Annwn (also called the "Gabriel Hounds", which link them with the flights of the Geese at this time of year). He rides out on a Wild Hunt, just like the other traditional figure in British lore, Herne (see October). His realm is supposedly entered through the hill of Glastonbury Tor, the mythical Apple Isle of Avalon, where he sits in judgement on the Dead until Doomsday, when the Tor will be opened and all shall go free. He is a type of Psychopomp in Traditional teaching, who guides the souls of those who have passed over to his realm and teaches the courageous Crafter the ways of the Fay. He may be approached with offerings of Apples, mead and/or cider on this day, placed at the hollow roots of old Apple trees, or, failing that, any deep hollows or caves that are sanctified by tradition and history in your area.

October

✣⍟✤⍟✣

The Sun rises at approximately 6:20 a.m. and sets at around 5:35 p.m. at the beginning of October.

This month, known to custom as The Golden Month and to the Saxons as the wine Month, is imaged as follows:

> *In a Garment of Yellow and Carnation, upon his head a garland of Oakleaves with Akorns, in his Right hand the Sign Scorpio, in his Left hand a Basket of Medlars, Services and Chestnuts; and any other Fruits then in Season.*

In some of the ancient Saxon calendars, this month bears the figure of a husbandman carrying a sack on his shoulder and sowing corn.

Seasonal Skies

October is one of the months when we can see the most dramatic changes in weather and countryside. The leaves fall and the newly-turned fields replace the corn and vegetables, although through this month many are still being harvested, particularly the Sugar Beets and Cabbages. The Autumn tones of the leaves are beautiful now, with gold, red, bronze and russet all jostling for attention; the wind shakes and buffets them and as each leaf falls, there is always a new bud being formed in its wake – life continues even as it ends. There is a feast of colours to be seen this month before the dearth of Winter as, in October, we are living on borrowed time when each balmy day may be the last. Tractors are turning over the fresh earth, setting the Winter Wheat in the ground for a head start on the next year, followed by masses of Seagulls swooping in their wake for the worms and other goodies that are unearthed. The late Autumn is the time when most of the wild creatures become gluttons in some measure and it is surprising if you watch them how much they can actually consume. By doing so they put on the extra layers of fat which are useful not only to help them withstand the cold weather to come, but also as a defence against the leaner times ahead. As the old saying goes, *"No hog looks up to the man who is thrashing down the acorns!"*

October is replete with weather lore, much of it concerned with inclement or windy weather.

> *A good October and a good blast,*
> *To blow the Hog acorns and the mast.*

This refers to the old practice of letting the pigs out into the Beech tree woods to forage for beechnuts, or mast, the practice being known as "pannage". This is still a legal right in some areas of the British Isles today, particularly for certain dwellers of the New Forest. It is said that October always has 21 fine days, but be aware of the signs in Nature as,

Many Haws, many snaws.
Many Sloes, many cold toes.

Also,

Many Hips and Haws,
Many frosts and snaws.

If there is a Full Moon in October without frost, traditionally there will be no frost until the Full Moon in November – which could make for a later Hallowmas observation. St. Luke's "Little Summer" starts on the 18th of the month, so called because there is often a spell of fine, dry weather in mid-October: *"On St. Luke's Day the Oxen may play."* This was also a day for choosing a husband, and in York it was called "Whip Dog Day", when children would run around the city with small whips chasing the dogs away. I have no idea if the two events are connected, or even if they should be! Many important fairs were held on St. Luke's Day, as it is traditionally the final burst of good weather before the hard times set in. The 28th is the Day of St. Simon and St. Jude, which, like St. Swithin's Day, has a reputation for bad weather. It is a time when the fine days traditionally break up, gales begin and sailors make for harbour at the first sign of wind; it can also mark the end of St. Luke's Little Summer. However, be of good cheer, for here is some traditional advice from yesteryear that may help with any weather emergencies this month.

The lightnings and thunderings will do no harme, if there be buried in the midst of the garden a kind of toade called a hedge toade, closed up in a pot of earthe. Others do hang in the midst of the garden, or at the fower coarners thereof the feather of an eagle or the skin of a seale. Others plant many Bay trees round about the garden. It is true that to breake or dissolve the thunder, accompanied with a great thick cloud threatening haile, there is nothing better than to ring the belles.

There, so now you know. (I have not been able to trace the origins of this sage advice, but I wouldn't really advise trying it.)

At Midnight in the second week of this month, the constellation of Andromeda has its culmination. Lying due South of the distinctive 'W' of Cassiopeia as you look to the South-East, the 'head' of Andromeda overlaps the constellation of Pegasus at the horse's navel. Both constellations share the bright star Alpheratz (which literally means "the Horse's Navel" in Arabic); this forms the North-Eastern corner of the "Great Square of Pegasus" and is the main luminary of Andromeda.

Classically, Andromeda is the daughter of the haughty Queen Cassiopeia, and is generally imaged as being chained to a rock as a sacrifice to the sea-monster Cetus, in punishment for her mother's vanity. She is rescued by the hero Perseus (whose constellation lies due East of her) riding the flying horse Pegasus, with whom she is so intimately linked. Some early depictions of this image have her standing between two trees and also as holding the chain, not being bound by it, and this gives the clue to the true meaning of this constellation. As daughter of the Great Queen Cassiopeia – whom we have already looked at – she is obviously not beholden to any man and needs no rescuing. It is actually She that does the entrapping of the Hero and initiates him into the Mysteries of the Feminine side of Nature. Therefore, the energies of this constellation can be worked with at this time of year, by both sexes, for greater understanding of these Mysteries, before they are finally put to sleep for the Winter, to rest until they have their resurgence with the Spring Tide in the new year. This mythic theme may be glimpsed in the traditional British Mummers or Guisers' plays of St. or King George rescuing Sabrina, the King (*sic*) of Egypt's daughter and killing the dragon in the process. If we view the daughter Sabrina as presiding over the situation and directing the event, the whole scenario takes on a completely different meaning to that normally given.

The Male Powers are generally to be seen at the forefront of most activities, but it is usually the Feminine Powers who are directing events behind the scenes.

From the 15th to the 29th of the month, the annual shower of the Orionid meteors may be seen, with the maximum generally appearing around the 20th-22nd of October. These occur as a result of the Earth passing through the dust of Halley's Comet, but also herald the return to the Northern hemisphere for the Winter months of the major constellation of Orion. These meteor showers originate close to the Eastern horizon, near Betelgeuse, and are generally not very bright or numerous, so keen eyes are required. Magically, this is an excellent time to welcome in the tide of the Lord of the Wild Hunt and may be combined with rites performed on the 18th for the Feast of Herne (see later in this month).

Also around this time (22nd), the influence of the constellation of Scorpius begins to come to the fore, with the Sun 'entering' this sign, astrologically known as "Scorpio". To be found in the heavens to the South of Ophiucus, Scorpius marked the Point of the Autumnal Equinox some 3,000 years ago, although due to precession it has now moved from that position. Its main luminary, Antares (meaning "Rival of Ares", which is the planet Mars) is a supergiant star, 400 times the size of our Sun and 170 light years distant. It is one of the four Royal Stars (or heavenly "Watchers") of ancient Mesopotamia, along with Aldebaran, Regulus and Fomalhaut. Scorpius is linked in Classical myth with Orion, who is slain by the venomous beast. This can be seen in the positions and movements of the constellations for, as Orion dies in the West, Scorpius rises in the East, and the subsequent rising of Orion in the East (at around this time), betokens the crushing of the Scorpion as it sets in the West. In British lore, Scorpius can be linked with the monster "Addanc" of Welsh mythology (scorpions being almost unknown in these climes), sometimes translated as "Beaver". Scorpius is known to herald the onset of the time of torrential rains, which may result in flooding later on. Likewise, the Addanc is a water monster who causes great harm by its actions, and the Beaver has also been known to alter significantly the course of waterways before it became extinct in these Isles. The esoteric meaning of all this may not be difficult to discern, as it can be seen to betoken the influx or earthing of the energies released at the Autumn Equinox, those of dissolution, decay and death. This indeed can be seen as disastrous by some, but worked with, in a mature and initiated manner, may lead to deeper insights into the Mysteries and how to apply them in the individual's life and evolution.

Fauna
Autumn is the time when many species of animal become fair game either for 'sport' shooting, for the pot or for 'culling' before the Winter. We have already seen that the Grouse hunting season begins in August, and this month – sometimes known as the "Hunter's Moon" – sees the start of both the Pheasant hunting season (1st), and Deer hunting begins at the end of the month. Natural Crafters understand that, although distasteful to some, hunting and killing is a fact of life and accept it for the necessity that it is, without over- or under-dramatising or romanticising the subject. Much of Craft lore derives from the magic, esoteric nature and spirituality surrounding the Hunt – indeed, one of the main Powers of the Craft is the Wild Hunter – and it would be hypocritical to practice rites based on this lore, whilst at the same time deploring the fact of its existence. Life feeds off Life; it always has done. This is part of the Natural Cycle of things and must be understood and accepted by anyone who wishes to call themselves a Traditional Witch or Crafter. This does **not** mean, however, that we should indulge in wanton slaughter purely for enjoyment's sake. Whilst in days gone by, the local Squire may well have been the the Master of the local convention as well, and could deal with the Hunt appropriately, those days are mostly

behind us. Today's "Masters" of the Hunt know very little, if any, esoteric lore and seem to kill for the pure joy of it. This is not part of Craft lore.

However, last month saw the start of the Partridge hunting season and by now it is in full swing. The Grey Partridge (*Perdix perdix*), surprisingly enough, is our only native, resident game bird, the Pheasant (*Phasianus colchicus*) being an introduced species and the Quail (*Coturnix coturnix*), a seasonal migrant. Known colloquially also as the "Girgirick", "Grey Bird", "Pairtrick", "Petrick" and "Stumpey", it is, as the latter suggests, a heavily-built bird, with short wings and a short, strong beak. They do not fly well or over long distances and feed mainly on the ground, which is where they make their nests, very simply from a few twigs or leaves. The hen generally lays 16-18 eggs in one clutch, but up to 22 is not uncommon. The nest is generally in the margin of some cereal field, very often Winter Wheat. They are mainly grain feeders – the adults almost entirely so, the young taking insects only for their first 10 days – and suffer particularly in our modern agricultural climate from the amount of pesticides used on the corn crops. They have disappeared almost entirely from Eire and large parts of Wales and South-Western England and recently from parts of Scotland. Most are bred especially for sport now, having never become naturalised in the wild, so stocks must be constantly replenished. The name "Partridge" comes via the French from Latin, but for such an important game bird, it seems never to have had an original English name. There have been several spelling variants, but the one we now use dates from around 1579. The Partridge is a rotund bird, brown-backed, with grey flanks and chest. The belly is white, usually marked with a large chestnut-brown horse-shoe mark in males, but also in many females. The only major and constant difference between the sexes is the so-called "Cross of Lorraine" on the females – these being marked with two transverse bars, as opposed to the one in males. These are present after around 16 weeks of age when the birds have moulted into adult plumage. As a game bird, the Partridge has always been known for its good eating and Henry VIII once issued a proclamation in order to preserve the bird over a large area, from his palace at Westminster to St. Giles in the Fields, purely so it could be hunted for the table. It is most generally roasted for the table, but here is a recipe from at least the18th century, hailing from Sussex, known as Partridge Pudding.

Ingredients:
  1 brace of Partridge
  4oz mushrooms
  8oz suet
  4oz rump steak
  1pint stock
  ½lb flour
  1 glass claret
  mixed herbs
  salt & pepper
  chopped parsley
  wet crust
  water to mix

Method:
Grease a quart pudding basin and line with the crust, leaving enough to cover over the pudding later. Flatten the steak and place it in the bottom of the pudding. Chop the Partridges into equal-sized, small joints, season with the salt and pepper, mix together with the parsley, mushrooms and herbs and add to the steak in the basin. Pour over the stock and the claret and cover with the suet crust, pinching the edges together. Tie a cloth over the whole thing and boil for three hours. This is a delicious savoury pudding for an Autumn feast, served with green vegetables and potatoes.

As you would expect for a native animal, the Partridge has been used for medicinal purposes, having been thought good to eat for consumptives, whilst the broth was used for jaundice, elephantitis and hectic fevers. The smoke of the feathers was thought to cure hysteric fits, apoplexy and vertigo; the gall bladder rubbed on the belly was said to aid in childbirth and, yes, you've guessed it, the liver and spleen were once used to treat epilepsy! Continuing with the theme of the hunt, October was once the month for the chasing of the Wild Boar (*Sus scrofa*), once it had fattened up on all the acorns and Beech mast that had dropped from the trees at this time of year. Known also simply as the "Wild Pig" or "Wild Swine" (which is slightly confusing as the Old English "Swin" actually meant "domesticated Pig", "Eofor" meaning "Wild Boar"), it is variously said to have become extinct in mainland Britain anywhere between the 13th and 17th centuries. It is likely that it disappeared from the wild at the earlier date, but remained in a semi-wild state in 'captivity' until the latter, as it used to be kept in large parks or fenced reserves from which it could not escape, for the purposes of hunting. The Boar was treated in much the same way as the Deer (both of which are members of the same biological group) and, originally, the term "venison" was applied equally to both, the term coming from the Latin "venari", meaning "to hunt". The Wild Boar is often smaller than its domesticated cousin, of which it is the ancestor, but can vary greatly in size. It is generally dark grey to brown or even black in colour, although white specimens have been known. It is covered in a long, bristly top coat with thicker, softer brown underfur. The males (confusingly called "boars" like their domestic relatives) have two upwardly-pointing canine teeth ("tusks"), which are generally used for rooting in the ground and for fighting; these are absent in the females ("sows"). The young are generally a much lighter brown/fawn colour, with darker longitudinal stripes down their backs, which they retain until half-grown, after which time they gain their adult colouration. They are omnivorous creatures, taking anything they can scavenge or kill (including lambs in some instances), but are mainly ground feeders. They forage in woodland for roots, tubers, nuts and seeds, as well as various forms of fungi, for which talent the domesticated Pig has been famously trained to hunt for truffles. Long known for the tradition of the Boar's Head during the Yuletide period, which has continued in more than one place up to the present day, the Wild Boar has been reintroduced into Britain as a food animal and its flesh is once more back on the menu for many people. It has a rich, gamey flavour, quite unlike the more normal pork most people are used to and can be an acquired taste, but is worth persevering with. There have been quite a few escapees from the farmed herds and there are now at least five breeding populations running wild in the South of Britain, spreading Northwards at quite a rapid rate. This is good for the general countryside, Wild Boar being great stewards of the Land in their foraging, encouraging seeds to germinate and turning over fresh soil, but can be quite damaging in other ways, not least to small farm livestock and small vehicles; they can make quite a dent in a car and will also attack humans if cornered, so go wary in the Wealds these days.

As a creature of myth and magic, the Wild Boar has long been honoured in these Isles for its courage and strength, and features on many ancient heraldic crests. It is also associated with such Otherworldly Powers as Freyr and Freyja, Fionn Mac Cumhaill and Diarmuid, Culhwch and Olwen and the "Allfather" Odin. It was greatly sought after as a familiar and 'totem' for those of a warriorlike persuasion, both physical and spiritual, and was also said to be one of the animals that accompanied the Lord of the Wild Hunt during his Winter rides. A Boar's tusk was and is greatly valued by Crafters as a charm of great power for good fortune and protection against malignant Otherworldly Powers and is said to give strength to women during childbirth. It is also highly valued for its abilities as a talisman to confer bravery and power in adverse situations. Boars' bristles were once avidly collected as magical items to bring on rain and storms by boiling them in fresh water in a large copper cauldron, and Boar's flesh was ritually eaten at certain times to impart strength and supernatural abilities when going into combat with rival magic workers. The blood was especially prized for making puddings for strength-giving preparations. Particularly associated with the Underworld and its Guardians, the Wild Boar was sought out as a guide and protector for those attempting contact with the Ancestors at this time of year, its broth being used as a potion to facilitate contact with departed kin.

Unlike most other members of the Crow family, the Rook (*Corvus frugilegus*), has less of a sinister reputation than would be expected. Called also "Brancher", "Brandre", "Cra", "Croaker" and "Percher", the Rook seems to have escaped most of the evil connotations that its cousins that have developed since the advent of Christianity to these Isles, and has retained more of the ancient respect and oracular attributes that most members of this family once possessed. Rooks are one of the larger Crows, being all black with a bare (i.e. white/feather-free) facial area around the bill in the adults. Unlike most other Crows, they feed mainly on insects, worms, larvae and grains, as opposed to the heavily carrion-based diet of their cousins. This may have lessened the ominous reputation imputed to those others of their clan who haunted battle grounds, death pits, gibbets and slaughter houses, giving rise to the associations of death, disease and disaster. The Rook is a very gregarious bird and always nests communally, forming what have come to be known as "rookeries". These are always high up in trees and can sometimes contain many hundreds, if not thousands of pairs. Before the advent of disease, the Elm was the tree of choice, but sadly, they must now make do with other tall trees. The nests are built mainly from branches and twigs that are broken off from the trees themselves, rather than being collected from the ground, but they are just as likely to be stolen from neighbouring nests as well. The noise from a Rookery can often be deafening as they are a vocal bird, with their cry of "kaah-kaah-kaah" echoing over the surrounding countryside, particularly during the calm, still days of Autumn, once all the muffling leaves have fallen to the ground. During October, they can often be observed indulging in the aerobatics that have come to be known as "shooting". Detecting thermals of warm air rising up from warm ground, or taking advantage of strong blustery gales, the Rooks let themselves be carried upwards with their wings outstretched to some quite amazing heights. As the whole flock ascends – an incredible sight *en masse* – individuals suddenly start to fall out of the sky, twisting, turning and spiralling, until they have descended back to tree-top height again. There is no known or obvious reason for this behaviour – other than sheer delight – but it has been suggested that it may be connected to courtship rituals in the younger birds, or possibly affirmations of position in status in the colony in older birds. Another strange habit of this bird is its habit of collecting in large groupings on the ground, known as a "parliament". Rooks can sometimes be observed to gather in large circles, as if having conversations amongst themselves. Folklore states sometimes two or three birds that have been standing in the middle can be seen either to fly away with relieved expressions on their faces, or be torn apart by the other birds, as if they had been undergoing some form of trial.

The name Rook comes to us from the Old English "Hroc", via the Middle English "Roc", although they have often been called just "Crow". Incidentally, the expression "as the Crow flies", actually derives from the Rook, as it flies in straight lines, whereas other Corvids do not usually do this. Rooks, like others in the family, are known to be highly-intelligent birds, even using simple tools on occasion, and have often been companions or pets to humans, having the admirable (?) ability to mimic human speech and 'talk' to us. They have been linked with prescience for centuries and many is the tale of their foreknowledge of disasters to come. They are said to dismantle their nests before a limb drops or a tree falls that bears it, or a whole colony may desert the rookery before a particularly savage storm. This desertion has long been considered a bad omen for those that owned the land and is said to presage a food shortage or famine. Rooks tumbling or flying very low indicates rain, and if they come in from the countryside and feed in town then a storm is on its way. If they fly high, then good weather is foretold. As with Bees, if there is a death in the family, particularly of the head of the household and that family owns land inhabited by a rookery, then the Rooks must be told, else they will desert and bring even more dire consequences.

For a bird that lacks the general opprobrium of other Corvids, and especially one of such high intelligence and far-sightedness, the Rook has often and traditionally been eaten in rural areas. As a mark of respect and in honour of its high status in Craft circles, I shall not this time give a recipe for consuming it, but shall just say that, contrary to some unfounded reports, you cannot gain second sight by eating roast Rook!

Hearth & Home
October is the month when the air can start to become really chilly in the mornings and evenings and most people start to think about putting on the heating for the house. For a Natural Crafter, this would ideally entail cleaning out the hearth and laying a new fire. For many people these days this is not possible, central heating having taken over from the old wood or coal fire in a grate or hearth, but it is quite possible – and many people do – to open up boarded or bricked-up chimneys and renovate or put in new fireplaces, or even to install a wood or multi-fuel burner. Failing this, there is a vast array of choice in outdoor fires

these days, from cast iron stoves, to pot-bellied barbecues and terracotta chimineas if you cannot have one indoors (although even these may be adaptable to indoors use, with a little forethought). A fire is an important part of Craft lore and no Witch worth their salt would think of having a home without one of some kind, or at least a representative of such. The hearth is the natural and traditional heart of the home and family and has inspired a vast amount of lore over the ages. Originally it would have been the place that the group, clan or family would have gathered at or around to cook their food, keep warm and to tell stories and swap news. Deceased family members were once buried beneath the hearth, so that they could remain close to the living. For the Witch it has always been a place of magic and somewhere to remember the Old Powers. Before starting a new fire, it is imperative that the remains of the old one be cleared out first; the hearth is the altar of the house and must be kept clean and well-tended. A new hearthstone must have a '+' marked upon it, or one made with iron (the poker) in some salt laid there; this is to bless the hearth from the beginning and to avert any ill luck. The chimney must be swept and cleaned, then the rest of the hearth cleared out and a new fire laid. Kindling (small pieces of wood or pine cones that will catch fire easily) is laid first, then larger pieces over that to get the fire going; larger logs can be added later when there is a good base on which to place them. There are many traditions about what type of wood should be burnt and what should not and these are neatly summed up in the old country rhyme that goes as follows:

Beechwood fires are bright and clear,
If the logs are kept a year;
Chestnut only good they say,
If for long it's laid away.
Make a fire of Elder tree,
Death within your house shall be;

But Ash new or Ash old,
Is fit for Queen with crown of gold.

Birch and Fir logs burn too fast,
Blaze up bright and do not last;
It is by the Irish said,
Hawthorn bakes the sweetest bread.
Elmwood burns like Churchyard mould,
E'en the very flames are cold;
But Ash green or Ash brown,
Is fit for Queen with golden crown.

Poplar gives a bitter smoke,
Fills your eyes and makes you choke;
Apple wood will scent your room,
With an incense like Perfume.
Oaken logs if dry and old,
Keep away the Winter's cold;
But Ash wet or Ash dry,
A King shall warm his slippers by.

This by no means covers all the woods traditionally available for lighting a domestic fire, but is a good place to start. (Try avoiding the modern lists that supposedly give ancient meanings for the 'sacred' trees – if these meanings were so special and magical for the old Druids or whoever, they wouldn't have committed them to writing for all and sundry now would they? Use your own intuition and the practices derived from folklore, rather than slavishly following a list that was probably devised by someone very recently; you'll probably have better luck with your practices that way.)

After the harvest was all in, many farm workers would ask the farmer if they could have a hedge to cut for Winter fuel and this would have been part of their wages for that season. A good tangle of Ash and Blackthorn were often favoured and they would work long into the night to get the wood cut and the logs stacked ready for carrying home.

Once the fire was lit, it had to be carefully tended; being a liminal place, it had the capacity for both healing and harming, so precautions had to be taken. It was thought unlucky for anyone other than a family member or longstanding friend to poke the fire and the well-being of absent family members could be determined by the action of the fire when poked. If the flames leap up the chimney, there will be an argument in the house, or a storm outside. Sparks at the back of the chimney indicate important news on the way and a fall of soot indicates bad luck (although a volume of soot suddenly falling indicates there is money coming to one member of the household). If the fire catches quickly without any help, then unexpected visitors will soon arrive. If it draws badly, rain is expected, and if it burns to one side a wedding is in the offing, whilst one that crackles indicates frost. Faggots thrown on the fire must always contain 13 sticks, but never Elder, as this is the Lady's especial tree and to burn it would court disaster. Placing the poker across the grate-bars in cross-form not only helps draw up a stubborn fire, but also keeps away any malignity that is attracted to the home. You must always wash your hands before tending the fire as dirty hands are an insult, implying disrespect, and the fire will go out. When retiring to bed for the night, the fire must first be "smoored" (banked) and another '+' made in the ashes, or an iron horseshoe placed there. This will avert any harm, stop anything untoward coming down the chimney and protect the house from all misadventure.

These practices are a mixture of folkloric memories and actual magic, but each Crafter will have their own ways of using their own hearth and fire. The Old Powers were often venerated with or beside fires and many Witches still practice their seasonal rites at their hearths. Scrying in the flames is a time-honoured method of foreseeing what is to come and it is sometimes very hard not to be drawn into a whole different world of flaming images when gazing into a warmly lighted hearth, so caution is required if you are not to fall in! Pungently-scented herbs, such as Bay or Rosemary, may be placed on the fire to aid focus and lift the mind, or else traditional scrying herbs such as Mugwort and Wormwood may be used. Fires are also a convenient focus for verbal and charm-based magic, if desired. The Crafter would sit before the fire and softly croon a chant of their own devising, whilst making or holding their charm; this may then be cast into the flames at the end, if this is appropriate, or placed in or by the hearth to absorb the magic of the flames. The hearth is also the customary place for practising image, doll or poppet magic, either for melting the wax needed to mould the image or for drying out the clay once the image has been made. This type of magic can be used for many purposes, not only the typical image of cursing or maleficia. The intent or desire is up to the Crafter alone and none else may know, until the results are obtained. Look after your hearth well, neglecting neither the fire nor the Powers and Spirits that dwell there and you will be amply rewarded for your care.

Flora

As the days are noticeably shortening now and Winter lies just ahead, things of the Dark begin to attract our attention and just such a thing is the Deadly Nightshade plant (*Atropa belladonna*). This plant has a fearsome reputation that can be seen in some of its folk names, which include "Banewort", "Dwale", "Devil's Cherries", "Divale", "Dwayberry", "Belladonna", "Poisonberry", "Sorcerer's Berry" and "Witch's Herb" and that reputation is generally richly deserved. It is a member of the Solanaceae family (which includes such favourites as Tomatoes, Potatoes and Sweet Peppers) all of whose members are poisonous in some parts to a greater or lesser degree. It is a shrubby herbaceous perennial plant, growing up to four feet in height and living on chalky and limestone soils and, although native, it is relatively uncommon in this country. It is a bushy plant with long stems, on which grow the ribbed, green leaves and the purplish-brown (or lighter), bell-shaped flowers, inside which the berries form. These are small and greenish at first, turning purplish-black later and growing to the size of small cherries, which they somewhat resemble in shape. The berries are at their prime at this time of the year and are ripe for picking – but with caution! All parts of this plant are toxic, the active ingredients being the alkaloids hyoscyamine, atropine, belladonnine and scopolamine; great care should be taken when harvesting any part of the plant, lest inadvertent poisoning occur – wear gloves. The effects on the human body if ingested can be quite violent, inducing nausea, dryness in the throat, dilation of the pupils, spasms of the gut, vomiting and increase of the heartbeat such that it can be heard several feet from the afflicted person. In larger doses (and three or four berries can be fatal in children) it causes hallucinations, coma and, if sufficient is ingested, ultimately death. No wonder the plant has such a reputation and you would think it would be actively avoided. In most cases it is, not even being used historically by poisoners as its effects are so recognisable (except in the case of an invading Danish army into Scotland in the 11th century. A truce was called and mead was offered to the invaders in which had been infused quantities of Belladonna. The entire army was slaughtered whilst under the effects of the plant and Scotland was saved). I must here recount an amusing – but also cautionary – tale that was told to me some years ago. The neighbours of a friend of mine had been observed dancing naked round the kitchen table one day and had then been seen to drop to the floor and fall fast asleep or into a coma. The paramedics were called and they were swiftly taken to hospital. On their recovery, the lady of the couple explained that she had made a 'blackberry pie' from fruits that they had picked in the wild, which they had eaten for lunch, after which they had started to feel quite strange. When questioned more closely, it turned out that the fruits they had picked and baked were not Blackberries at all, but Deadly Nightshade. The lady expressed surprise at this as she thought that all dark fruits were "Blackberries" and could be eaten without harm. Let that be a warning to you all!

However, the plant has been used in many beneficial ways throughout the centuries and still is to this day. The folk-name "Dwale" comes from the Middle English word meaning "dulling" or "stupefying" and gives us our word "dull" and this refers to its soporific and pain-relieving effects in small quantities. It has been used medicinally in poultices to reduce tumours and ulcers, as a stomach sedative, to relieve the pain and symptoms of osteoarthritis and to aid the circulation in cases of pneumonia and typhoid fever. It was used by Roman and Italian ladies in a dilute tincture form to dilate the pupils and increase the beauty of the eyes, hence "Bella Donna" meaning "Beautiful Lady"; it is still used for this physical effect by modern eye surgeons, in the treatment of eye diseases. A tincture of the plant has been successfully used in small doses to protect against infection from scarlet fever, and it is also a very useful antidote in cases of poisoning by other plants.

This leads me on to another of its more nefarious uses and that is in the famed Flying Ointment of Traditional Witchcraft. These ointments, as mentioned previously, were often composed of incredibly toxic ingredients and great care and skill was needed in their preparation. One of the other ingredients, which caused similar effects to Deadly Nightshade, was often Aconite or Wolfsbane, and you would think that a combination of the two would definitely be fatal. However, used carefully, not at all, as one herb is the antidote to the other! Of course, these ointments contained other ingredients which were mitigating, strengthening or supportive herbs for all the others, but it was and is a highly-skilled job compounding them safely and effectively. If you have not been fully trained or are not working under the guidance of someone who is, then my advice is to leave well alone. There are reasons why these things are kept secret! However, Belladonna has other magical uses, which, if used carefully, are a lot safer than Flying Ointment. An incense containing the berries, and burnt in the open air, can be used in rites for contacting the Ancestors or the Departed, particularly at the Dark of the Moon at this time of year. A watery solution or tincture may be used to pour over certain fetishes in rain-making rites, and the dried root carried about the person is said to bring good fortune to gamblers. It is a plant easily attracted to negative or malevolent energies and, if desired, can be used to contact spirits of this nature for works of revenge or destruction. Finally, it may also be used in the same way as the famed root of the Mandrake plant, in that a spirit servant or familiar may be bound to the root and used to do the Crafters' (magical) bidding, as long as it receives sufficient care and payment.

Moving further into the darker realms, the Alder (*Alnus glutinosa*), is one of our native trees with a definitely ambiguous nature, but more of that anon. This tree, known also as "Aller", "Orle", "Waller", "Scottish Mahogany" and "Whistlewood", grows mainly in damp, marshy or boggy areas, or by the banks of rivers and streams. It is a great water-lover and its presence is a sure sign of moisture, although it can also appear to be growing in quite barren conditions, as it has very deep taproots which search out underground moisture and raise it up. It is very resistant to rotting in water, the wood being oily and resinous and for this reason has long been used for the pilings that hold up bridges and riverbanks and also, in the industrial North, for workers' clogs. In the distant past it was used as the foundations for the Scottish and Irish Iron Age lake dwellings, known as "crannogs". The city of Venice was practically built on Alder and this wood underpins the famous Rialto Bridge over the Grand Canal.

The tree bears both catkins (male) and cones (female), the catkins being greenish in colour and appearing before the leaves and staying on the tree for nearly the whole year. The cones form in small clusters, resembling tiny fir cones and appear in the Autumn. The leaves are blunt and saw-edged, rarely symmetrical and, when young, are sticky and shiny above and whitish beneath. The cut wood is soft and light in weight, being white when first cut, but quickly turning a reddish-brown colour when exposed to the air; this resembles fresh blood, and dries to a pinkish colour. This is the reason it has earned the name of "Scottish Mahogany". The small branches and twigs from the tops of the tree, being slow to split and easy to work, were often turned into whistles and small flutes, giving it another of its alternative names, "Whistlewood". Although it does not burn well and gives out little heat, Alder is one of the best woods for making charcoal. Groups ("carrs"), of this tree were often planted near gunpowder works in the past, to use as a ready source of charcoal, as one of the main ingredients of the explosive mixture. The bark, twigs, catkins, chippings and leaves all yield dyes of different colours, giving red, green, brown or black depending on the part used, and both the bark and leaves have been used in the tanning of leather. The bark was once an essential ingredient in the preserving of fishermens nets and cordage. In folk medicine, Alder leaves have been used as dressings for minor burns and been placed in shoes to avoid soreness on long walks. A decoction of the twigs was used to treat gout and as a gargle and also for green wounds and ulcers. A horseman's recipe from the 19th century for stopping 'the wind' in his charges goes as follows:

A Quart of Milk, 2 handfuls of the inside bark of Alder and cut it fine – pint of honey. Boil the bark in the Milk and put the Honey in after it Boiles give him no water after.

Official herbal medicine has used the Alder mainly for the treatment of burns and inflammations, and also as a gargle and mouthwash for ulcers, but it also has another unique usage – the leaves attract Fleas! Scatter the leaves on the floor and, after a while, sweep both the leaves and the fleas away. Carrying Alder wood was supposed to protect against the little vermin and the leaves were often rubbed on horses to repel them as well.

Turning to the magical and mythological aspects, the Alder is one of the prime trees of the British Isles, although generally much neglected. It appears in the modern "tree alphabet" lists with various attributes and also lends its name to one of the so-called "tree months" of the year. As mentioned earlier, that these lists existed is beyond question, but that we have the original meanings used by our ancestors is open to serious doubt. These things were supposed to be part of the secret, inner teachings of the Bards and Druids, so it is hardly likely that they would commit them to writing for all and sundry. Much more likely that these generally available interpretations are a deliberate blind to put people off the scent and conceal the inner meanings that were actually used. Lists vary in their interpretations anyway, one list rarely agreeing with another entirely, and they cannot all be right. Far better to use one's own magical experience, intuition and experimentation to find out what each particular tree/plant means for the individual and how they should work with it.

The Alder is associated in myth and folklore with the Underworld Power of Bran, with the Faere Folk and with the vital elements of Fire and Water. All of these make it an exceedingly powerful tree, but one of which to be wary. It is considered unlucky to unnecessarily cut an Alder as they are protected by the Fay, and it is dangerous to attract their attention. They are known to very much favour the green dye obtained from its leaves and they do not take kindly to intervention from humans for no reason. The fact that it 'weeps blood' when cut binds it very closely to the mythos and magic of the dying and resurrecting Powers and those energies of the life forces of the Underworld. Remember, it is a favoured source of charcoal for fire-making and this always creates a link with the Fire in the Land. Its close association with water also links it with the Underworld Powers, as rivers, streams, wells and lakes have always been viewed as entrances and crossing places to the Otherworlds, and gifts of propitiation were and are still cast into the waters of these places. Using an Alder whistle or flute with knowledge and experience can conjure up a strong wind or storm, which may equally be used for benefit or harm. However, using Alder wood as an incense can help dissolve harmful energies and disperse malevolent forces; using it without care however can cause dissension, even between the closest of friends. Traditionally, hanging a branch of Alder in your home will bring it and you under the protection of powerful spirits, which can both attract good fortune and dispel negative energies. The bough is best picked during this month, just before All Hallows, when both cones and catkins are present, representing the balance of opposing forces in control. So, it can be seen from the foregoing that, although a tree of immense power, value and significance, the Alder is of an ambivalent nature to humans and it is only with wisdom and caution that one should work with its energies.

Against the stark backdrop of leafless trees and windswept skies, the spiky Teasel (*Dipsacus fullonum*), creates a striking spectacle. Commonly known as "Venus' Basin", "Barber's Brush", "Brushes and Combs", "Card Thistle" and "Church Broom", it is a biennial plant, with a tall, rigid, prickly furrowed stem, which reaches heights of four to five feet. At the top of the stem, it bears globular flower heads, which lengthen out to a cone-shape when in full flower. At this time of year the flowers are past and what remains is a spiny ball, which children of yesteryear used to make toy Hedgehogs from. The whole plant is very harsh and prickly to the touch, so be very careful when collecting; there are tiny spines that can stick in the fingers like fine hairs and worry themselves into the flesh, so gloves are advised. The stem is bare below the head for some distance, apart from the spines, then pairs of leaves, either side of the stem begin to appear and these get larger as they go down the stem. In the lower, larger pairs of leaves the bases are conjoined around the stem and form deep cups, which hold rainwater and dew deposits, sometimes as much as two or three wineglassfuls. This gives the plant one of its alternative names of "Venus' Basin", which I shall speak more of later. The English name "Teasel" is from the Anglo-Saxon "taesan", with the meaning of "to tease cloth", and this is what the main practical use of Teasel has been for centuries, giving it some of its other folk names. The spiky flower heads are a mass of stiff spines and in a subspecies called "Fuller's Teasel" the spines are slightly curved at the top, forming a hook or comb. These were collected and attached to wheels or the insides of revolving drums into which woollen cloth was placed and the whole rotated. The flower heads then combed the wool, raising the "nap" on the fabric, without tearing the cloth which a fixed, metal comb would otherwise have done. This practice has only recently been abandoned for man-made alternatives, but it is still used sometimes for delicate materials and for the green baize of billiard tables.

To return to the water collected in the 'cups'; this was used in folk medicine to treat sore eyes, improve the complexion and to remove warts. As a cosmetic and eyewash it was highly valued by country people and there was more than a tinge of magic about it, the water appearing as if miraculously in the cups and remaining for some days. This gives us the clue to its main magical use, which is as an aid to scrying and clairvoyance. A word of caution here: the plant comes under the auspices of the Faere Folk and, as we know, they are jealous for their own and don't like interference from us mortals. Therefore, obtaining the water must be done with care and respect. Approach the plant on a clear night of the Full Moon, taking some sweet offering with you, such as honey and milk or sugar-water. Pour the offering out on the ground at the base of the plant, stating your request that you wish to take some of the water for the purpose of clairvoyance and that you would like the permission and blessing of its Guardians to do so. Wait a few moments and, if you do not receive any obvious reply in the negative or intuitively feel that the request has been refused, then carefully tip some of the water in the cups into a container, bow in respect stating your thanks, turn and walk away without looking back. The water thus obtained should either be used to bathe the eyes before scrying, or a cloth may be soaked in the liquid and bound around the forehead or eyes for the attempt at clairvoyance.

The main medicinal use for the plant is for the cleansing action of its roots, these containing the healing properties, specifically at this time of year when all the beneficial constituents have been drawn below ground for Winter. They are used in the treatment of abscesses and cankers, fistulas and warts as an external remedy, or, internally, for strengthening the stomach by creating an appetite and for removing blockages in the liver and as a remedy for jaundice. Externally a poultice of the root would be used and placed on the abscess etc. but internally an infusion, or more correctly, a decoction would be used. I have mentioned decoctions before but not fully explained them, so I would like to remedy that here.

A Decoction is a preparation obtained by bringing to the boil and simmering dense plant material in water, as opposed to an infusion, which just involves pouring boiling water over the softer plant material and letting it steep for a while. A decoction is made mainly from the dried roots of plants, their essential "virtue" having retreated there in the Autumn and over the Winter months, but it is also made from barks, dried berries and any woody part of a plant for which an infusion would not suffice. Once a plant has dried out, it needs more vigour to obtain any benefit from it, hence the boiling and simmering. This would be applicable to things like Oak bark, Burdock root, Hawthorn berries and, of course Teasel root. A decoction is usually made from one ounce of the cut or crushed herb to one pint of water, brought to the boil and then simmered until the volume is reduced by a third. It should be made in a covered vessel to prevent any of the volatile ingredients escaping. The mixture is then strained, cooled and taken in prescribed doses as required. As this is an aqueous preparation it will only last a day or two, so fresh should be made at regular intervals. Of course, as well as medicinal decoctions, preparations can be made in the same manner for magical purposes also and used as washes.

Times & Tides

For those that follow the old Julian calendar, the 10th of the month is (Old) Michaelmas and so their Goose will be on the table this day. St. Michael is seen as one of the greatest of the Archangels, a warrior of Light and protector against the Dark, so those of the older persuasion combine this feast with rites for safekeeping during the darker months ahead. No contradiction is seen in honouring an ostensibly major Christian saint in this way, as he is accepted as one of the great Beings of Light and above such things as religious terminology. His origins go back further into history than the Judaeo-Christian Bible in any case and his archetype can be seen in many ancient cultures.

The 14th of the month is known as Winter's Day and is derived from the old Norse Vinternatsblot, or Winter's Night Feast and is important to those whose traditions have derived from the North of Europe. It was the time in centuries past – at the opposite end of the year to Sommarsblot on April 14th – when the trading fleets and other shipping would hang up their sails for the year; the weather was now considered too inclement for seafaring until the Winter was over. This is the time to reflect on the past season's ventures, give thanks for projects and journeys achieved and to begin planning for next season's ventures and look forward to what they might bring.

A few days later on October 18th comes the Feast of Herne, which some Crafters consider a major event and a foreshadowing of the darker tide to come. There has been much discussion about the origins of this great Power. Shakespeare mentions a version of the legend in *The Merry Wives of Windsor* and it is said to be based on a true event in the reign of Richard II or Henry VII, so it was clearly old even during his time. Most modern pagans simply see Herne as a version of the Horned One, but to those of Traditional or Natural Craft He is very important indeed. He is an individual in His own right and of major importance in the flow of the natural energies throughout the year and in some of the inner Mysteries of Craft workings. It is likely that Herne, or Hran as He is sometimes known, is a memory or version of the Northern European Odin or Woden, in that his attributes almost entirely revolve around the Wild Hunt and sacrifice, both physical and metaphysical and the Mysteries and energies that go with it. He does, however, contain echoes of some even more ancient and savage Power, which is not to be ignored. He is honoured as the Psychopomp, the soul guide leading the discarnate spirit of the dead from one state to another, and is also instrumental in opening up the Crafter to deeper forms of inner initiation than can be achieved by worldly teachings alone. He is the Wild Hunter, the Dark Rider and is the harbinger and foreshadower of the manifestation of the Winter Tide at All Hallows. Indeed, depending on what time Hallowmas manifests in the year, He may embody the actual earthing of the energies released at the Autumnal Equinox. He is generally not Called by the fainthearted, but by those who wish to achieve a deeper vision and experience of their Craft, or for a specific reason, and is always approached with extreme caution. Once Called, there is no knowing what may happen. For those who may wish to attempt this, I offer the following suggestions.

On the night of the Feast, go alone to some remote place, Wildwood or windswept heath. Take with you a forked Staff (preferably of Holly or Ash), a Stag's Skull with horns (or as close as you can get), a Cup with dark wine to fill it and a Bowl with meat to place in it. Create your space, standing the Staff in the ground at the North, just inside the edge. At the foot of the Staff, place the Skull, then dig a shallow hole before it and place the Cup and Bowl either side of it. Circle the hole, Cup and Bowl around with dark stones that you have collected from nearby before starting your rite. Stand before the Staff and Call upon Herne in your own words, stating the reason why you wish to encounter Him. You may keep the following image in your mind for the Call and the duration of the rite if this will help. See a fearsome, black hunter astride a large dark horse, the shimmering form of a translucent, white Stag's skull and antlers superimposed over His own face, which is that of a dark-skinned man sporting wickedly sharp horns. His eyes glow and flicker and He bears a long hunting spear in His right hand. After you have made the Call, move the Staff to the centre of the space and circle it with a rhythmic, stamping, forceful step, to the left or widdershins, chanting the following rune:

> *Hran, Hran, Come, Come,*
> *To lead the Hunt, to lead the Hunt.*
> *Master, Master, Come, Come,*
> *To be the Hunt, to be the Hunt.*

(This may seem childishly simple, but the intent is the motivating factor and the monotonous beat of the chant and the stamp of the feet as you circle should produce both a mental and physical effect that is most mesmerising. The words can, and often do, change of their own accord; don't be surprised if you end up uttering some guttural and primitive sound – this is perfectly natural and to be expected.)

Keep this up, all the while focussing on His image, until there is a palpable 'shift' in the atmosphere and His presence is felt. (This is sometimes accompanied by the sound of baying hounds, a high wind in the trees, or the faint sound of a hunting horn in the distance.) At this point you must fling yourself down on the ground, full-length, in front of the Stag Skull. Breathe deeply and fully from the stomach and gaze intently **through** the eye sockets. What happens next is entirely in the hands of the Powers that be and none can say beforehand.

Once your experience is over, rise and dedicate your feast in the name of Herne. Take some of the meat and drink some of the wine, leaving a portion for libation. When you are ready, place the remaining meat in the hole before the Skull and cover it over with the stones surrounding it; dedicate it to Herne. Take your Cup and fling the remaining wine to the winds, with words of thanks for your experience. Take up the rest of your equipment and depart, not looking back as you leave.

This rite is not for everyone and takes courage, dedication, application and focus. If it is not appropriate for you at this time, you may honour this time simply by recognising it with a feast of your own. The main meal should consist of game meat of some kind – venison would be most appropriate – in honour of the Hunter; this is not a festival for vegetarians!

On the last, full weekend of the year the clocks are turned back one hour, so they are once again set to Greenwich Mean Time; this means we gain an extra hour, which makes it slightly lighter in the mornings for a while, but darker earlier in the evenings. Although an artificial measure of time and the reasons for this change are materialistic and political in origin, it is most timely at this period. It reinforces the feeling of the Dark encroaching and focuses the mind of the Crafter on the times and tides to come.

As we near the end of the month, we enter Hollantide, Hallowtide or the beginning of the time of Hallowmas, All Hallows Eve. This is one of the three "Spirit Nights" in the year and is traditionally considered to be the most powerful. Before it occurs – and the energies of dissolution, decay and death are fully manifested – there is a kind of 'foreshadowing', where some of the forthcoming energies 'leak through' so to speak, and create a type of eldritch atmosphere. Part of this foreshadowing is the energies leaked from the realms of the Good Folk, or the Underworld, before the portals are fully opened at Hallowmas and they ride forth in their quarterly procession. These energies inspire unease and fear for those that don't understand them and this leads to atavistic actions, almost automatically. Most people can feel this and react instinctively with traditional practices, which include protective and propitiatory actions. The "Punkie" lantern, customarily made from a hollowed-out turnip, swede or mangold and fitted with a lighted candle, is one of these and is an apotropaic device intended to protect the household or bearer. It represents at one and the same time the Lord of Death, whose time is coming upon us, the human head or skull, long considered the seat of the soul, spirit or essential essence of the human being, and the divine Light or spark that resides in each of us. This symbol is employed specifically as a defensive barrier against those outside Powers and Spirits that are feared, and placed at liminal points around the home to facilitate this. Alongside this, propitiatory gestures are made towards the Good Folk and their kin, to ensure that they do not feel slighted and turn their wrath against mortal kind. A traditional practice is the making and leaving out of cakes or buns, known as "Soul Cakes" in many areas. These are also placed at liminal points around the house, such as thresholds, window sills, fireplaces and the like, along with bowls of milk and bread, as offerings to the spirits in the hope of ensuring their good will.

Bonfires, or Bone-fires, are also kindled at this time (the origin of the modern Bonfire/Guy Fawkes Night) which are considered powerfully protective measures against all malignancy. The fires are traditionally made of nine kinds of wood – which vary in type around the country – except Oak or Elder, and are kindled without the use of metal. Again, these are situated around the house, farm or property and flaming brands maybe taken from them to circle the buildings and people themselves.

The very Eve of Hallowmas itself, just as the tides are beginning to flow in a different manner and the veil is thinnest, is a time of divination and foreseeing. It is known to some as "Nutcrack Night", due to the preponderance of divinatory techniques and folk-practices using nuts that are performed on this night. These are generally conducted in a fairly light-hearted manner, using hazel nuts, chestnuts and the like, to determine one's future lover, spouse or fortune. Apples are also employed at this time, using the shape of a falling peel or a bursting skin in the fire to determine much the same events as with nuts; the popular practice of "bobbing for apples" is derived from this.

The true Witch or Crafter, as inheritors of the mantle of the Hedgewitch – the crosser of boundaries and the rider in the Dark – will normally attempt something a bit more arcane however. This is the time to take advantage of the drawing back of the veil between the worlds and search in the Dark for that which may have more meaning. At this 'time-between-times', when all is chaos and the rules are reversed, it is possible to slip through the cracks in time and space – if you dare – and learn those secret things that are normally hidden. It is time to light the incense composed of Belladonna, Rosemary and Mugwort and gaze into the depths of the Cauldron, step through the portals of the black mirror, or let slip the spirit with the tendrils of smoke that drift upwards from the censer and journey to the Well of Wyrd, where all futures are displayed and destinies are set.

On the brow of the hill the King Stag lifts his antlered head and bellows deeply in the summons to the rut, as the gates of the Hollow Hills swing open and the Master and the Dame, Rulers of the Otherworld, set forth on their timely parade.

Hallowmas has arrived.

Selected Bibliography and Suggested Reading List

Allen, R. H., *Star Names: Their Lore & Meaning*, Dover Publications

Baker, M., *Folklore & Customs of Rural England*, David & Charles

Bartram, T., *Bartram's Encyclopedia of Herbal Medicine*, Robinson

Bates, B., *The Real Middle Earth*, Pan

Briggs, K., *A Dictionary of Fairies*, Penguin Books

Briggs, K., *British Folktales & Legends: A Sampler*, Routledge

Buczacki, S., *Fauna Britannica*, Hamlyn

Conway, D., *The Magic of Herbs*, Harper Collins

Cornelius, G., *The Complete Guide to the Constellations*, Duncan Baird

Davies, O., *Popular Magic: Cunning-Folk in English History*, Hambledon Continuum

Evans, G. E., *Ask the Fellows who Cut the Hay*, Faber & Faber

Evans, G. E., *The Crooked Scythe*, Faber & Faber

Evans, G. E., *The Farm and the Village*, Faber & Faber

Evans, G. E., *The Pattern Under the Plough*, Faber & Faber

Evans, G. E. & Thomson, D., *The Leaping Hare*, Faber & Faber

French, C. N., *A Countryman's Day Book: An Anthology of Countryside Lore*, J.M. Dent & Sons

Gary, Gemma, *The Black Toad: West Country Witchcraft & Magic*, Troy Books

Gary, Gemma, *The Devil's Dozen: Thirteen Craft Rites of the Old One*, Troy Books

Gary, Gemma, *Traditional Witchcraft: A Cornish Book of Ways*, Troy Books

Gray, W. G., *Seasonal Occult Rituals*, Skylight Press

Grieve, M., *A Modern Herbal*, Tiger Books

Gwyn, *Light from the Shadows*, Capall Bann

Harte, J., *Explore Fairy Traditions*, Explore Books

Hatfield, G., *Hatfield's Herbal: The Curious Stories of Britain's Wild Plants*, Penguin Books

Bibliography

Hatsis, T., *The Witches' Ointment: The Secret History of Psychedelic Magic*, Park Street Press

Hole, C., *British Folk Customs*, Hutchinson, Book Club Associates

Howard, M., *Liber Nox: A Traditional Witch's Gramarye*, Skylight Press

Howard, M., *The Sacred Ring*, Capall Bann

Huson, P., *Mastering Witchcraft*, iUniverse

Hutton, R., *The Stations of the Sun*, Oxford University Press

Jackson, N., *The Call of the Horned Piper*, Capall Bann

Jackson, N. & Howard, M., *The Pillars of Tubal Cain*, Capall Bann

Jacob, D., *A Witch's Guide to Gardening*, Taplinger Publishing

Lambeth, M., *A Golden Dolly: The Art, Mystery & History of Corn Dollies*, John Baker

Mabey, R., *Flora Britannica*, Sinclair Stevenson

Pearson, Nigel G., *The Devil's Plantation: East Anglian Lore, Witchcraft & Folk-Magic*, Troy Books

Pearson, Nigel G., *Treading the Mill: Workings in Traditional Witchcraft*, Troy Books

Pennick, N., *Secrets of East Anglian Magic*, Capall Bann

Rohde, E. S., *A Garden of Herbs*, HardPress Publishing

Roud, S. & Simpson, J., *A Dictionary of English Folklore*, Oxford University Press

Schulke, D., *Viridarium Umbris: The Pleasure Garden of the Shadow*, Xoanon Publishing

Simpson, J. & Westwood, J., *The Lore of the Land*, Penguin Books

Stewart, R. J., *Where is Saint George? Pagan Imagery in English Folksong*, Blandford Press

Watson, Giles, *A Witch's Natural History*, Troy Books

Wilson, S., *The Magical Universe*, Hambledon Continuum

Index

A

Aconite, 351
Addanc, 337, 338
Adder, 207-208, 226
Aegir, 151
Aesculapius, 299
Ague, 159, 171, 182, 324
Aldebaran, 177, 337
Alder, 117, 352-355
All Fools, 157
Altair, 257
Ancestors, 27-29, 31, 39, 58, 73, 122, 137, 276, 328, 343, 352, 354
Andromeda, 120, 134, 273, 312, 336
Apple/Crab Apple, 54, 74, 84-85, 87-88, 195, 234, 257, 271, 308-310, 316-317, 330-332, 347, 363
April Fools, 157
Aquarius, 78, 92, 121
Aquila, 92, 257
Arcturus, 214
Aries, 107, 120, 122, 131, 134-135, 141
Armada, 91, 321
Artemisia, 129, 261-263
Arum Lily, 173
Ash, 74, 95, 114, 119, 145, 190, 197, 207, 212, 347, 360
Aspirin, 171
Autumnal Equinox, 154-155, 314, 328, 337, 359
Avalon, 330, 332

B

Badger, 48-49
Barn Owl, 250-251
Bat, 137, 210
Bay, 55-56, 86, 129, 228-229, 310, 335, 349
Bean King, 86
Bede, 70, 113, 153, 160, 163, 245
Bee, 141, 222-224, 227, 235-236, 312
Beechnuts, 334
Beehive, 235-236
Beeswax, 203, 223, 229-231, 242, 246, 286, 323
Belladonna, 272, 349-350, 352, 363
Bells, 67, 115, 172-173, 256
Ben Jonson, 281
Besom, 145-147
Blackberry, 303-305, 350
Blackbird, 138-139
Blackthorn, 31-32, 133, 197, 272, 347
Blind Days, 132
Bluebell, 172-173
Bonfire, 363
Boötes, 90, 186, 213-214
Boscobel Oak, 195
Box, 55, 83, 86, 126, 216
Bramble, 303-304, 317
Bran, 64
Brandy, 206, 266, 291, 304
Broom plant, 143, 145
Bumble Bee, 222-223